FROM OMAHA TO OKINAWA

FROM OMAHA TO OKINAWA

THE STORY OF THE SEABEES

WILLIAM BRADFORD HUIE

BLUEJACKET BOOKS

NAVAL INSTITUTE PRESS
ANNAPOLIS, MARYLAND

To the memory of my friends,
the Forty-two Seabees of the 133rd Battalion
who died on D-Day at Iwo Jima,
this book is dedicated.

(Names on page 63.)

Originally published by E.P. Dutton & Company, Inc.

First Bluejacket Books printing, 1999

Library of Congress Cataloging-in-Publication Data

Huie, William Bradford, 1910–1986.
    From Omaha to Okinawa : the story of the seabees / William
Bradford Huie.
        p.   cm.
    Originally published: New York : E. P. Dutton, 1945.
    Includes index.
    ISBN 1-55750-348-6
    1. United States. Navy. Construction Battalions—History.
2. World War, 1939–1945—Naval operations, American.   3. World War,
1939–1945—Campaigns—Pacific Area.   I. Title.
D769.55H82   1999
940.54′26—dc21   98-54793

Printed in the United States of America on acid-free paper ∞

06 05 04 03 02   8 7 6 5 4 3 2

CONTENTS

FOREWORD

From Omaha to Okinawa: The Story of the Seabees was published in the autumn of 1945, just a few weeks after the Emperor of Japan announced surrender on 14 August and only a few days after the "Instrument of Surrender" was signed on the battleship *Missouri* in Tokyo Bay on 2 September 1945. This volume is in some ways a continuation, a sequel, to Huie's *Can Do! The Story of the Seabees,* which was published to great acclaim in 1944, going through eight printings in the first two years.

In that first volume, Huie had some very specific goals. Because the Seabees did not exist on 7 December 1941 and had been brought into being in a great rush as the need for military, especially naval, facilities of all kinds became dramatically evident, he needed to explain who the Seabees were, what it was they did, and why they were so crucial to the war effort. Huie told of how the first Seabees were all volunteers, usually experienced men who had left high-paying jobs in the various construction trades; how their average age was thirty-one while the average age of the Marines they landed with at Guadalcanal and elsewhere was only twenty years and six months. In that first volume Huie was dramatizing for his readers the horrific conditions under which the early operations of the war in the Pacific, and to a lesser extent Italy, were being waged. Part of his job was to educate his reader, to explain how complex and how huge the job would be. He was writing of the darkest days of the war, and patience and confidence were needed. Miracles would certainly be achieved; they would just take a little time.

FOREWORD

In that first volume Huie laid out the "Roads" theory. The Seabees would be building five great "Highways," three across the Pacific and two across the Atlantic. The war would be won on the battlefields, it is true, but it would also be a production war and then, since the matériel manufactured in America would have to be shipped to the fronts, stored, and distributed, it would be a *construction* war also. The Seabees would make every landing, build the piers and docks to bring the matériel ashore, and then, often still under enemy fire, build the ammunition dumps, tank farms, airfields, warehouses, water systems, roads, and finally the housing for millions of men.

Huie explained the nearly magical properties of the pontoon, that steel box five by five by seven that could be configured into barges, docks, causeways—nearly anything! He explained the need for and praised the work of the "special" stevedore battalions who unloaded thousands of American ships in the Pacific, again, sometimes while under enemy attack.

In *Omaha to Okinawa*, Huie does not feel the need to go into all these issues in much detail, mainly because he is assuming his readers have read *Can Do!*

Here, in *Omaha to Okinawa*, Huie picks up the story in the late spring of 1944. The tide has turned. Where the first volume has the tone of explanation and a call for patience, this volume has the tone of accomplishment and celebration. The reader will notice that *Omaha to Okinawa* is laced with astounding statistics. Huie is proud to relate, for example, that on Guam, the Seabees moved eighteen million cubic yards of earth, constructed a refrigeration system of five hundred thousand cubic feet, and developed a water system that could pump nine million gallons of fresh water a day. On Tinian the Seabees moved enough coral to make five Boulder Dams; in fact, just the building of the B-29 bases in the Marianas Islands represented a construction project larger than the building of all the dams in the United States—TVA,

FOREWORD

Boulder, Grand Coulee, Shasta, all of them put together. In his descriptions of Seabee accomplishments, Huie compares the work on Tinian to the construction of the Panama Canal and that on Saipan to the building of the Pyramids.

What would have been the largest construction achievement ever on Okinawa was rudely snatched from Huie's narrative when the Japanese surrendered. There is almost a wistful quality to his narration as he discusses what the Seabees would have built had the military needed Okinawa as a staging area for invasion of the Japanese home islands: fourteen hundred miles of paved road, much of it four-lane, twenty-two airdromes, and so on. Huie writes, "Our development of Okinawa was to be comparable to the total development of Rhode Island from virgin forest land."

In Huie's first volume, the centerpiece was certainly the battle for Guadalcanal, the first major "comeback" of the Pacific War. In this volume the two main events are the battle for Iwo Jima and the invasion at Normandy. Although vastly different in scale, each was noteworthy for the ferocity of the fighting and for the technical achievements of the Seabees in overcoming daunting natural obstacles.

The battle for Iwo Jima became perhaps the best-known Pacific island conflict because of the famous flag-raising. The fighting on Iwo Jima was especially ferocious and the construction there especially difficult, largely due to the terrain. Because Iwo was a volcanic island, it was laced with caves. Also, because it was volcanic, there was no coral reef, no calm or protected water. The landings had to be made on some narrow stretches of beach with huge swells and surf, where the water became hundreds of feet deep only a few feet from shore. The Japanese artillery and mortars had these small stretches of beach zeroed in. Under concentrated fire, the Seabees rigged floating causeways, blew up wrecked landing craft that were in the way, and drove their bulldozers up over

9

the three "terraces" that rose from the beach. The sand was thick with the dead. One bulldozer operator reported to Huie: "There were so many dead men in front of the ship that there was no way for me to unload and operate without crushing their bodies. . . . I had no choice but to go over them."

On the first landing strip "liberated" at Iwo Jima the Seabees showed astounding heroism. As Japanese snipers fired away at them, men of the 31st Battalion lined up at intervals of about two feet and crawled the length of the runway picking up every tiny bit of shrapnel. Huie explains: "The smallest sliver of shrapnel can explode a plane's tire and wreck it. A runway over which a battle has been fought must be combed between the fingers before it is safe."

Because of the rough surf, the "terraces," the network of volcanic caves, and the determination of the Japanese Imperial Marines, Iwo Jima became the most "expensive" piece of land ever obtained by the United States. Ultimately, forty-three hundred men were killed, and twenty thousand were wounded—550 killed and 2,500 wounded for every square mile of isolated volcanic rock.

Conditions in the English Channel were different from Iwo, but just as daunting, with huge waves, strong tides and currents, and terrible weather. Huie spends a good deal of time, in a surprisingly interesting way, discussing the different experiments conducted by the United States and Britain in England and Scotland to invent new piers and loading platforms for the wide, shallow beach at Normandy. Engineers tried a series of ingenious devices: piers that rose and fell with the tides, rubber roadways to serve as bridges between pier and shore, the "Bubble Harbor" using compressed air to create a calm harbor for unloading, the "lie low," gigantic rubber bags, like the floats at bathing beaches, from which 750-ton cylinders of concrete would be suspended in the water. These plans were all abandoned, some reluctantly, some with great relief.

FOREWORD

What finally were invented and settled on were the phoenixes, bombardons, pierheads, and floating steel bridges that would, together, create the artificial harbors for landing millions of tons of matériel after the beaches were secure. For the landing itself, the "Rhino" ferry was invented, a flat barge of six pontoons propelled by outboard engines, which could carry eighty trucks and jeeps or ten Sherman tanks and land in three feet of water. These rhinos delivered fifteen hundred vehicles to the beach on the first trip in, and all were manned by Seabees.

The story of the Normandy invasion has been told many times. Huie's particular contribution is to tell how it could not have been accomplished without the inventiveness, flexibility, and courage of the construction battalions.

As with his previous book, Huie's narrative of Seabee accomplishments and their courage is heavily laced with stories of Seabees at play. A large part of the enjoyment of this book comes from his tales of Seabees moonshining on Guadalcanal, manufacturing Japanese "souvenirs," especially hara-kiri knives, in their machine shops on Saipan, giving a Christmas party for Japanese children from the prisoners' compound ("kids is kids"), dancing the night away with WACS at Hollandia, brawling on leave in New Zealand, and just generally behaving like sailors. And Huie knew them well, for he had been one of them for two long years, on all five "Roads" in every theater of the war except the Russian.

Huie had been inducted into the Navy on 24 April 1943, then allowed to enlist voluntarily in the U.S. Naval Reserve and given the rank of chief carpenter's mate. His real assignment, however, was not carpentry; it was writing. Huie was sent by Vice Adm. Ben Moreell, to whom he reported directly, to a series of Seabee training centers and other installations. His job was to observe Seabees being trained, come to know how they thought, get their stories, interview men

11

who had been serving since right after Pearl Harbor, and then, in newspaper pieces, magazine articles, and finally in *Can Do*, to tell the story of the Seabees and make sure they got all the publicity and credit they so fully deserved.

Huie worked tirelessly at his own "education" through the second half of 1943. In January 1944 Huie was commissioned a lieutenant (jg), USNR. He continued his interviewing and his traveling to Seabee sites in the Pacific and, while still an active duty officer, published *Can Do!* in 1944. Admiral Moreell was well pleased. When Huie applied for release from active duty on 7 October, his request was granted and Huie, on 3 February 1945, was given the rank of ensign (permanent) in the U.S. Naval Reserve. He immediately exchanged his naval officer's uniform for that of a war correspondent for *Stars and Stripes* and went to work on his second Seabee book. As a correspondent, Huie traveled extensively throughout the Pacific, was in England for the Normandy Invasion, and went ashore on the first LST to land on the beach.

Throughout these months Huie interviewed Seabees, took many of the photographs that so enrich this volume, and continued to write. He was virtually a compulsive writer.

Huie had already been writing for much of his life. After graduating from his Hartselle, Alabama, high school first in his class in May 1927, William Bradford Huie, born 13 November 1910, went on to the University of Alabama, where he graduated with a major in English and a Phi Beta Kappa key. Huie would go on to write for the *Birmingham Post*, become the co-founder of the *Cullman Banner*, and then associate editor of the *American Mercury*, H. L. Mencken's old magazine, which Huie would later buy. His best-selling autobiographical novel *Mud on the Stars* was published in 1942, and this book, along with his impressive credentials in journalism, is why Admiral Moreell wanted Huie as an information officer.

FOREWORD

Huie published *From Omaha to Okinawa* not as an officer but as a civilian and, as a professional writer, was delighted to be able to receive the royalties from the book. In fact, more than one reviewer at the time of publication commented on how Huie might have written too hastily and, in any case, might have delayed publication until after the censorship concerning much of the Okinawa campaign had been lifted, so that he could tell the story of our superb advance intelligence on Okinawa. Huie knew, however, that with the war over, readers' interest in the war would diminish. To maximize sales, he published as quickly as he could.

But Huie's own interest in his war never diminished. Although he would achieve great success with many volumes concerning life in his native deep South—*Wolf Whistle,* which told the hidden story of the Emmett Till murder, *Three Lives for Mississippi,* concerning the slain civil rights workers in Philadelphia, Mississippi, *He Slew the Dreamer,* about the assassination of Rev. Martin Luther King Jr. by James Earl Ray, and a novel, *The Klansman,* which unmasked the working of the Alabama KKK—Huie's best work always seemed to concern, in some fashion, World War II. Using Lt. Cdr. James Madison, USNR, as a protagonist, Huie published the rather comical story of a Honolulu prostitute in *The Revolt of Mamie Stover* (1951), *The Americanization of Emily* (1959), in which Madison lands on Omaha Beach, and *Hotel Mamie Stover* (1963), the story of a free-love hotel in the Hawaiian Islands. His *The Execution of Private Slovik* (1954) revealed the story of the only American soldier shot for desertion since 1864! This last book is widely considered to be one of the best pieces of investigative reporting ever done, surpassed perhaps only by Truman Capote's *In Cold Blood.*

Huie never lost his zeal for writing or for the U.S. Navy. He kept his reserve commission until he was discharged,

13

again a lieutenant (jg) on 30 June 1961. Huie stayed actively interested in issues pertaining to naval warfare, the disputes between the services, and issues affecting our military policies during the Cold War. One of his last major works was a novel, *In the Hours of Night* (1975), based on the life and controversial death of James V. Forrestal, secretary of the navy.

William Bradford Huie died at his desk while writing his autobiography, *Report from Buck's Pocket*, in 1986. His first wife of twenty-eight years, Ruth Puckett Huie, had died in 1973. Huie was survived by his second wife, Martha Hunt Huie, whom he had married in 1977. He would be very pleased, but I think not surprised, to see the huge revival of interest in his war, occasioned by the fiftieth anniversary of V-J Day and D-Day the sixth of June, events which were the most important in his life.

DONALD R. NOBLE

ACKNOWLEDGMENTS

For their assistance in the preparation of this book, the author is indebted to many of his friends in the Seabees: particularly to Bernard R. Cordes, Los Angeles, Calif.; Herman F. Mertens, Omaha, Nebr.; Hy Freedman, Boston, Mass.; and Louis C. Higdon, Chillicothe, Miss.

I

ROADS' END

I WONDER if old King Dobie is resting peacefully? Dobie was an ancient Marshallese native, didn't have a tooth in his head, and reminded you of some grinning black gargoyle. The Seabees of the 110th Battalion found him on Eniwetok, and he became the adoring slave of L. L. Mize (Boatswain's Mate First, Atlanta, Ga.). Dobie mastered all the more elegant Seabee obscenity, and he could sing a sweeter *You Are My Sunshine* than the Governor of Louisiana. His act, demonstrating how the Japs had dived for holes when the American planes had come over, was always good for a belly-laugh.

But poor Dobie! Those C-rations got him down, and he began to waste away with "spam stomach." His ears were pierced, so D. D. Blackwood (Boatswain's Mate First, Portland, Ore.) made him some outrageously large brass earrings which Dobie wore about proudly, announcing that he would be buried with them on.

Later, when Dobie died, he was given a military funeral; four Seabees sang *You Are My Sunshine* over his grave; and a headboard was erected with this inscription:

HERE LIES KING DOBIE. HE WAS A WARM FRIEND OF THE SEABEES, AND HE DIED WHILE VALIANTLY RESISTING AN ATTACK OF SPAM STOMACH. MAY HE REST IN PEACE.

17

For the V-J Day celebration I imagine my good friends Bill Linton (Carpenter's Mate Third, Dallas, Tex.) and J. E. Starley (Carpenter's Mate Third, Almagordo, N. M.) "cooked off" a batch of cane squeezin's out on Saipan. Linton and Starley were the ace distillers of the 39th Seabees. They once "worked off" thirty gallons of apricot grog for a Christmas celebration on Maui, but on Saipan they made "L & S Cane Squeezin's" their specialty. While Jap planes were raiding Saipan, these two masters-of-moonshine kept a well-stocked cellar under their tent floor; and while other men cowered in open foxholes, Linton and Starley sat in their cellar and radiated courage.

For twenty American dollars I once purchased a pint of this "Squeezin's" from Linton and Starley on their personal guarantee that I'd be stiff for twenty-four hours and would dream only of Betty Grable. Two days later they insisted on refunding my money when I reported that I had dreamed not of Grable, but of Paulette Goddard.

"We've built a business on that Grable guarantee," they argued. "We can't have a dissatisfied customer going around reportin' a failure."

"But I'm not dissatisfied," I contended. "I'm Goddard-minded. I got more than my money's worth."

We compromised by my accepting another pint of "Squeezin's."

I wonder if the natives on Malaita are still giving the Rebel Yell and goddaming-the-Yankees at sundown?

In the Solomons only a few Americans ever were sent over to Malaita, but Red Eubanks (Paul G. Eubanks, Motor Machinist First, Atlanta, Ga., 61st Seabees) was one of them. While Red lived among the natives he taught them a Rebel Yell more fearsome than anything heard at Gettysburg. The

18

yell was a sort of Tarzan scream which ended with a defiant: "God-ud-dam the Yankees!"

Red told the natives that the yell was part of the American religion; that they must give it each day at sundown. And religiously, at every sundown for months, Red walked to a hilltop near his tent and did his Tarzan, and his yelling would set off a wild symphony of hideous screams which reverberated throughout the island as the natives sounded off and passed it on.

When I visited Malaita, Eubanks and the war had moved far northward, but the natives still were observing his ritual faithfully. Each sundown they played their symphony of yelling and goddaming. One night, after the yelling and goddaming had subsided, I called a huge black native and asked him what the yell meant. He rolled his eyes piously heavenward and answered " 'Merican God." Then he leaped high into the air and screamed: "God-ud-dam the Yankees!"

I suppose that with peace here my old hunting companion, A. W. Sineath (Chief Boatswain's Mate, Lakeland, Fla., 72nd Seabees) has quit potting Japs on Guam. Sineath, a quiet, powerful fellow, former Florida State Highway patrolman, had the most efficient method for liquidating Japs I ever saw.

The 72nd's camp area on Guam was on the edge of the "boon docks"—that's Marine and Seabee for wilderness or the place where Japs hide. It was an ideal position for sniping at foraging Jap stragglers. For months after Guam had been pronounced "secure," Sineath would go out each night around midnight and select a stand on the camp perimeter. He'd have a searchlight, a carbine, and his blacked-out pipe. Usually, sometime before daybreak, at least one Jap would try to sneak into the camp in search of food. Sineath would switch on his light and catch the Jap in it.

19

Invariably, the Jap would run and thus expose himself, and—bingo!—there was one more dead Jap for Sineath's collection.

"If the Jap would sit still when the light hits him," Sineath explained, "I'd have trouble seeing him in the brush. But, just like a rabbit, he'll run every time."

At the last count Sineath had buried 67 Japs around the 72nd's camp.

G. Rolando (Carpenter's Mate Second, Buffalo, N. Y., 113th Seabees) was a double-talk artist who could double-talk in four languages. He figured that Americans had been taken for several million bucks in the world souvenir market, so when he saw the Filipinos selling their mimeographed "guerilla money" to Americans for as much as five dollars for one worthless bill, he decided to do a little reciprocal trading. He designed some "Maine & Vermont American Guerilla Money" and persuaded a yeoman to mimeograph a bale of it.

Rolando then began telling the Filipinos that the Republicans were the American guerillas, and that they issued this money with the big elephant on it in the states of Maine and Vermont. He'd either sell the American Guerilla Money for good pesos, or he'd trade it for Filipino guerilla money, then sell the latter to Americans.

Rolando planned to buy a postwar business with his profits.

I wonder if my old pal (Chief Commissary Steward, Dallas, Texas, 102nd Seabees) ever resolved his dilemma about Filipino women?

Bill Thomson, a big, blond, boisterous baker, was the "Casanova of Subic Bay." He was devoted to that old dictum: "The blacker the berry, the sweeter the juice." At Hollandia he baked 1742 cakes for his friends who had established beachheads with the Wacs, but Slater himself spurned the Woman's Army. He took his own cakes to the native women.

In the Philippines, however, I found Bill Thomson in a horrible quandary. Most Filipino women are small, and it's difficult to tell on sight whether a particular subject is a child of twelve or an old woman of eighteen.

"Why, hell's fire," Bill Thomson complained, "these Filipino women are so small that when one of 'em walks up to me I don't know whether to pat her on the head or pat her on the—bustle."

I wonder what became of that luxurious portable "head" —Navy for latrine—that the Seabees built especially for Betty Hutton on Eniwetok?

It was a little gem that would have warmed Chic Sale's heart. After Betty had gone, the Seabees put it on exhibition, and for the price of one beer chit you could go in and contemplate the very spot where the beautiful, powdered Hutton bottom had been. Over the stool was a reverent sign:

HATS OFF, MATES!
BETTY HUTTON SAT HERE!

My war is over. As I write these words I am sitting at my home in Maryland, scratching my jungle rot and nursing my hangover from V-J Day. My back still shows the marks of those king-sized Okinawan fleas, and my doctor is still combing me for Philippine flukes and amoebae. But I'm home. I've got the three luxuries that every GI dreams of repossessing: a bed, a white woman, and a flush toilet. The

21

bed is thick and soft and white; the woman wears shoes—
but not in bed—and is more desirable than any gal who ever
haunted an officers' club; and the flush toilet is a magnificent
bowl, so magnificent that if it were on Iwo Jima the war
might have to wait while the general and the admiral fought
over which one was to get it for his quarters.

Yes, I'm home. My war wasn't a hard one; I wasn't important. I was a graybeard of thirty-two, and the demand
was for youth. Sure, I could jump *in* a foxhole just like the
twenty-year-olds; but next morning they could jump *out* and
I couldn't. Also the demand was for men who could use
their hands to make machines run, and after devoting a
lifetime to telling stories from atop bar stools, I could use
my hands for little else than manipulating an "idiot stick"—
a shovel—or lifting a glass. But on a goodly number of battlefields from Omaha to Okinawa—Omaha Beach in Normandy,
not the fair city in Nebraska—I was among-those-present.
So when the grandchildren come to me and ask: "Grandpop,
what did you do in the great war?" I can reply solemnly:
"Boys, I lived through it!"

I'm home and I'm glad. I also feel a little guilty at being
so comfortable while so many of my friends are still out
there in those cheerless, Godless, womanless islands where,
at the same moment, you can be standing in mud up to your
bottom and choking from the dust in your face. The Pacific
was so damn lonely; you felt so far away; there was nothing
but filth, bugs, disease, and oppressive weather.

My particular friends are the Seabees, and this book is
mostly about them. While I was in the Navy—both as an
enlisted man and an officer—they were my gang; and when
I traveled as a civilian correspondent, I lived with them
wherever possible, not only because I liked them, but for
the more practical reason that they lived better than anybody else in the service. Because most of the Seabees are

old construction hands long accustomed to making themselves comfortable in wilderness, and because if they haven't
the equipment they can make it, you always will find the
Seabees living better, eating better, and drinking better
than any Army, Air Corps, or Marine unit. Only the Seabees could serve you ice cream on the Balingiga River in
the Samar jungles; only the Seabees could cool your whisky
with flaked ice on Iwo Jima on D-plus-10.

If you have read my first Seabee book, *Can Do!*,* you
already know that I am a Seabee partisan in the good-
natured argument as to who won the war. You already know
that before B-29's could make their flights the Seabees had
to help take an island and then build an airfield on it; that
before PT boats could make their forays the Seabees first
had to blast a base for them out of some coral-choked inlet.
You already understand that while the Army made some of
the landings and the Marines made others, the Seabees made
them all. On every beach and island where the American flag
was raised in this war, the Seabees were in there taking their
licks, griping, and wisecracking, and asking only that we "get
on with the goddam war so we can go home." They are the
real "Sons of Beaches," the mud-and-guts boys who moved
mountains and stamped Japs with their boot heels.

The Naval Construction Battalions were organized very
quickly after Pearl Harbor, and much of their early work
was secret. Consequently, there was public confusion as to
who they were. They wore the initials "C. B."—for construction battalion—on their Navy blues, and from this came
"Seabee" as an organizational name. Then men called themselves "Confused Bastards." They had to explain the "C. B."
to everybody, and when the first Seabees reached New
Zealand to rest after Guadalcanal, they found the C. B. an
actual operational handicap.

* *Can Do!* The Story of the Seabees; E. P. Dutton & Co.; $2.75.

23

Every woman in New Zealand seemed to know that "C. B." on a British sailor's sleeve meant "confined to barracks for clap," and the Marines—damn their buttons—had spread the slander that it was the same with Americans. This resulted in no few altercations while the Seabees induced the Marines to correct the misunderstanding, and afterwards the New Zealand women were so eager to compensate the injustice that they deserted the younger, inexperienced Marines for the more mature Seabees.

Now, of course, the whole world knows that the Seabees were America's un-secret weapon; the Bulldozer Boys; the cream of our heavy construction industry gone to war. When the Navy called for volunteers who could whip jungles and Japs, two hundred thousand of these men left Grand Coulee, left the Northwest woods, left the East River tunnels, and left the road and bridge gangs of the country, picked up their rifles, and got going in a hurry. With little military training, they proved to be natural fighters: just tough, hard-working, hard-cussing Americans with a staggering ability to get the job done, and with a sense of humor that could survive jungles, ensigns, and *snafu*.

Their favorite definition for themselves: A Seabee is a soldier in a sailor's uniform with Marine training and doing civilian work at WPA wages.

It is incredible how much these Seabees—these roisterous construction stiffs in shorts and jungle greens—accomplished in three and a half years. The Seabees were the answer to America's strategic problems. Until this war, all of our military preparations had been defensive. We were a continental power, and if we were to have war, our enemies would have to cross oceans and attack us.

Then suddenly we were catapulted into two great wars. We were required to *project* our industrial and military might around the world, and this projection had to be along five routes: the North and South Atlantic routes to Europe, and the North, Central, and South Pacific routes to Asia. Five great chains of bases had to be built, and the Seabees— along with the Army Engineers—had to build them.

Now the bases are completed and the war is over, and only by traveling these five Highways to Victory can you realize the magnitude of the accomplishment. You would have to see the scores of airfields carved out of tundra, rock, sand, and coral, the naval bases blasted and dredged out of rock and mud, the great docks and artificial harbors, the tank farms, warehouses, ammunition dumps, and accommodations for men by the millions. You would have to see all this to realize what American sweat, ingenuity, and mechanical know-how can do when the chips are down.

Completed, the five great highways form one of the dividends of victory. They are ready to carry the commerce of peace, and their very existence assures the quick destruction of any would-be aggressor of the future.

I've traveled all of these highways, and I've visited and shot the breeze and made landings with the Seabees who were building them. I've found the Seabees profane and inspiring, always ready to provide a good effort, a good drink, and a good yarn.

In *Can Do!* I told of the frantic recruiting of the Seabees in the desperate days after Pearl Harbor, of their being rushed without training and with little equipment to the New Hebrides to build the air and naval bases from which we struck at Guadalcanal. I told of the Battle of Henderson Field and of the slow, muddy climb up the "slot" of the Solomons. I described the tremendous Alaska-Aleutian projects which seem to have been completed so very long ago; and I told of the Seabees' adventures in the West Indies, Newfoundland, Iceland, North Africa, Sicily, and Salerno.

Here I propose to pick up where I left off in *Can Do!* I

want to relate in some detail the Seabee experiences on the Normandy beaches, in New Guinea, the Marianas, and the Philippines, at Iwo Jima and Okinawa. And, above all, I want to sample the robust good humor of these Americans who grubbed through so much mud so many miles for victory.

II

IWO JIMA

FIVE minutes before the Japs pulled their last big "banzai" on Iwo Jima, a strange little drama was enacted. The principal character was a rat terrier dog, white with a black head and a black spot amidships. He was a Japanese dog. Several times the Marines and Seabees had seen him with the Japs. Once when a Marine spied him alone he had whistled to him and invited him to come over to our lines, but the dog had spurned the invitation and run back to his Jap masters.

Now the Japs had been driven to the fringe of caves on the north end of the island. In their "spider nests" they were hopping themselves up, preparing for their last screaming, drunken, death-seeking charge.

Two hundred yards across the sulphurous waste, the Americans waited. A dirty, red haze hung in the afternoon air. The silence, tense and expectant, was broken only by an order being passed or by a quiet, under-the-breath: "Yeah, yuh bastards, come on out and get it!"

Suddenly, at the mouth of a Jap cave, a small cloud of dust appeared. Something had come out of that cave in a hurry and was racing out across No Man's Land toward the Americans.

It was the dog. He was deserting—but fast! The Japs saw him, and I think that the sight of their little dog deserting them at the end must have stabbed every Jap to the heart. They began to fire at the dog resentfully, and

27

when the bullets began to knock up dust around him, the dog really poured on the coal. He was running a frantic, heart-straining race to save his life.

At first, suspecting that the Japs might have tied explosives to the dog, the Marines were ready to use a flame-thrower on him if he neared our lines, but when it became apparent that the Japs really were trying to kill him, the Marines decided to risk his being "mined" and began to cheer him on. And when, with his last ounce of energy, the dog leaped into one of our foxholes, there was a great, spontaneous shout from the Americans.

Five minutes later the Japs pulled their banzai. All banzais appear futile and ridiculous to Americans, but this particular banzai appeared more futile and ridiculous than usual. None of the Japs seemed intent on reaching the American lines; they just ran, screamed, and grenaded their own guts out in a supreme gesture of hopelessness. Our flame-throwers incinerated the few who came near.

Had the dog's desertion affected the morale of the Japs? Had it made them feel lonelier, more forlorn, more anxious for death? I believe it did. Several Marines and Seabees told me that they believed the incident had taken the wind out of the Jap sails.

Why did that dog leave the Jap cave when he did? What strange impulse entered his brain? Was it something like the impulse which causes birds to migrate? It's unnatural for a dog to run *away* from people he knows and *toward* people he does not know. Did he sense death around him, and did the urge for self-preservation cause him to do this unnatural thing?

I wish I could report a happy ending to this little drama, I wish I could describe how the dog romped and played with his American saviors. But the drama ends only with a problem.

When the dog leaped into the American foxhole, he lay there whimpering, exhausted, his heart fluttering from fear and supreme effort. Edgar D. Renninger (Seaman First, Tiffin, O., 62nd Seabee Battalion) took him, deloused him, named him "Banzai," and began trying to restore his health and confidence. Health was easy; C-rations are good for dogs. But confidence was something Banzai had lost. When you spoke to him he would shiver pathetically and lick your hand. The more and kindlier you talked to him, the more he shivered.

Maybe the Japs had been cruel to him. Maybe he felt guilty over his desertion; or maybe he lost his soul by not standing and dying. Or maybe he was a victim of battle shock; I have seen battle-shocked men shiver and cower in a similar manner.

I asked Renninger if he thought Banzai would ever romp again, and he said he hoped so. He said he had noted some improvement, and that he and his friends were using all the good dog psychology they could think of. But I'm afraid Banzai will always shiver.

Banzai's case strikes me as being the case of the whole Jap nation. I have seen Jap prisoners react just like this dog. Maybe it's true that they had to die. If they are ever going to quit shivering, if they are ever going to be reclaimed, then a lot of Renningers are going to have to do one helluva psychological job.

I don't like beer. I'm sorry; I've tried desperately to like it, but I'm just one of those folks who loathe the stuff. You can take it and pour it all back in the horse as far as I'm concerned. Probably because of this failing, I have been something less than enthusiastic about all the effort, all the shipping, and the millions of tax dollars which went into the "beer program" in the Pacific.

The Seabees had to clear and convert entire islets into beer gardens. When ever the fleet was at Ulithi, ten thousand men a day were transported from their ships to Mogmog and back again for the sole purpose of guzzling beer. Thousands of cubic feet of refrigeration were diverted to beer; it was an immense cargo item; hundreds of men devoted their entire time to handling and guarding and dispensing beer. Beer was such big business in the Pacific that more than a few of us were appalled by it.

The incident of the arrival of the first beer on Iwo Jima, however, went a long way toward justifying the great to-do about beer.

Iwo Jima probably is the ugliest, filthiest island on earth. Everything about our operation there was difficult, dirty, and horrifying. That coarse, volcanic grit filled your shoes, cascaded down your neck, cut your face and eyes. The all-pervading odor was a mixture of incinerated or decaying flesh, sulphur fumes, sweat, excrement, and that sickening, pink "whorehouse powder" which the Japs smear on their stinking bodies. Sleep was impossible, and men deteriorated into incredibly filthy moles with split fingernails, swollen lips, begrimed faces, and comatose eyes.

After endless days of this existence, a magic word was passed. Beer! There'd be beer on the island tonight! The 31st Seabees would handle it! The very report had revival qualities; little knots of men everywhere took comfort from the fact that beer would be "on the island" even if the supply didn't reach out to them.

At headquarters of the 31st Seabees, M. Leslie Harris (Chief Storekeeper, Greenville, Tex.) took two thousand dollars in cash to buy the beer and called for a fifty-man armed guard to accompany him to the beer ship.

"Why all the guards, Les?" he was asked. "Money don't mean nothing on this island."

30

"Hell, it ain't the money I'm guarding," Harris replied, "but I may need a regiment to guard the beer."

With his money, ten trucks, and his guards, Harris proceeded to the beach and loaded on his beer. Then the truck caravan began to wind slowly, halting at intervals, through lines of dull-eyed, dirty-faced men who now were cheering, laughing, and scrambling. Four guards, with clubs and tommy guns, stood on each truck as the cans were passed out.

Harris and his boys distributed 24,000 cans of beer that evening. It was warm beer, one can to a man, and still not enough to go around. But I'll never forget the effect.

Many of the men drained their cans in one gulp as they stood at the truck. Others moved off into little groups and drank more slowly. A few took their cans and walked back to their foxholes and sat alone in the twilight. I watched one of these youngsters who sat alone.

He contemplated that can of beer as fondly as though it had been a letter from home. Tears cut trenches through the dirt on his cheeks. He sipped the beer slowly through his chapped, swollen lips and let it trickle down his dust-dry throat. He sniffed and wiped his face on a dirty sleeve.

I thought, with that can of beer in his hand that kid isn't on Iwo Jima. He's not filthy and exhausted, with a foul stench in his nostrils. Hell, no! He's sitting somewhere in a garden, all fresh and massaged and manicured and clean. A band is playing "The Missouri Waltz," and he's smelling his girl's perfume and holding her hand and laughing with her. That's what beer has: the power to transport a man all the way from Iwo Jima to Sioux City. To the man who must make filth his element, beer is his link with the good life.

That night I scribbled in my notebook: "I would rather have been the man who brought the beer to Iwo Jima today than to have taken Quebec."

The battle for Iwo Jima will be the war's classic example of triphibious assault against an "impregnable" island citadel. It is also the perfect illustration of how the Marine-Seabee team operated in moving across the Pacific, and it demonstrates how heavily our engineering superiority weighed against the Japanese. If you would understand just how we wrested an island from our enemies and converted it so quickly into a base from which to project our power, you must understand Iwo Jima.

All the natural characteristics of Iwo Jima favored the Japs. The island is a labyrinth of caves, a volcanic fortress surrounded by fierce, deep water. It is shaped like a pork chop, and lies north and south on a direct line from Tokyo to Saipan and halfway between the two.

As you approach Iwo by air from Saipan—and our bombers approached it in this manner for sixty-four consecutive days before the landing—the first thing you see is Mt. Suribachi. Suribachi is a 556-foot volcanic cone, brown-streaked with sulphur, and it fills the southern or little end of the pork chop.

Now stand with me for a moment atop Suribachi. Three-fourths of the sulphurous cone is surrounded by turbulent water, and off to the north stretches the rest of the pork chop. Directly beneath us, at the base of Suribachi, the island is half a mile wide and reasonably flat. Then it widens gradually, twists westward to our right, and the terrain rises. Five miles away is Kitana Point, the northernmost end of the island. At this wide end of the pork chop, which contains most of the island's area, the terrain has risen to a height of 100 or more feet, and precipitous bluffs fall off to the sea. Thus the pork chop is five miles long, two miles wide at its greatest width, and one-half mile wide at the base of Suribachi, which forms its little end. Its total area is slightly less than eight square miles.

The Japs had worked on three airstrips. The one nearest the base of Suribachi was a fighter strip. The second, near the center of the pork chop, had a longer runway for the Jap bombers which had once annoyed us in the Marianas, and the third, far up on the north end, had not been completed.

Another characteristic is important. Whereas most of our Pacific landings were against islands surrounded by coral reefs, Iwo Jima is a volcanic island and has no reef. Reefs have been handicaps in several landings, as at Tarawa, and I shall have more to say on this, but at Iwo the *absence* of a reef made a landing more difficult. There is no protected water at Iwo, no beaches in the usual sense. The ocean bottom falls away rapidly, and only a few feet from the shore line the water is hundreds of feet deep. This makes for tremendous swells and a treacherous surf. When you step ashore you sink above your shoe tops in the coarse, volcanic sand.

As you stand atop Suribachi, it appears incredible that the island could be assaulted successfully if it were defended by a skillful and courageous garrison. There are only two stretches of shore line where unloading is possible. These are the east and west shores of the narrow portion of the island. On the east shore—which we chose—there is a stretch of about 3500 yards between the base of Suribachi and the beginning of the cliffs. In this stretch the land rises from the sea in a series of three terraces. It is apparent, however, that even here a landing party would be vulnerable to fire from every section of the island. Guns from Suribachi and from the high north end would be firing down upon the landing party, and mortars—with which the Japs are most efficient—could lob shells on every square foot of the landing area.

That, in fact, is exactly what happened. Iwo Jima was

manned by 20,000 of the Mikado's finest troops and Imperial Marines, and no Japs ever conducted a more skillfull or courageous defense. They had the men, the guns, and all these natural advantages. Yet Iwo Jima was taken.

How was it taken? "The Marines took it," is the simple answer, but that takes a little explaining.

The public is generally familiar with the term "task force" as applied to the fleet. A naval "task force" is a group of ships designated to perform a particular task. The number and types of craft in the task force depend upon what the task is. If the task were a carrier strike against Tokyo, most of the ships would be fast carriers escorted by equally fast cruisers and destroyers. If the task were a bombardment of an enemy-held position, the task force would contain few carriers but there would be battleships, heavy cruisers, and their destroyer screen.

What is not so generally understood is that an assault force moving against an objective like Iwo is also organized as a "task force." Such a task force is made up of all the specialist units required to destroy the enemy and convert the island into an American offensive base as quickly as possible.

The base on which an assault task force is built is either an Army or Marine division. The Third, Fourth, and Fifth Marine Divisions were chosen for the Iwo task; the Fourth and Fifth for assault and the Third to be held in reserve. But note this. Each of the assault divisions was then "re-enforced" with additional specialized units necessary to this particular task. Since the task was to grab the airfields and convert Iwo into a mammoth "aircraft carrier," the Fourth Division was "re-enforced" with the 133rd Seabee Battalion, and the Fifth Division was "re-enforced" with the 31st Seabee Battalion.* There were other "re-enforcing" Navy units such

* A Seabee battalion: 1079 men and 32 officers.

34

as communications, medics, radar specialists, etc. Then the three "re-enforced" Marine divisions were formed into the Fifth Amphibious Corps and additional "re-enforcing" units were added to the corps. The 62nd Seabee Battalion (airstrip specialists) and one-half the 70th Seabee Battalion (pontoon specialists for the landing) were among the corps re-enforcements.

Thus, while the Marines spearheaded the assault, there were about four thousand Seabees in the assault phase whose job it was to land the heavy equipment, get the airstrips in working order in the shortest possible time, and proceed with the development of the island. But because the Seabees, along with the other Navy specialists, were components of the "re-enforced" Marine divisions and the amphibious corps, their presence was often obscured by the vast Marine publicity machine.

I am not trying to take credit from the Marines. They were the best friends the Seabees had in the service. Give them full credit. They were the indomitable youngsters who handled the bayonets and flame throwers and who suffered the most cruel casualties. But other Navy units besides the Marines were on the beaches at Iwo Jima. The 31st and 133rd Seabees were in the first waves; the entire 133rd Battalion had reached the beach by four P.M. on D-Day; and the 133rd's casualties—twenty-five per cent— were higher than many Marine units suffered.

In addition to the four Seabee battalions involved in the assault—the 70th, the 133rd, the 31st, and the 62nd—six additional battalions arrived in the second echelon. These were the 8th, 90th, 95th, and 106th Battalions for heavy construction; the 23rd Stevedore Battalion to handle cargo; and the 301st "Harbor Stretcher" Battalion to aid in creating the artificial harbor.

This was a *construction army*, an army which carried with it many more shiploads of equipment than the Marines carried; an army composed of the country's most skilled machine-users; an army fully capable of mopping up all the Jap stragglers while it worked. When one thousand Seabees per square mile moved onto an island with the kind and volume of equipment that they carried, and when they began using 10-ton bulldozers where the Japs used hand carts, then the real superiority of America became apparent.

Originally, every member of the 70th Seabee Battalion was a Northeasterner from Maine, Massachusetts, New Hampshire, or Vermont. They were specialists in fighting the surf, in using the Navy's ubiquitous, many-purpose steel pontoon to help land equipment and supplies over any beach anywhere.

In *Can Do!* I described how the Navy pontoon, this miraculous five-by-seven-by-five-foot steel box, was developed by the Navy Civil Engineer Corps. It was one of the war's really significant devices. It will be ranked with the jeep, the duck, the LST, and the bulldozer when we classify the machines which helped us confound our enemies. Put together like building blocks, these pontoons can be used to make a barge, a pontoon causeway for a landing operation, or a stationary pier. There are a hundred lesser uses for them. You saw them everywhere. Their assembly both in this country and in the islands was a tremendous industry. The Navy had five Pontoon Assembly Detachments (known as PADs) in the Pacific which did nothing but make the pontoons from sheet steel, and there are five Seabee "pontoon" battalions (the 70th, 81st, 111th, 128th, and 302nd) which assembled and operated barges, causeways, and piers.

Veterans of the 70th Battalion had the barge and causeway job at Iwo Jima. They had seen long service in North Africa, and the famous Ten-o-Five and Ten-o-Six Detachments formerly were companies of the 70th Battalion. Ten-o-Six carried the causeways in at Sicily, Salerno, and Normandy, and Ten-o-Five was at Anzio and Southern France.

To handle the job at Iwo the 70th sent a picked detachment of fifteen officers and 285 men. They carried twenty-five barges and six sets of causeways. The barges were the three-pontoon-by-seven-pontoon assemblies—22 x 38 feet—each equipped with one outboard propulsion unit. The causeways were the standard two-pontoon-by-thirty-pontoon strings—14 x 175 feet—and two strings composed a set. Both the barges and the causeways were carried on the LSTs and LSMs by the side-carry method. The barges weigh about twenty-five tons and a causeway set weighs 130 tons, but they are carried slung on the sides of the landing craft so they can be dropped into the water as the craft approaches the beach.

As our assault force moved in toward Iwo Jima on the morning of February 19, 1945, here was the picture. We were going to land on the east side of the island along the stretch between the base of Suribachi and the beginning of the cliffs. Thus Suribachi was on our left and the beginning of the cliffs was on our right. The landing area was about 3500 yards long, and for landing purposes this had been divided into seven "beaches." Each "beach" was about 500 yards long. The "beaches," reading from left to right as we approached the island, were Green Beach—nearest the base of Suribachi—then Red-1, Red-2, Yellow-1, Yellow-2, Blue-1, and Blue-2. Men in the first wave would mark the beaches with colorful banners, and each landing craft had its orders as to which beach to land on.

H-Hour was nine A.M., and as the waves began to form and make for the beaches, the problem of the "great unknowns" haunted every man in the operation. No matter how effective your intelligence is, there are always "unknowns" in amphibious warfare, and in the planning of the

assault on Iwo Jima, our intelligence had been able to provide little more than aerial photographs. How deep was the
water at the beaches? Where would our landing craft
ground? Would ducks and trucks be able to negotiate the
sand without matting? Would the ocean bottom be sandy
and hard as at Normandy, or muddy and soft as at Leyte?
What about wind, surf, and swells? These are considerations
as vital as the unknowns concerning enemy strength and gun
positions. A miscalculation—as witness what happened at
Tarawa when we misjudged the depth of the water at the
reef—can be disastrous.

The first grave threat at Iwo came from surf and swells.
The small craft, LCVPs and LCMs taking in the first waves,
began to broach * on all beaches. Because of the deep water,
the boats were having to push very near the beach before
they dropped their ramps and unloaded their men, and
waves coming in behind the boats were smashing many
of them onto the beach. Moreover, some of the coxswains—
the youngest kids in the Navy—proved none too steady
under the intense mortar fire. The result was that broached
boats, many of them without coxswains, were cluttering the
beach and threatening to prevent additional waves of supplies and re-enforcements from landing.

Two steps were ordered to try to stop the broaching and
clear the beaches. The 70th Seabees were ordered to attempt
to rig floating causeways, and sappers of the 133rd Seabees
began blasting the broached boats to pieces.

A mile off Red-1 Beach a detachment of the 70th led by
T. J. Duffy (Chief Carpenter's Mate, Brooklyn, N. Y.) and
R. F. Morgan (Shipfitter First, Concord, N. H.) prepared to

* As a landing craft approaches a beach, it is imperative that it be
kept at right angles to the beach. If it veers it may become unmanageable and be driven, sideways, aground. When it does this, it is said
to have "broached."

38

bring in the causeways. They dropped the two 175-foot strings off the LSM; then, using ducks, they arranged the two in the famous "slide-rule" position alongside the LSM. Rough water made this a most difficult job of seamanship, and the heavy steel causeways threatened to bash in the sides of the ship. But with the Seabees riding the causeways and holding the sea chains as tight as possible, the LSM started for the beach full speed.

One man, C. L. Branch (Carpenter's Mate Second, Cleveland, Okla.), was washed overboard and managed to avoid being crushed between the ship and the causeways by diving under the causeways. A second man, W. J. Brunner (Seaman First, Boston, Mass.), had his leg mangled between the causeways and had to be given first aid while the causeways were going in. Machine-gun fire was hot, so the men lay face down on the causeways.

At the beach an epic battle was waged. Defying the zeroed-in mortar fire, the Seabees rammed one end of the causeway onto the beach and hooked two bulldozers to it to hold it in place. But the fight had only begun. The causeways had to be held at right angles to the beach so that they wouldn't broach and so that craft could use them as an unloading platform and thus not have to come so close to the treacherous beach. To hold the offshore end of the causeways, the Seabees had brought two 3000-pound sea anchors which they now "bulled" into the water.

The anchors were not heavy enough; they began to slip, and the sea was so furious that the bulldozers could not hold the onshore end. Desperately, Duffy obtained a line from an LST to his offshore end, but the battle was lost. The line snapped, and 130 tons of causeway was hurled onto the beach, making kindling wood out of several LCVPs.

Another problem had developed on the beach. As fast as the Seabees would accumulate a fuel dump on the beach, the Japs would drop a "widow maker" into it, and up she'd go. The Japs had every square foot of land area zeroed-in, so we had to have a fuel dump set up offshore. On LST 761, E. B. Gandy (Chief Shipfitter, West Los Angeles, Cal.) was ordered to try to convert his causeways into an offshore fuel dump.

The LST pushed in to within 400 yards of Yellow-1 Beach, and Gandy and his crew dropped the causeways. But instead of arranging them in the "slide-rule" position for a run to the beach, Gandy made the two causeway sections fast to one another, forming a steel platform 28 x 175 feet. He and his six men "bulled off" four 3000-pound sea anchors, and these anchors proved sufficient to hold the big, barge-like platform in place. The platform was then loaded with 400-pound drums containing high-octane gasoline, and Gandy and his men dispensed this fuel to ducks and amtracks with hand-operated pumps.

For seven days and nights Gandy and those men lived and worked on that fuel dump, just 400 yards off the beach. At any moment one Jap shell could have sent them all to Kingdom Come. The men handled the 400-pound drums by main strength; they had no lifting equipment. They had no fires to heat coffee, no hot food during the seven-day stretch. At night there could be no lights. They were rammed by an LST during the third night. Part of the time they were protected by a smoke screen. Holes were smashed in all the outside pontoons by amtracks coming alongside to get fuel.

Gandy told me: "That's the first gasoline station I've ever run without competition."

On the second night the 70th made one more effort to establish a pontoon pier. The fight lasted most of the night. A net tender was employed to try to hold the offshore end of the assembly, but the skipper of the tender cast off the

40

lines when he began to drag anchor and slide toward the beach himself. The entire pontoon assembly then broached and was lost.

The 70th had the same heartbreaking experience with its twenty-five pontoon barges. These barges had been successful at every other Pacific beachhead, but they couldn't operate in the water around Iwo. The first attempt was made just before H-Hour, when LST 779 pushed in and dropped two barges. These barges were handled by two of the battalion's ablest seamen: Earl Smith (Carpenter's Mate Second, East Machias, Me.) and Arthur W. Lyon (Carpenter's Mate Second, Boston, Mass.). But it was no use. As the barges approached the beach, four feet of water would smash over their sterns, and they would broach. Their propulsion units did not have enough power to hold them in such water.

Of the 25 barges taken to Iwo, only four were successful. These were four which had been assigned to hospital LSTs. Moored alongside the LSTs, the barges served as platforms over which wounded men could be transferred from small boats to the LST. Even this process was difficult in the rampaging sea. The small boats would plunge up and down at the platforms, but the Seabees and corpsmen managed to snatch the wounded men out of them; the litters were lifted from the barge onto the weather deck of the LST by a "cherrypicker" crane.

R. E. Dingle (Chief Shipfitter, Ottumwa, Ia.) and P. G. Purcell (Machinist's Mate, Shop, First Class, Rock Island, Ill.) operated these hospital barges.

Thus many of our landing devices which normally operated between Liberty ships and the beach were failures at Iwo. But there was some compensation. Because the water was deep, our big LSTs and LSMs could drive in clear to the water's edge and drop their ramps "in the dry." This was seldom possible in our Pacific war. These big landing ships proved heavy and sturdy enough to withstand the surf and swells without broaching, and they saved the day.

The 133rd Battalion, attached to the Fourth Marine Division, led the way for the Seabees at Iwo. The first Seabee to hit the beach was A. W. Barker (Chief Carpenter's Mate, Fort Smith, Ark.), a stockily-built former deputy sheriff. Barker, leading the security section of A-Company, landed at nine-seventeen, just behind the first Marine wave, on Yellow-1 Beach. The Marines were pinned down at the second terrace, 50 yards from the beach.

These Seabee "security sections" were supposed to form a second line behind the Marines, and to prevent any infiltrating Japs from reaching our dumps at the beach. Normally there are about forty men in such a section. There are fifteen BAR men, and each BAR man has one assistant. The others handle two 50-caliber machine guns and carry grenades.

"All we needed was grenades," Barker said. "We could throw a grenade as far as we could see."

Of the thirty BAR men and assistants in this section, three were killed and fourteen were wounded. The men killed were: Thomas J. Herman (Carpenter's Mate Third, Detroit, Mich.); Oscar C. Leaser (Carpenter's Mate Third, Pontiac, Mich.); and Julius C. McCarty (Water Tender Second, Graybull, Wyo.).*

A seven-man engineering detachment from A-Company was sent in to mark the beach. It was led by William L. Freitas (Carpenter's Mate First, San Francisco). Freitas and four others were hit, and only two men escaped injury. The two who escaped were George W. Priegnitz (Elec-

* The 133rd's total casualties at Iwo will be found at the end of this chapter.

trician's Mate Second, Elgin, Ill.) and Henry J. Prokoff (Carpenter's Mate First, Milford, Mich.).

A thirty-man shore party from A-Company, led by D. Davis (Chief Carpenter's Mate, Merchantville, N. J.), reached Yellow-1 Beach at nine-thirty with the first artillery. They were bringing in four 37-mm antitank guns in LCVPs. The problem at the beach was gunfire and broaching boats. Already so many craft were piled on the beach that Davis had great difficulty in finding a spot to land the guns. Ducks were stalled in the soft sand and could not get out of the water.

When the Seabees finally worked the four boats to the beach, they found the unloading of the guns in the boggy sand a backbreaking task. The seven-man crew handling the first gun was wiped out by a mortar shell at the very moment they pushed the gun onto the beach. Two of these men, Robert Pirie (Carpenter's Mate First, South Lynnfield, Mass.) and Neldon A. Day (Motor Machinist, Shop, Second, Moab, Utah) died under the gun they had brought in. Day was the battalion's ace softball pitcher, a drummer in the band, and was saving money to be married. Pirie was a modest, timid little fellow, the last man in the world you'd expect to see bringing in the first heavy gun to Yellow-1 Beach on Iwo Jima.

After they reached the beach, the A-Company assignment was to unload guns and ammunition, build dumps, pass the wounded into the boats, then get the boats off the beach. In all, the 150-man A-Company had sixty casualties. Two of these were twin brothers: Allen C. and Robert R. McCully, both Seamen First of Allison Park, Pa. The twins were hit by the same shell-burst and were evacuated together.

The 133rd's medical section came in as two groups. The junior medical officer, Dr. Francis C. Robinson (Lieut., MC,

43

USNR, Beaver, Pa.) landed on Blue-2 Beach with Jerome A. Brunswick (Pharmacist's Mate First, New York City) and six other corpsmen. Dr. Robinson was hit almost instantly, and the corpsmen sent him back out in the same boat in which he had landed.

The senior medical officer, Dr. Herbert R. Toombs (Lieut.-Comdr., MC, USNR, Westfield, Mass.), and the dental officer, Dr. Wilmer F. Lange (Lieut., DC, USNR, Cranford, N. J.), landed on Yellow-2 Beach with six corpsmen. A single shell virtually eliminated this party. Lawrence E. Betts (Pharmacist's Mate Third, Long Island City, N. Y.) was killed, and the two doctors were wounded seriously, along with Vincent J. Kelly (Chief Pharmacist's Mate, Williamsville, N. Y.); Robert J. Bell (Pharmacist's Mate, Third, Long Island City, N. Y.); and Maynard Kolakowski (Hospital Apprentice First, Glen Lyon, Pa.).

Most of B-Company, led by Lieut. Milton H. Birger (CEC, USNR, St. Louis, Mo.), landed on Blue-2 Beach, which quickly became known as "Blew-to-Hell" Beach. It was on the extreme right flank, next to the bluffs, and thus directly under the Jap guns emplaced on the high part of the island. B-Company suffered 30 casualties within the first few minutes, some of them from our own shells which were ricocheting off the cliffs. Chief Warrant Officer Thomas Y. McKinney (CEC, USNR, San Angelo, Tex.) was killed as he stepped off the boat.

Jess E. Simpson (Shipfitter First, Burbank, Cal.) did a strange thing. No sooner had he reached the beach than he turned to his friend, R. F. Heyn (Machinist Mate Third, Detroit, Mich.). "Here, Heyn," he said, "take my wallet; I won't be needing it." Heyn took the wallet reluctantly, and before he could protest, a machine-gun bullet had killed Simpson instantly.

C-Company's security section of 42 men was led by Chief

Warrant Officer Edwin E. Blythe (CEC, USNR, Charlotte, N. C.) and J. H. Wilson (Chief Electrician's Mate, Augusta, Ark.). Blythe and Wilson had pushed in to the first anti-tank trench when a shell-burst killed Blythe and knocked Wilson flat. Wilson led the section to the top of the third terrace and dug in at the edge of the airstrip. Two men were killed the first day: Leon M. Newsome (Seaman First, Franklin, Va.) and Robert J. Olson (Seaman Second, Anchorage, Alaska).

C-Company's beach party, led by Warrant Officer Marvin E. Smith (CEC, USNR, Yorkville, Ill.), landed on Yellow-1 at twelve-twenty, and was ordered by the beachmaster to run ammunition to the airstrip. The sand was so boggy that our vehicles could not operate, so these Seabees had to load themselves with grenades and ammunition and go scrambling over the terraces. To reach the airstrip, they had to go "over-the-top" three times because of the three terraces.

A very brave lad set the pattern for this ammunition run, and the men of the 133rd will never forget his courage. He was John C. Butts, Jr. (Shipfitter Third, Salt Lake City, Utah). Butts, a strapping fellow of twenty-four, with a wife and one child, made four runs to the airstrip and carried grenades right into the front lines. On his fifth run a Jap sniper killed him as he went over the top of the third terrace. His two buddies, J. E. Cashatt (Machinist Mate Third, Hamilton, Mo.) and Roy E. Cameron (Machinist's Mate First, Shawnee, Kan.) divided his ammunition load between them and carried it onto the airstrip.

A. J. Benard (Machinist's Mate First, Escanaba, Mich.) is a brawny bulldozer operator, veteran of many big construction jobs. His assignment was to bring in two big cats, two tanks, and two retrievers. Coming in on the LSM, Benard's biggest cat was hit and damaged, and he had to repair it hastily with garden hose and copper line ripped out of a refrigerator. When the LSM grounded, Benard was ready to unload, but he almost fainted when he saw what he had to do.

"I was so horrified," he told me, "that I thought I would fall off my cat. There were so many dead men in front of the ship that there was no way for me to unload and operate without crushing their bodies. I didn't think I could do it, but the ship already had been hit and the skipper was anxious to get off the beach. I had no choice but to go over them."

Benard and his two assistants, Frank A. Schimke (Machinist's Mate Third, Manistee, Mich.) and Lewis Rohde (Machinist's Mate Third, Salinas, Cal.), used their big machines to pull stalled vehicles through the sand; to dig revetments for dumps; and to bury both Japs and our own men. While Benard was digging the first cemetery on the island, his cat was hit by a mortar shell.

D-Company, led by boyish Lieut. W. H. Shears (CEC, USNR, Hutchinson, Kan.), landed next to the cliffs on Blue-1 and Blue-2 Beaches. There the Japs were particularly successful in setting off our ammunition dumps, and D-Company suffered many casualties.

Samuel A. Farmer (Chief Carpenter's Mate, Ada, Okla.) had been entrusted with a bottle of brandy on the ship, and the bottle was to be raffled off to D-Company. But when Farmer was shot in the leg, he said: "To hell with the raffle; this brandy can never be put to any better use." Then he drank the entire bottle.

A terrible retribution came to Russell G. Dalin (Machinist's Mate Third, Glendale, Cal.). Dalin was called "The Deacon" because he never gambled, but on the ship going to Iwo he backslid and won heavily at craps, so he wasn't surprised at what happened on the beach: his "dice arm" was blown off.

46

Cat operators were most unpopular because the Japs would use their big machines as targets, and Marvin A. Nottingham (Machinist's Mate Third, Big Horn, Wyo.) qualified as the "most cussed man on the beach." On the first night, Nottingham had to start his cat to pull guns up to the third terrace. The starting motor on these machines is much louder than the regular motor, and Nottingham had trouble starting. While his starting motor roared, again and again, like an airplane, great oaths were hurled at him from all over the beach, and the Japs began to send over mortar shells.

The 133rd's Headquarters Company—the "telephone girls," yeomen, cooks, bakers, etc.—landed at four P.M. One man from this company, Norman V. Dupuis (Ship's Cook First, Peshtigo, Wis.), was killed the next day while passing up ammunition for a machine-gun unit. Two others were wounded: Henry J. Goss (Ship's Cook Second, Exeter, N. H.) and John H. Mills (Ship's Cook Third, Childress, Tex.).

Henri Dupre (Chief Commissary Steward, Culver City, Cal.) was chef at Chicago's Palmer House for many years. More recently he catered for MGM's stable of darlings at Culver City. But on Iwo Jima he was operating twenty-four-hour coffee stations on the Yellow and Blue Beaches.

"Worse than Chicago, isn't it, Henri?" I asked him.

"The crowds are worse here," he answered, "but the gunfire is more accurate in Chicago."

Cleveland Washington (Steward's Mate First, Philadelphia, Pa.) was the first Negro to reach the beach. On the ship he had won $400 shooting craps, then began worrying about the Japs getting his money. Just before he left the Liberty ship, he had mailed $50 back to some church in Los Angeles and divided the rest of his money among seven of his friends so they could hold it for him.

47

"I was plenty brave out there in that VP," Washington told me. "All the time we was stalling around out there I kept saying: 'Let's go on in!' But just as we come up to that Blew-to-Hell Beach I looked over there and there was a man just blowed all to hell. I had to look again because I couldn't believe my eyes. I mean that man was blowed to bits! Then I lost my nerve. When they pushed me out of that boat, I just fell down in the water and knelt by a log and prayed. While I was kneeling and praying, a Marine major come by and yelled: 'You goddam Seabees, get out of the water and get up on that goddam terrace.' I didn't think I could move, but somehow I got up on the terrace, and there I seen where the blockbuster had busted.

"I jumped down in that big hole and started digging it deeper. A dog come up and smelled me to see if I was a Jap, then the dog started digging, too. Some of the other boys was in the hole with me, and an officer come up and yelled again: 'You goddam Seabees, you gotta carry ammunition up to the airstrip.' The other boys looked at me, and they knew I couldn't go, so the chief ordered me to stay there and guard the hole. I dug that hole so deep that I was afraid I'd be A. O. L. getting out. I stuck my head so deep in the sand when one of them blockbusters come over that a Seabee pulled me out, afraid I'd smother. I got so much of that sharp sand in my ears that for days, whenever I ate, I could hear grinding. The doc had a helluva time getting all that sand out of my head."

Another of the 133rd's cooks, Claude L. Wallace (Ship's Cook Third, Bridgewater, Me.), was halted in the darkness one night by Abe Levine (Seaman First, Brooklyn, N. Y.) and asked for the password. The password was presidents—any President of the United States. Wallace was so frightened that he could only shout his name: "Wallace."

"Okay, pass," Levine replied. "But, goddamit, the password's presidents, not vice-presidents."

On another night when the password was presidents, Levine threatened to shoot a wise-guy who answered: "Fillmore."

"Listen, wise-guy," Levine roared, "one more crack like that and you're a dead pigeon. When you give me the password, you give me Roosevelt, Washington, or Lincoln. Them's the only presidents I remember."

The 133rd Battalion was commanded by Lieut. Comdr. R. P. Murphy (CEC, USNR, Oakland, Cal.). Its number indicates that it was one of the last construction battalions to be formed. Before being attached to the Fourth Marines for the Iwo job, the battalion had seen brief service in Hawaii.

The veteran 31st Battalion was one of the Seabee "Honeymoon Battalions," so called because it spent a year in Bermuda building our naval and air installations. The 31st joined the Fifth Marines at Camp Tarawa on the island of Hawaii, and spent several months training there in the rain, wind, and red dust of Parker Brothers' big ranch.

The 31st landed on Green Beach, the left flank beach which began at the very base of Suribachi. A demolition party led by James L. Price (Chief Carpenter's Mate, Bunkie, La.) reached the beach at nine-twenty-two. Each member of the party was laden with a demolition kit containing TNT, blasting caps, and prima-cord. Their assignment was to blast obstacles out of the path of the landing craft, to blast landing craft off the beach, and to remove enemy mines. Others in this party included P. A. Paris (Gunner's Mate First, Colorado Springs, Col.); W. A. Stark (Machinist's Mate Second, Appleton, Wis.); David Boles (Gunner's Mate

49

Third, Los Angeles, Cal.); and Thomas E. Gilham, the photographer whose pictures of Iwo Jima appear in this book.

One of the most hazardous jobs which these men performed was the removal and disposal of our own duds after one of our ammunition dumps had been exploded by the Japs. Contrary to general belief, an ammunition dump does not go up in one big explosion when it is hit. It keeps popping for an hour or more. On a small island like Iwo, where every inch of ground has to be used, our explosive experts have to go into the dump and remove the unexploded shells, and no shell is quite so unpredictable as one which somehow has survived a dump explosion.

To combat the soft sand, the 31st began landing heavy cats on Green Beach about noon. Bales of steel "pierced plank" had been strapped to slides, and these slides had been loaded on LSMs. The cats were supposed to drag these heavy slides off the LSMs onto the beach where the Seabees could lay the "pierced plank" into roadways from the landing ramps up over the terraces.

The first cat to reach the beach and begin unloading the "pierced plank" was operated by Ben Massey (Seaman First, Plainview, Tex.). Massey was hit in the neck by machine-gun fire almost immediately, and he was carried back to the ship by Hollis Cash, Jr. (Machinist's Mate Second, Calera, Ala.). Cash took over the cat and completed the unloading.

A second bulldozer was brought in by William DeRamus Machinist's Mate Second, Billingsley, Ala.), but DeRamus, too, was hit by shrapnel which tore the blade off his machine. His place was taken by James D. Ballard (Machinist's Mate Third, Austin, Tex.).

When the Japs hit the first ammunition dump, Bernard P. Bobbitt (Seaman First, Littleton, N. C.) qualified as the luckiest man on Iwo Jima. He had eleven holes in his body from gunfire and shrapnel, but not one of the holes was in a vital spot.

On the fifth day the 31st began clearing the No. 1, or South, airstrip. It was here that the Seabees lost all respect for the Jap snipers. The most spectacular part of an airfield clearing operation is when the men line up at intervals of about two feet between shoulders and begin to crawl the length of the runway, picking up minute bits of shrapnel. The smallest sliver of shrapnel can explode a plane's tire and wreck it. A runway over which a battle has been fought literally must be combed between the fingers before it is safe.

When the men of the 31st lined up and began the combing process, the Japs began to snipe. But the combing went on. Only one man was hit: Emanuel R. Steed (Seaman First, Alabama City, Ala.); he was shot in the leg.

On the following day the 62nd Battalion brought its heavy equipment onto the South strip, and on D-Day-plus-10, while the battle still raged on the north end, the field was listed as operational for fighter planes.

As soon as Iwo was declared "secure," the Marines began to move out to make room for the Seabees and all their equipment, and for the Army Air Force units which were coming in to operate the Mustangs and night fighters and service the crippled B-29's.

This term "secure" needs explaining. When our high commands declared an island "secured" they only meant that all organized resistance had been broken; that all the enemy's heavy weapons had been knocked out or captured and his principal sources of supply liquidated. But "secured" did not mean that the island was free of Japs. There were still plenty of Japs around, armed with grenades and rifles, to be killed or captured.

On Iwo, long after the last Marine had left the island, the Seabees still were killing as many as twenty Japs a night. Where had these Japs hidden? Well, the island is a labyrinth of caves, and the Seabees were digging it up, blasting it, leveling it, picking it up, and moving it. In this process they would open up the caves where the Japs were hiding, and out would run the fugitives. It was like plowing into a rat nest and watching the rats run out. A Seabee with a tommy gun would be perched on top of a bulldozer or carryall, and when a cave was opened and Japs scurried, he'd give them the business.

When a Seabee battalion landed, the men lived for a while like prairie dogs on the beach. Then they would begin preparing their permanent camp site by leveling and grading the assigned living area. Most of the permanent camp sites were on the north end, in the "badlands" or "boon docks." As soon as a battalion began working on a camp site, it posted guards around the site and stretched "trip wire" attached to regularly spaced "trip flares." Thus the guards would sit in their dugouts at night and wait for a Jap to come sneaking in, looking for food. The Jap would trip over a wire, set off a trip flare, and find himself bathed in light. But his consternation would be short-lived, because the Seabees are the "shootingest bastards" in the service. They never shot less than a clip at any Jap.

In fact, it was bruited about the Pacific that the Seabee method for doing guard duty was to lay down a constant curtain of fire—just in case. There are men, including myself, who would rather have met a Jap any night than a Seabee guard.

The battalion which did most of the Jap-killing during the mopup on Iwo was the famous "Shooting Eighth." The Eighth was an old Dutch Harbor outfit; they were at Dutch when the Japs were threatening to come in there. They were a tough bunch.

The Eighth set up the first fuel tanks and laid the first fuel lines at Iwo. They had to use net tenders in that rough water to lay their lines out to tankers; no smaller craft could handle the lines. They picked the wildest section of the "badlands" for their camp site, and sent their patrols up there to exterminate the Japs.

The Japs got in the first lick. They ambushed the Eighth's survey party and killed C. A. Van Eps (Carpenter's Mate Third, Callender, Ia.). Two other men were wounded: E. F. Young (Machinist's Mate First, Toledo, O.) and F. C. Mc-Gowan (Chief Shipfitter, Jacksonville, Fla.). Then the Eighth's cave blasters went into action.

I accompanied one of these cave-blasting outfits on several patrols. It was led by G. E. Barber (Chief Gunner's Mate, Lubbock, Tex.) and L. J. Byfield (Chief Gunner's Mate, El Paso, Tex.). Both Barber and Byfield were rangy, 40-year-old Texans, veterans of years in the potash mines. Both were graduates of the Navy's Mine and Demolition School at Hawaii. Two of their rugged associates in the cave-blasting business were S. Bencich (Gunner's Mate Second, Kellogg, Idaho) and E. A. Bennett (Gunner's Mate Second, North Hollywood, Cal.). Bencich, too, was a bearded ex-potash miner.

Of all the cold-blooded, methodical, tobacco-chewing Jap annihilators I have seen in the Pacific, this Barber-Byfield outfit impressed me as being the most fearsome and efficient. They had a system that never failed.

Entering the "boon docks" on Iwo, Barber and Byfield always carried along a couple of Jap prisoners. They'd approach a cave mouth stealthily and cover it with tommy guns. Then they'd send in one of the prisoners, waving a strip of toilet paper, to see how many Japs were in the cave and whether or not they wanted to surrender. If the Jap prisoner did not come out in ten minutes, Barber and Byfield moved a charge of dynamite into the cave mouth— 500-pound charges were not uncommon—and set off a blast which rocked the island and closed the cave.

If the Jap prisoner came out and reported no Japs in the cave, Barber and Byfield blasted it shut just the same. The Jap might be lying. If the Jap prisoner reported that Japs were in the cave but wouldn't surrender, Barber and Byfield sent in the second Jap prisoner to try to persuade his countrymen.

"I like to give the little bastards two chances," Barber told me, "but it makes me no difference whether they come out or not."

If the Japs in the cave decided to surrender—and some of them did—then the prisoner explained how to go about it. This process of surrender was more or less standard and rather intricate. First, the surrendering Japs had to remove their clothes *while they were in the cave*. If a Jap came out with his clothes on, there was too much danger that he might have a grenade hidden on him, so each Jap took off his clothes, grasped either a surrender leaflet or a piece of toilet paper, and proceeded slowly out of the cave mouth, with his hands up and waving the toilet paper.

This toilet paper, of course, was the white symbol of surrender. Since white flags were not plentiful, all cave-blasting outfits carried along a roll of toilet paper to provide the Japs something white to wave.

It was always a tense moment when the Japs started coming out of the cave; there was so much danger of treachery. Trigger fingers were tight as the naked Japs filed out, lined up, and turned around for inspection. Then the Jap prisoner brought out the clothing, shook out each piece, handed it to Barber, who shook and examined the clothing,

54

then passed it on to the Jap owner. Eventually the Japs were clothed again, and they marched ahead of the patrol.

"I usta' could smell Japs," Barber said, "but now I smell like 'em myself."

When I was with Barber and Byfield, they had killed about ninety Japs and taken a score of prisoners. Barber showed me in his notebook where one Jap prisoner had printed the English words: HELP ME.

"Some of 'em are kinda pitiful," Barber explained. "This Jap here probably saved my life. He pointed out a Jap who was just about to fire at me. I hate to be soft, but it's pitiful to think that men can be so caught in some web that they'll act like these Japs. Yet it'll boil your blood to see some of the things the ratty little bastards will do. It always makes me want to kill 'em when I find 'em with American cigarets. I know that they got those cigarets off'a dead Marines."

Barber told me about the biggest cave he had blasted. He went into the cave himself and kept the Japs driven back while Byfield and the others rigged a 500-pound charge. Then he ran out, and they set off the charge.

"The charge didn't close up the mouth, the cave was so big," he said. "Two Japs come running out after the blast, and I tommy-gunned 'em. Two more come out and fell on their faces, yelling 'ditty koy,' so we let 'em surrender. Then I went back into the cave, and I never seen such a mess o' Japs. That blast had smashed their backbones, their jaw-bones, and some o' their skulls. One of 'em threw a grenade at me, so I finished killing 'em."

One of the two Japs from that cave who surrendered explained that he had been able to escape in the "confusion" caused by the blast; that the confusion had prevented his officers from killing him.

"You create more confusion," he told Barber, "and more Japs escape and surrender."

55

This same Jap said to Barber: "You come in cave; you very brave man."

"Naw, I'm just crazy," Barber replied.

I asked Barber if he had picked up any of the Japanese language.

"I just know 'ditty koy,'" he drawled. "It means something like 'Do you want to surrender?' That's all the goddam Jap I need to know. If he wants to surrender, okay; if he don't, okay. It makes me no difference."

Barber had a valuable collection of souvenirs which included a fine Japanese clock, a jeweled hara-kiri knife, and a pair of powerful binoculars. "I figger I'll get some of that purty silk up around Tokyo," he said, "and then I'll take all this stuff back to Texas to my wife and kids."

Two of my friends of the Eighth Battalion, who had better not be identified, bought themselves some barber tools in Hawaii. For sixty days on the ship coming to Iwo, they generously gave the Marines free haircuts.

"That was a nice gesture," I commented, "but you should have charged a little something for all your work."

"Naw," they explained. "You see, we never cut any hair before. We were just picking up a new trade, so we didn't have the nerve to charge for it."

The 62nd Battalion held its "Stateside Sweepstakes" while I was on Iwo. The battalion had been overseas two years, and its 703 "original men" were qualified for Stateside furloughs under a new Navy rotation plan. But under the plan only about twenty-five per cent of the men a month could leave the battalion. The 62nd could send 200 of the 703 men home by the "next available transportation." How were the 200 to be selected?

At first the commanding officer called in the doctors and the chaplain, and the group attempted to select 200 men on the basis of age, family difficulties, physical condition, etc. But they soon gave this up and decided that the only fair and satisfactory way to select the 200 would be by public drawing.

The announced "Stateside Sweepstakes," with its 200 priceless awards, was the biggest news on Iwo Jima since the island had been "secured." The pharmacist's mates supplied 703 capsules; the yeomen, working under an armed guard and the watchful eye of the chaplain, put the 703 names in the capsules; and the cooks supplied a wire basket— for cooking potatoes—to hold the capsules.

The drawing was done from the back of a truck, while the entire battalion crowded around and hung on the announcement of each name. The names were drawn, one by one, by Chaplain C. E. Godwin (Lieutenant, CEC, USNR, Ahoskie, N. C.), and he read each name over the loudspeaker as he drew it.

I'll never forget the drama of that drawing. It was late afternoon, and most of the men were dirty from a day's work on the Central, or B-29 Airstrip. I stood on the truck and looked down into their begrimed, anxious faces. A chance to go home! Can you imagine what two years on Pacific islands means? Two years of haunting loneliness? Filth? Bugs? Disease? Two Christmases away from home? There were many men in that crowd who had children they had never seen. Others had lost their wives; their whole worlds had changed back there. Now, each time the chaplain's hand dipped into that basket, there was a chance for each man to go home.

There were wisecracks as the men tried to relieve the tightness in their throats.

"I can't go, chaplain; my laundry's out."

"Don't draw my name, chaplain; I got a package in the mail."

Some of the men whooped when their names were called; others wept without shame. Some of them steeled themselves against disappointment with remarks like: "Aw, if there was just 201 capsules in there, I couldn't win."

The first name drawn was that of Milton J. McKinnon (Carpenter's Mate First, Chicago, Ill.). When he came up for me to make his picture, I asked him how he felt. He just shook his head and swallowed and wiped his eyes.

The second name drawn was that of John J. Mingarelli (Seaman First, Chicago, Ill.). He was a brash youngster with a fancy beard, and his friends were pounding him on the back.

"Think of all those shortages back in Chicago," I kidded him. "You don't want to go back there, do you?"

"Hell, man," he answered, "there ain't no shortage of what I'll be looking for!"

The man in charge of all the work on Iwo Jima was Commodore Bob Johnson (CEC, USNR, Chicago, Ill.). He is a lanky, sun-browned construction veteran with close-cropped, iron-gray hair and an easy-flowing chuckle which may erupt into a whoop if the story is funny enough. In the early days on Iwo, he lived in a "gopher hole" near the beach. He wore the Seabee "greens"—coarse, loose-fitting pants and coat—and the green cloth cap. Frequently he was mistaken for a Seabee chief petty officer, and this pleased him. One evening he and I sat on a pile of sandbags and discussed the job.

58

"You know," he said, "this is the most expensive piece of real estate the United States of America ever purchased. Forty-three hundred of the finest lads who ever bore arms for our country are buried here. Another 20,000 were wounded. That means we paid 550 lives and 2500 wounded for every square mile of this volcanic rock. Pretty expensive, huh?"

"Yes, sir," I replied. "And it adds up to a lot of responsibility, doesn't it?"

"That's what I'm driving at," he said. "It's up to me and these 7000 other Seabees to see that the country gets value received. The men realize the responsibility; they were here and saw what the island cost. That's why they work so hard. We're going to make this island the most efficient aircraft carrier in the world.

"First, we've got to complete the grading. We've got *three million yards* of grading to do. It would take the Japs ten years to move that much dirt. We'll do it in a few weeks because we've got the equipment and the men who know how. We're working on three airfields now. The Central field, for B-29's, will have an 8500-foot runway plus plenty of taxiway and hardstands for those big planes.

"We've got to have plenty of space for the Mustangs, since this is their main base for the Tokyo run. We'll take care of hundreds of those fast babies. Then there are the night fighters. Those Black Widows are ugly airplanes, but we've got to have them to keep those Bettys from sneaking down here some night and setting us afire.

"Eventually these three airfields will have expanded so much that they'll all be one big airfield. In fact, I laughed and told the General that we might as well level the whole damned island off, blacktop it, and then just paint the airstrips in.

"Along with the airstrips we are building some roads. There'll be twenty miles of paved road and twenty miles of secondary road. We'll blacktop the roads, the airstrips, and taxiways. That blacktopping is a pretty big job. We'll have to mix and pour about as much asphalt here as we'd have to handle at home if we paved a road thirty feet wide and 100 miles long."

"Do you have enough men to complete all this on schedule?" I asked.

"Yeah," he answered confidently. "The 62nd is the 'lead battalion' on the Central airstrip. They are a great outfit. The 31st—just as good—is 'lead battalion' on the North strip; and the 133rd, in spite of losing a fourth of its men, will finish the South strip. All the other battalions are contributing earth-moving equipment and personnel to the airstrip jobs.

"The 90th Battalion will build the two big tank farms. You can imagine how much gasoline we'll need here. The 95th will concentrate on housing; we've got to house and feed all these pilots and ground crews. The 106th will build the housing and installations for the Naval Operating Base.

"Then we've got to have a harbor and some piers so we can bring Liberty ships in here and unload them. We've got to build a breakwater first. The 301st Battalion—they're harbor specialists, you know—will sink some concrete block ships; then the 8th Battalion will drive sheet piling along both sides of the sunken ships and fill in over the ships with dirt and rock. The 8th will also build the piers, and the 23rd Special—stevedores—will handle the cargo.

"There'll be a lot of little jobs to do. Our fresh-water supply is a problem. We're distilling about 50,000 gallons a day now, and we're using 350,000 gallons of saline water a day to 'bind' our airstrips. We're going to sink twenty 160-foot wells on the island to get fresh water. But we've got some old Texas oil-well boys who can handle that chore without any trouble."

"You make it all sound mighty easy," I said.

He chuckled. "Well, it is easy when you've got the organization and the men and the machines. This kind of war is right down the American alley. They say England won Waterloo on the 'playing fields of Eton.' I say we won this war when we built Boulder Dam, the TVA projects, the skyscrapers, and all the other big things we've got. While we were building our country we trained the men and developed the machines and acquired the know-how to do just the kind of job we have to do here on Iwo Jima."

The morning before I left Iwo Jima I rode over to the big, cross-shaped Fifth Marine cemetery. I strolled down the long aisles of white crosses, looking for the men I had known. On many of the graves Marines and Seabees already had placed pieces of the yellow, volcanic rock bearing crudely chiseled names, birth dates, and some inscription like: "In memory of my buddy," or "a true comrade." The longest inscription was: "Reach down, dear Lord, for this Marine who gave his all that we might live." The shortest inscription was on the grave of Phil Pittser of the 133rd Seabees, a youngster from Springfield, Colorado. It said: "A good guy."

The thing which affected me most, however, was the birth dates. There were many 1925's and, since they had fallen in February, 1945, these men were less than twenty years old. There were even more 1926's—less than nineteen when they had died. And there were some 1927's—barely eighteen!

"My God!" I thought. "I was leaving high-school when these kids were born!"

I felt very old as I walked out of that cemetery.

That afternoon I rode up to the top of Mt. Suribachi. The 31st Battalion had completed the road. Where the Marines had once spent four bloody days scaling the peak, we could now zip up in a jeep. The jeep driver was Irving Katz (Carpenter's Mate Third, Brooklyn, N. Y.), who is a former Brooklyn cab driver. Because Katz was constantly taking the wrong road and losing himself, I had dubbed him "Wrong-Way Katz," and had ribbed him by pitying all the poor fares who would be overcharged when they rode with him in Brooklyn. He had explained to me, however, that Brooklyn cab drivers always know where they are when they are in Brooklyn, but when they have to be away from Brooklyn they just naturally don't give a damn.

With Katz and me were Bernard R. Cordes (Chief Specialist, Los Angeles, Cal.) and the bearded, philosophical, aforementioned photographer, Tom Gilham. Cordes, a Seabee correspondent, was a former Los Angeles *Times* man; and Gilham had had an adventurous career which included service with the Army on Corregidor.

As the four of us stood on Suribachi and looked north across the pork chop, we could see the B-29's coming back from Tokyo. We could pick out the big ships which had feathered propellors indicating dead engines, and we watched them swing wide into the Iwo "traffic circle" and come in to land on the Central airstrip.

"Those 29 crews really love this island," Cordes remarked. "I've seen them jump out of their damaged planes and hug the ground."

"Sure," Gilham said. "This place is the difference between life and death for them. A lot of them went in the drink before we got this strip."

We drove back down to the Central field, and I hitched a ride on a B-29 going back to Guam. As we took off and circled back over the island, the engineer punched me and pointed down to that ugly mass of sulphurous wasteland.

"That's the sweetest little island in all the world," he said. "Three days ago we landed here all shot to hell. We couldn't have stayed aloft another ten minutes. Now we are as good as new. Yessir, that's a sweet place."

The 133rd Battalion's total casualties at Iwo Jima are as follows:

KILLED IN ACTION

OFFICERS

Chief Warrant Officer Edwin E. Blythe, CEC, USNR, Charlotte, N. C.

Chief Warrant Officer Thomas Y. McKinney, CEC, USNR, San Angelo, Tex.

MEN

Joseph M. Benson, CM2c, Logan, Utah.
Lawrence E. Betz, PhM3c, Long Island City, N. Y.
Norman L. Bondurant, MMS3c, Buffalo Gap, S. D.
John C. Butts, Jr., SF3c, Salt Lake City, Utah.
Walter S. Coleman, CM3c, Burlington, Ia.
Francis J. Craig, CM3c, Rhinelander, Wis.
Paul A. Davidich, MM2c, Helena, Mont.
Neldon A. Day, MMS2c, Moab, Utah.
J. D. De Money, EM1c, Houston, Tex.
Norman V. Dupuis, SC1c, Peshtigo, Wis.
Elza J. Evans, MM1c, Spiro, Okla.
Glenn C. Floe, CM2c, Tacoma, Wash.
Hans Gatterer, EM1c, Bellaire, N. Y.
Robert A. Geer, S1c, Jewett City, Conn.
John B. Grudzina, S1c, Milwaukee, Wis.
Marvin C. Haynes, Jr., SF3c, Cairo, Ill.
Thomas J. Herman, CM3c, Detroit, Mich.
Arthur A. Herron, S2c, Montgomery, Ala.
Oscar C. Leaser, CM3c, Pontiac, Mich.
Robert J. Martin, Ptr3c, Elwood City, Pa.
Julius C. McCarty, WT2c, Graybull, Wyo.

Orie Millard, Jr., S1c, Everett, Wash.
George F. Mitchell, S1c, Harrisburg, Pa.
Herbert G. Moxey, CM2c, St. Louis, Mo.
Leon M. Newsome, S1c, Franklin, Va.
Harry A. Noll, CM1c, Reading, Pa.
Robert J. Olson, S2c, Anchorage, Alaska.
Joseph A. Peck, MoMM2c, Erie, Pa.
Robert Pirie, CM1c, Lynnfield, Mass.
Philander F. Pittser, Jr., S1c, Springfield, Col.
Malcolm Rose, F1c, Bingham Canyon, Utah.
Leonard F. Sale, Jr., S1c, Los Angeles, Cal.
Jess E. Simpson, SF1c, Burbank, Cal.
Earl E. Smull, Cm3c, Wilkinsburg, Pa.
Casper W. Tomasetti, SF3c, Ebensburg, Pa.

WOUNDED IN ACTION

OFFICERS

Lieut. Paul F. Cook, CEC, USNR, Cincinnati, O.
Lieut. (jg) Leslie R. Fleming, CEC, USNR, Elbridge, Tenn.
Lieut. Donald H. Greenfield, CEC, USNR, Centralia, Ill.
Lieut. (jg) Robert G. Jones, CEC, USNR, Kohler, Wis.
Lieut. Wilmer F. Lange, DC, USNR, Cranford, N. J.
Lieut. Roy B. O'Brien, CEC, USNR, Washington, D. C.
Lieut. (jg) John J. Rath, SC, USNR, Steubenville, O.
Lieut. Herschell H. Richmond, ChC, USNR, Wellsburg, W. Va.
Lieut. Francis C. Robinson, MC, USNR, Beaver, Pa.
Lieut. Sam R. Stanbery, CEC, USNR, New Orleans, La.
Lieut.-Comdr. Herbert R. Toombs, MC, USNR, Westfield, Mass.
Warrant Officer Owen S. White, CEC, USNR, Nesom, La.

MEN

Herman J. Abbott, GM1c, Van, W. Va.
J. L. Abernathy, MM1c, San Angelo, Tex.
Morton Aclander, PhM3c, Brooklyn, N. Y.
John F. Archipoli, EM2c, Huntington, N. Y.
Russell Armitage, SK2c, Auburn, R. I.
William B. Armstrong, SF1c, Akron, O.
Harry T. Ashworth, EM1c, Fall River, Mass.

IWO JIMA

Dennis C. Barnett, CCM, Rio Dell, Cal.
John Bas, MM2c, Brooklyn, N. Y.
Clarence A. Bassinger, MoMM2c, Alief, Texas.
Louis A. Bean, CCM, Eugene, Ore.
George J. Beaudin, MM3c, Lowell, Mass.
Albert J. Belanger, SF1c, Whitinsville, Mass.
Robert J. Bell, PhM3c, Long Island City, N. Y.
Edward J. Bergeron, MM2c, West Swanzy, N. H.
Randall R. Bickell, CM1c, Harrisburg, Pa.
John Billman, Ptr2c, Philadelphia, Pa.
Kenneth D. Blair, MM3c, Tucson, Ariz.
Sidney W. Blakeway, S1c, Moorhead, Minn.
Richard W. Blomstrand, CM1c, St. Paul, Minn.
James L. Boso, CCM, Summersville, W. Va.
Charles J. Boyle, MM2c, Hinsdale, N. H.
Kenneth M. Bryan, MMS3c, Horseheads, N. Y.
T. Bell Caperton, CCM, Leland, Miss.
Ralph W. Carey, SF3c, Anderson, Ind.
O. Lawton Chandler, BM1c, Anaheim, Cal.
Lyman Cobb, S1c, Alameda, Cal.
Charles W. Cole, Jr., MM3c, Mishawaka, Ind.
William M. Coney, SF3c, Jersey City, N. J.
Clifford K. Connor, EM1c, Trinity, Ala.
Joseph Coppola, MM2c, Port Chester, N. Y.
Victor D. Cortez, SF1c, Dearborn, Mich.
Albert C. Cothren, WT3c, Lawton, Okla.
William H. Courtney, S1c, Stockton, Cal.
Orbin Curnutt, MM3c, Fruitvale, Texas.
Russell G. Dalin, MM3c, Glendale, Cal.
Joseph A. Damico, S1c, Windber, Pa.
Harry C. Davis, MM1c, Duchesne, Utah.
Howard A. Day, CM1c, Glencoe, Okla.
Theodore R. Demyttenaere, CM1c, Westport, Conn.
Estell Dunlap, MM3c, Lyndon, Ill.
John R. Enders, EM1c, Utica, N. Y.
Charles D. Euston, SF3c, Lebanon, Pa.
Sam A. Farmer, CCM, Ada, Okla.
Edward T. Feeney, CM3c, Wheeling, W. Va.
Jack W. Ferguson, SF1c, Yale, Okla.
Phil J. Finazzo, Ptr3c, St. Louis, Mo.

Philip Franz, CM3c, Locust Valley, N. Y.
William L. Freitas, CM1c, San Francisco, Cal.
Richard D. Fries, S1c, Sioux City, Ia.
Earl M. Gehm, MM3c, Montclare, Pa.
Sidney Gelman, S1c, Pittsburgh, Pa.
Edward Gillis, S1c, North Wilmington, Mass.
Herbert M. Gold, MM3c, Brooklyn, N. Y.
George C. Gordon, MoMM2c, Pensacola, Fla.
Henry J. Goss, SC2c, Exeter, N. H.
G. Daniel Greene, CM2c, Oglethorpe, Ga.
James T. Greene, EM3c, Villa Park, Ill.
Vernon C. Greenwell, S1c, Harvey, Ill.
Merrill G. Guest, EM1c, San Diego, Cal.
Charles A. Gulyas, S1c, Toledo, O.
Daniel T. Gustafson, Cox, Boston, Mass.
Richard L. Gutierrez, S1c, Los Angeles, Cal.
James M. Hall, S1c, Rincon, N. M.
Owen S. Hammond, M1c, Lewiston, Me.
Clyde Y. Harris, MaM3c, Caldwell, O.
Milton H. Harth, MoMM3c, Minneapolis, Minn.
H. Clarence Hartwig, SF3c, St. Louis, Mo.
Orrin C. Harvey, EM1c, Chicago, Ill.
Gerald R. Hedrick, S1c, Mansfield, O.
Gerald O. Heinz, SF1c, Streator, Ill.
Donald E. Higbee, SF2c, Laurel Gardens, Pa.
John T. Hinson, S2c, Great Falls, S. C.
Earl R. Hocking, S1c, LaSalle, Ill.
Royce D. Holley, S2c, Marks, Miss.
Richard R. Hopkins, S2c, Port Arthur, Tex.
L. Byron Hunter, CEM, Shelton, Wash.
Clifford S. Hupp, S1c, Lowell, O.
Frank T. Jelinek, S1c, Riverside, Ill.
Stephen J. Jerebic, CM3c, Chicago, Ill.
William L. Johnson, S1c, San Diego, Cal.
Albert C. Jones, MM3c, Detroit, Mich.
Richard D. Jones, S1c, Cumberland, Md.
George W. Jozwick, S1c, Baltimore, Md.
Frank P. Kelly, SF2c, Newport, R. I.
Vincent J. Kelly, CPhM, Williamsville, N. Y.
Fred H. Kettering, Ptr3c, Pittsburgh, Pa.

John W. Knerr, MM3c, Pitman, Pa.
Maynard Kolakowski, HA1c, Glen Lyon, Pa.
William J. Konop, S1c, Minneapolis, Minn.
Edward J. Kowalski, F1c, Jefferson, O.
John R. Kromer, CSF, Oklahoma City, Okla.
Ernest L. Kubosh, EM1c, Texarkana, Tex.
Elmer F. Kuether, SF1c, Milwaukee, Wis.
Stanley A. Kukas, S1c, Dowagiac, Mich.
Andrew Kurtz, S1c, Munhall, Pa.
Harold O. Laird, MM3c, Arcadia, Cal.
Dominick J. Lippre, SF2c, Philadelphia, Pa.
Elmer M. Lepley, MM2c, Cumberland, Md.
Robert A. Mann, S1c, Oxford, O.
Charles Mantovani, CM3c, Lower Falls, Mass.
Charles Marchese, CM1c, Lawrence, Mass.
Alfred D. Marlin, CM3c, Westport, Conn.
Dean S. Marshall, BM1c, Milwaukee, Wis.
Edward M. Maull, MMS1c, Buffalo, N. Y.
Blair C. McCann, MM3c, South Boston, Mass.
Allen C. McCully, S1c, Allison Park, Pa.
Robert R. McCully, S1c, Allison Park, Pa.
James J. McGovern, CM3c, Providence, R. I.
Cecil R. Means, MM3c, Charleston, W. Va.
Walter Mehrholz, SF2c, Chicago, Ill.
Fred E. Miller, S1c, West Unity, O.
John H. Mills, SC3c, Childress, Tex.
William G. Molina, GM2c, Flagstaff, Ariz.
Marshall R. Music, BM1c, Tacoma, Wash.
Charles A. Napier, Jr., SF1c, Litchfield, Ill.
Robert G. Nelson, EM1c, Talbot, Ind.
Charles W. Nielson, MoMM3c, Fairview, Utah.
William G. Olitsky, BM2c, Bronx, N. Y.
Harry H. Olson, CM3c, Huntington Park, Cal.
Thomas E. O'Malley, SC1c, LeSueur, Minn.
Edward F. Pasquette, S1c, Holyoke, Mass.
Donald W. Parrott, S2c, Philadelphia, Pa.
L. D. Peyton, MMS1c, Houston, Tex.
Michael Potoshnik, Jr., SF2c, Moxee City, Wash.
Allen E. Powell, CM1c, Portland, Ore.
Oscar L. Prewitt, CM1c, Glendale, Cal.

Floyd J. Pysnik, MoMM1c, St. Paul, Minn.
Charles L. Railey, CM2c, Redding, Cal.
Leo W. Rawlinson, F1c, Dallas, Tex.
Daniel T. Raymond, MM3c, Bayonne, N. J.
Eldridge W. Reynolds, SF3c, Max Meadows, Va.
Walter J. Reynolds, CM3c, Portland, Ore.
Thomas E. Robinson, SF3c, Rockland, Mass.
Norman C. Rodgers, Jr., CM2c, Takoma Park, Md.
Robert F. Salter, EM1c, Gloucester, Mass.
Elmer P. Sample, MMS2c, Lancaster, O.
Robert B. Sanders, CM3c, Altadena, Cal.
Carl J. Scott, S1c, Portland, Ore.
William R. Scott, Cox, Portland, Ore.
Robert R. Shank, MM1c, Poughkeepsie, N. Y.
Joseph B. Sharp, CSp, Toledo, O.
Russell J. Siemers, WT3c, Brooklyn, N. Y.
James G. Sigalos, S1c, Chicago, Ill.
Lowell O. Sims, MM3c, Wanatah, Ind.
Victor W. Sleuter, CM1c, Sacramento, Cal.
Howard C. Smith, CM1c, North Syracuse, N. Y.
William J. Smith, MM3c, Trenton, N. J.
Douglas J. Spenningsby, CM3c, Huron, S. D.
Lawrence M. Starr, GM3c, Huntington Beach, Cal.
Leon H. Strickland, MMS2c, Savannah, Ga.
Fred A. Stuhl, CM1c, Millville, N. J.
Andrew Sulock, MM2c, Syracuse, N. Y.
Alfred R. Teehee, SF3c, Peru, Kan.
Raymond E. Templin, F1c, Watseka, Ill.
Anthony J. Terico, GM1c, Houston, Tex.
Francis J. Tighe, F1c, Indianapolis, Ind.
William J. Tigue, S1c, West Chester, Pa.
Clinton J. Trefethen, MM3c, Kerby, Ore.
Walter A. Truty, MMS1c, Chicago, Ill.
Arthur J. Vaeth, S1c, Irvington, N. J.
Robert J. Vetter, M3c, Bayshore, Cal.
Leonard F. Vilet, SF2c, Riverside, Ill.
Edward F. Wasilius, SF2c, Wilkes-Barre, Pa.
James B. Welch, CM1c, Stockton, Cal.
James E. Wilson, CM3c, Charleston, W. Va.
Karl E. Zakrison, BM1c, Buffalo, N. Y.

III

TINIAN

OF THE three islands we developed to form the gigantic American base in the Marianas, Tinian received the least publicity. Guam, as headquarters of the Pacific Fleet and the 21st Bomber Command, was constantly in the news, and Saipan got all the early credit for the B-29 operations. Yet Tinian's story is as dramatic as either of the others, and in some respects is even more interesting.

Tinian was simply an aerial artillery pedestal; it was an aircraft carrier for B-29's. It had six great 8500-foot runways, hardstands * for many hundreds of B-29's, and all the necessary taxiways. Its builders called it "the greatest military airdrome in the world." Everything on the island—its vast bomb dumps and fuel storage, its artificial harbor, warehouses, and machine shops, its highways and communications—was there to serve the B-29. Like Iwo Jima, Tinian was an "all Seabee job." The Army Engineers assisted the Seabees on Saipan and Guam, but Tinian, as a construction job, was an exclusive Seabee gift to the B-29's. Fifteen Seabee battalions had a part in the gift.

Tinian is the "Manhattan of the Pacific." It is almost exactly the same length as Manhattan Island—about eleven miles—and is only slightly wider at its greatest width, about

* A "hardstand" is the parking place for an airplane. It must be as hard-surfaced as a runway, since the B-29's 70 tons of weight is concentrated on its tripod landing gear.

five miles. It covers approximately forty-eight square miles and has thirty-four miles of shore line, mostly rocky cliffs. Most of the island is flat. Its northern tip lies three miles southwest of Saipan, and it extends along a north-south line.

In the Japanese development scheme, Tinian was one big sugar-cane plantation. Its 15,339 inhabitants, mostly Okinawans, had been brought in by Nanyo Kohatsu Kabushiki Kaisha, the Japanese South Seas Development Company, which operated very much like the old British East India Company. Tinian, like Saipan, had its big syrup mill, a narrow-gauge railroad for hauling cane to the mill, and a few roads.

The railroad's rails, incidentally, were made in Birmingham, Alabama, twenty-five years ago by the Tennessee Coal, Iron & Railroad Co. The Seabees, some of them former employees of the T. C. I., ripped up the rails and used them for telephone and power line poles.

The island's shopping center was Tinian Town, and this was knocked flat during the assault. However, one monolith of an interesting prehistoric ruin was preserved. In 1565 the Spanish historian, Miguel Lopez Gusuby, found 12 pillars on Tinian which bore inscriptions indicating that they were remains of the prehistoric Taga race. Between then and 1900, all but two of the monoliths crumbled, and an American bomb destroyed one of these. The Seabees, however, took steps to preserve the last of these monoliths, which still bears the ancient Taga inscriptions found by the Spanish historian.

Despite its lack of any semblance of a harbor and despite the coral cliffs which surround most of the island, our planners found Tinian desirable because: (1) It was flat; (2) it contained an abundance of coral for roads and runways; and (3) there appeared to be plenty of fresh water. Long before we invaded the Marianas the planners, too, had noted

70

Tinian's resemblance to Manhattan. They had dubbed it "Tinimanhat," and had begun laying out its roads according to the Manhattan street scheme. When they were through Tinian had a Broadway running down its north-south axis; Broadway and 42nd Street was the nerve center of the island; North Field was "up in Harlem"; and West Field and the harbor were over along Riverside Drive. If you lived below 23rd Street you were pretty far "downtown," and if you were up around 96th Street, everyone knew you were an "uptowner." There was a Radio City, a Wall Street, an India House, a Battery, and a Park Row, all located in the same relative positions that they occupy on Manhattan.

In the assault phase, when it was imperative that traffic not go astray, the east side perimeter road was marked with red signs, the west side with green signs—just like New York subway guides.

The thousands of Americans who have never been to New York but who have lived on Tinian will find Manhattan's streets no puzzle when they reach that tight little isle.

Saipan was "secured" on July 9, 1944, and Tinian was invaded July 24, 1944, in a shore-to-shore operation from Saipan. Elements of the 2nd and 4th Marine Divisions, "re-enforced" by the 18th and 121st Seabee Battalions, handled the assault. A detachment of the 302nd Pontoon Battalion, Seabees, assisted in the landing. The Marine story has been told—the island was secured in nine days—but the Seabee story, which involved an improvised landing device, is told here for the first time.

Landing on Tinian presented several difficulties. First was the matter of the coral cliffs. There were no flat beaches. It was desirable that the landing be made on the northern

71

end of Tinian, the sector closest to our kick-off point on Saipan. Yet intelligence had disclosed only two very narrow breaks in the cliffs, and these were guarded heavily by the Japs.

It is extremely dangerous to attempt a large-scale landing through narrow, bottleneck beaches. Suppose the beaches become clogged with smashed or broached landing craft, as even the 3500-yard stretch at Iwo threatened to become? Heavy swells at Tinian made this more than a possibility. Suppose there is delay in cutting the "access roads" from the narrow beach out to the main road or to open country and traffic snarls? Suppose enemy artillery has the narrow beach zeroed-in, and your own wrecked equipment halts the flow of your supplies and re-enforcements? These are some of the nightmares of amphibious planning. A narrow beach is an open invitation to disaster.

If Tinian was not to be another Tarawa, the first men and vehicles would have to go in over cliffs. Two sectors of "cliff" were selected where the precipitous rise from the water's edge ranged between six and ten feet, and the Seabees were ordered to devise a method whereby tanks and trucks could scale this height.

Commodore Paul J. Halloran (CEC, USN, New York, N. Y.), commanding all Seabees moving to Tinian, sketched out a heavy scaling ladder or ramp which he thought might work. He showed his sketches to Leslie G. Smith (Chief Carpenter's Mate, Los Angeles, Cal., 121st Battalion), and Smith completed the plans. Fifty-four hours later, Seabees of the 18th and 121st Battalions had built the first experimental "tank ladder" out of materials salvaged from the Jap sugar mill on Saipan.

This ramp, or "tank ladder," had to be heavy enough to support a Sherman tank. It had to be so devised that some amphibious vehicle could carry it from Saipan across three miles of open water to the Tinian cliffs, and there it had to be set in place, under fire, in not more than two minutes!

The Seabees proposed to carry the ramp on an LVT (landing vehicle tracked, commonly called an "amphtrack"). They had built the ramp to fit over the LVT's bed. The long supports of the ramp, or tank ladder, were two 10-inch I-beams each twenty-five feet long. The crosspieces, or rungs of the ladder, were wooden beams resembling railroad crossties. They were six by fourteen inches and fourteen feet long. But note this: The crosspieces, or rungs could not be fastened to the I-beams in the regular manner of building a ladder, because the I-beams had to run diagonally down the sides of the LVT so that the top of this tank ladder would be high enough to reach over the brow of the cliff.

The problem can be visualized if you will imagine you are carrying a ladder to set against a building at a forty-five degree angle, and you have to carry the ladder before you at the forty-five degree angle. You can see the difficulty. The rungs near the top of the ladder will not be in your way, but the rungs on the bottom portion of the ladder will have to come out to make room for your body.

The Seabees completed the top four feet of the tank ladder by bolting the heavy crosspieces to the I-beams. Then they strung the remainder of the crosspieces on cables, at six-inch intervals, to form a sort of articulated mat, and this mat lay on top of the LVT.

To counterbalance the portion of the ramp which protruded beyond the bow of the LVT, to keep the LVT stable in the water, and to keep it from tipping forward the moment it hit the sand, the Seabees hung heavy bundles of steel Marston mat over the stern of the craft. The result was an LVT with four feet of completed tank ladder sticking out over its bow, with the steel beams extending diagonally along its sides, with a heavy platform of crossties draped over its entire length, and with bundles of steel matting hanging over its stern. That was the strange contraption which the Seabees unveiled before Lieutenant General Holland M. Smith and Vice Admiral Richmond Kelly Turner as their answer to the Tinian cliffs. The contraption was named the "Doodlebug."

There was much shaking of heads as the Doodlebug took to the water on a test run and headed for a Tinian-like sector of the Saipan coastline. But the Doodlebug never missed a lick. As it ran into shallow water its treads dug into the sand. Coming up out of the water it smashed into a sheer eight-foot cliff. The forward end of the tank ladder dropped down and gripped the top of the cliff with specially designed grippers. Then, like a snake pulling out of its skin, the LVT backed away from the cliff, and two things happened: the after ends of the I-beams disconnected themselves from the LVT, dropped into the sand, and held fast; and the articulated mat of crosspieces was laid down the full length of the I-beams, thus completing the tank ladder. Then, while the onlookers cheered, the LVT scaled its own ladder and halted atop the cliff.

To make certain that the ramp was strong enough, and to be sure that the articulated mat would not slip off the I-beams, Admiral Turner ordered that 100 vehicles be run over the ramp in one hour. The ramp stood the test and was accepted.

During the next few days the 18th and 121st Battalions, working with the 2nd Amphibian Tractor Battalion, built ten Doodlebugs. Four-man Seabee crews were trained to ride on top of each Doodlebug to make sure that the ramp was placed properly and to repair it if necessary.

Then on D-Day, H-Hour, at Tinian the Japs, who could never be certain what the Seabees would think up next, saw these Doodlebugs approaching. The sight reminded you of the Romans approaching some barbarian wall with scaling ladders. The Seabees rammed their Doodlebugs against the cliffs. The scaling ladders were there and tanks and trucks were quickly pouring in upon the Japs. As they emplaced and maintained the ramps, the Seabees were working under the cliff, and thus were safe from Jap fire and suffered no casualties.

The first crew to get a ramp in place was led by R. M. Hensley (Carpenter's Mate First, Elkton, Va., 18th Battalion). The other three men in the crew were W. Y. Hundley (Electrician's Mate First, Eunice, La.), Roy O. Schanhals (Shipfitter First, Elgin, Tex.), and Bob Bonnaud (Chief Shipfitter, Los Angeles, Cal.). These three 18th Battalion veterans also had been on the first ammunition barge to reach the Jap pier at Tarawa.

The second ramp was emplaced by a crew led by H. D. "Pop" Niday (Chief Carpenter's Mate, Houston, Tex.), another fabulous character of the 18th Battalion, who will be mentioned subsequently.

Hundreds of vehicles passed over the ramps during the first hour of the invasion. The Marines were able to outflank and kill the Japs defending the two more desirable sectors of beach where there were no cliffs. When this was done, the ramps and the cliff sectors of beach were abandoned.

Meanwhile, Seabees of the 302nd Pontoon Battalion had anticipated our securing the two sectors of flat beach and were ready with two pontoon piers, each 300 feet long and forty-two feet wide. These piers had been assembled at Saipan and towed across the three miles of water.

Shortly before noon a crew headed by the 302nd's commanding officer, Lieutenant Commander Bill Dallas (CEC, USNR, Plainfield, N. J.), began to work one pier in toward the beach. The Japs raked the pier with shellfire, and one Seabee was killed: John De Luca (Boatswain's Mate Second,

Chicago, Ill.). Another was badly wounded: Lieut. W. M. Beaton (CEC, USNR, Lawrence, Mass.). When this pier was emplaced, it was found that there wasn't enough water for LCTs to reach it, and it had to be moved several times. To prevent any interruption of the landing during this delay, James J. Gores (Shipfitter Second, White Deer, Tex.), operating a waterproofed bulldozer, dug a channel up to an old Jap pier so that LCTs and pontoon barges could reach it.

The second pier was brought in by a crew directed by Lieutenant Commander Jack McGaraghan (CEC, USNR, Eureka, Cal.), a veteran of many Pacific landings. This pier was emplaced without incident, and by the morning of D-plus-1, both piers were in full operation.

On the third day North Field—the Jap airdrome—was secured, and the Seabees made it operational within a few hours. Thenceforth all wounded were evacuated by air as C-47's shuttled back and forth from Saipan.

Altogether, the Tinian landing was perhaps the smoothest of all our amphibious undertakings—this despite the fact that all of our invasion impedimenta moved through the narrowest beach bottleneck employed on any landing.

Now that the war is over, perhaps the Brookings Institution will employ a host of statisticians and begin the job of computing how much the B-29's cost the United States. The statisticians can start with the plane cost: one million dollars apiece. The crew cost: at least $300,000 per eleven-man crew. The fuel cost: one railroad tank car of 100-octane per plane per trip. Then add the base cost—Tinian, Saipan, and Guam, plus Iwo Jima—and the figure will make the World War I debt look like peanuts.

Ponder these thoughts for a moment:

1. To bombard Japan with B-29's, we spent more money

and energy than were spent to build all the railroads in the United States.

2. The combined B-29 bases in the Marianas represented a construction job larger than the building of all the dams in the United States—TVA, Boulder, Grand Coulee, Shasta, all of them put together.

3. The amount of coral moved by the Seabees *on Tinian alone* would make five Boulder Dams.

4. To build the six great 8500-foot runways on Tinian, the Seabees moved 14,000,000 cubic yards of coral, enough to fill a solid string of railroad coal cars reaching from Los Angeles to New York.

5. The cost of dropping each 500 pounds of bombs on Japan was more than the average American earns in a year.

It is difficult to illustrate the magnitude of these construction projects because they were so much larger than anything ever attempted before. The development of Tinian, for instance, dwarfed the Panama Canal as a construction project. It made the building of the Pyramids look like a children's exercise.

The development of Tinian began about August 1, 1944, with two battalions—the 18th and 121st—on the island. On December 21st there were thirteen battalions of Seabees on the island; the first 8500-foot runway was completed ten days ahead of schedule; the first B-29's had landed; and the general development of the island was proceeding at full speed.

On April 2, 1945, the fourth 8500-foot runway was presented to the Army Air Force. Hundreds of B-29's were operating from Tinian. All the B-29's formerly based in China and India had been transferred to Tinian. The artificial harbor was nearing completion. Liberty ships could dock and disgorge cargoes where once there had been no harbor and no piers. There was enough housing on the island to house an entire city of 50,000 people. There was more fuel storage on the island than we had at Pearl Harbor before the war.

But Tinian was not completed on April 2nd. The work was "leveling off." Three of the battalions were to move on to Okinawa during the summer of 1945, but the development program was to go on. Two more 8500-foot runways were to be added. Then all six of the great runways were to be block-topped, a little job of milling and laying 500,000 *tons* of black-top—asphalt mixed with coral. More housing had to be built for the Japanese and Korean natives. More fuel capacity was needed.

It was believed that Tinian might be finished by the end of 1945, seventeen months after its development had begun.

The big job at Tinian was earth-moving. A B-29 strip is one and five-eighths miles long and 165 yards wide. It was a vast expanse of coral when completed. It was a ferment of machinery while the Seabees were building it. The hills had to be cut; the valleys had to be filled. Endless layers of material were spread on, and each layer had to be rooted, crushed, kneaded, scraped, and rolled. The great "strip" was the center of activity.

Two or three miles away was another busy spot: the coral pit. Here the borers swarmed over a coral "face" with their coughing, sputtering machines. The blasters—powdermen like Johnny Hartline (Gunner's Mate First, Palatka, Fla., 13th Bat.) and T. E. Hilliard (Gunner's Mate First, Lake Wales, Fla., 13th Bat.)—were busy tamping the charges in. Hartline and Hilliard fired 5000 holes at one time, containing 40,000 sticks of dynamite. They set off one twenty-three-ton powder charge. The coral is soft, spongy, and tricky.

It absorbs much of the blast, so double charges have to be used.

When the coral had been blasted, it was churned by heavy bulldozers to break it up, then the big shovels went after it, loading it into the dump trucks. As many as 275 dump trucks were hauling coral out of one pit on Tinian. The "haul road" to the airstrip was a race track, so heavily guarded that not even the general's jeep could use it. The trucks, in a ceaseless roar, pounded over it so furiously that the drivers had to have periodic vacations to prevent their kidneys from being ruined.

Not all the coral was hauled in trucks. In the "cuts" on the strip, the big "pans"—with one caterpillar pushing and one pulling—took many cubic yards in a gulp, waddled forward and vomited the coral on a "fill." Turnapulls, which are pans with their own motive power, can pick up five cubic yards and race cross-country with it.

All this machinery working added up to a maintenance nightmare. Victor Bass (Chief Machinist Mate, Watertown, N. Y., 67th Bat.) and Chester W. Harris (Shipfitter First, New Orleans, La., 67th Bat.) used 1000 pounds of welding rod a month repairing heavy equipment. Tires wore out in a week. At one time 100 dump trucks had to sit idle awaiting the arrival of additional tires on Tinian. To save rubber, a field mess hall was built beside the strip so that the men would not have to be transported to and from their camps for noon and midnight meals.

Earth-moving means dynamite and machinery—and men who know how to use them. During the thirty-six days the Seabees were building the first strip on Tinian, they moved 700,000 cubic yards of earth and coral and drove 900,000 truck miles. This was more earth-moving than the Japs had been able to do in the entire Pacific since 1941.

The 18th Battalion had the distinction of being the battalion with the longest period of overseas service. When I visited them on Tinian in April, 1945, they were on their thirty-second month out of the States. They had a great batch of stories.

In the early days, when we were making war on a twenty-four-hour basis, several Seabee battalions served as integral parts of Marine units. They were Seabees, but they were also Marines. They were a battalion in a Marine regiment. The 18th Seabees were the first to be so assigned. On September 12, 1942—a month after we had landed on Guadalcanal—the 18th was assigned to the 2nd Marine Division and transferred to the Marine base at Norfolk for outfitting.

The 2nd Marine Division, however, was not ready for action; the 18th Seabees were. Moreover, the demand for Seabees was much more urgent than the demand for Marines, so on September 19th, wearing their new Marine uniforms, the 18th Seabees embarked for the South Pacific. On a brief stop-over in Cuba, they fired their rifles for the first time.

The battalion spent a few days assembling equipment at Noumea, New Caledonia, and on December 12th—right in the middle of the long campaign—they arrived at Guadalcanal. They were the third Seabee battalion to arrive on Guadal; the pioneering 6th, which had fought the Battle of Henderson Field, and the 14th were already there.

"The Japs gave us a reception," Pop Niday, the aforementioned chief from Houston, Texas, told me. "The bombers came over, and our star gunner, 'One Shot' Usher (James F. Usher, Gunner's Mate First, Hershey, Pa.), opened up with his 20 mm and shot the landing gear off of a parrot.

"We went to work building Fighter Strip No. 1. We all had the Tropical Trots, so we spent our nights racing for the head, dodging shots from our guards as we ran. After four months, when we had finished the strip, we went down to New Zealand—that beautiful land of stike-and-aiggs, two-bit whores, and twenty-dollar whisky. There we fought 'The Battle of Cuba Street' and taught a few folks that CB did not mean 'confined to barracks for clap.'"

The 18th Seabees—or Marines—went to New Zealand to rejoin the 2nd Marine Division, which had arrived there for training. It was decided there that the 18th Seabees should not be Seabees any more, so they were redesignated as the 3rd Battalion, 18th Marine Regiment, 2nd Marine Division.

I explain this in some detail because several Seabee battalions went through this now-they-are-Marines-now-they-ain't routine, and it was a source of confusion. It's true that some Seabee battalions were Marine battalions for long periods; a lot of Seabees wore Marine uniforms; Seabees were "attached" to Marines in every operation. But the Navy insisted that the two organizations remain separate.

In the 2nd Marines the Seabees were known as the "Sergeants Battalion" for an interesting reason. All the early Seabees were volunteers and skilled men. Their average age was around thirty, so they came into the Navy as "rated" men, with their rates ranging all the way up to chief petty officers. Therefore, when they put on Marine uniforms and translated their Navy "rates" into Marine noncommissioned ranks, all of the Seabees were sergeants. There were no privates.

This angered the Marines in the other two battalions in the 18th Marine Regiment because, since only privates do guard duty, the 3rd Battalion—the Seabees—could not do its share of guard duty, and this meant extra duty for the 1st and 2nd Battalions.

"We spent seven months in New Zealand," Pop Niday went on. "We were the first Americans to get leave down on the South Island. The boys thought it was heaven: sheep and women were everywhere. Gin was only $1.75 a quart, T-bone steaks were 16 cents a pound, and taxis were reasonable. But the Americans soon fixed this; we drove the prices up to a proper extortion level.

"Coal was our big problem, because down there it was as cold as north Texas. Coal was rationed—one bucket per tent per day—so everybody had to cut a trap door in his tent floor and fix a secret coal bin under the floor. The coal was sooty as hell. There wasn't no use in blowin' reveille because the whole camp was waked up every morning by the boys beating soot out of stove pipes. Some of us put '03 shells in the stoves to blow the soot out. This would blow burning soot all over the camp, and a lot of times we'd have to run out in the cold air in our shorts to put a fire out on the tent.

"Then we'd have to drink a Shellshock Cocktail—port wine and gin—to get warm."

In November, 1943, the 2nd Marines hit Tarawa, and the Seabee contingent was in there, too. The first Seabee to reach Betio beach was Commander L. E. Tull (CEC, USNR, Delmar, N. Y.), the bronzed, fifty-year-old ramrod who has commanded the 18th Seabees through all their tribulations. With him was Carl L. Catt (Carpenter's Mate First, Monticello, Miss.).

The Seabees' chief assignment was to unload ammunition and bring it to the beach on their pontoon barges. The first barge, carrying thirty tons of ammunition, attempted to reach the Jap pier shortly after the first waves had gained a toe hold. This barge was manned by Bob Bonnaud (Chief Shipfitter, Los Angeles, Cal.), W. Y. Hundley (Electrician's Mate First, Eunice, La.), and Roy O. Schanhals (Shipfitter First, Elgin, Tex.). These are the three, mentioned before, who placed the first invasion ramp against the Tinian cliffs.

Just as Bonnaud and his men approached the pier with the explosive ammunition, Jap artillery set the pier afire, and the barge had to stand off. Shells were falling all around the barge, and one shell hit would have set off the whole thirty tons of ammunition. Unable to reach the beach, Bonnaud held his barge in position and transferred the ammunition to amphtracks which took it on in. Then Bonnaud's barge—and others like it—operated a shuttle service between the reef, where they took ammunition from Higgins boats which could not get over the reef, and the amphtracks near the beach.

"On the fourth day," Bonnaud told me, "we got a load of camp stools and billiard tables, so we said 'to hell with it,' the invasion is over, and we went to sleep on the barge."

The first bulldozer on the beach was handled by R. W. Isbell (Chief Carpenter's Mate, Joaquin, Tex.). Isbell pushed over Jap pillboxes, dug gun positions, buried Marines, and buried 1100 Japs.

The airfield was made operational on the fifth day, and the following day the Japs bombed the field and set some of our planes on fire. Three Hellcats were pushed out of the fire and saved by A. R. Turregano (Electrician's Mate Second, Miami, Fla.) and E. X. Shook (Shipfitter Second, Philadelphia, Pa.).

The 18th stayed on Tarawa forty days and aided the 74th Seabees, who had brought in full equipment, in rebuilding the airstrip and developing the island.

"We lived in that native village," I was told by H. S. "Sea Gull" Wright (Yeoman Second, Wichita Falls, Tex.). "The natives wouldn't go back to it because the Japs had lived there, so the island commander gave it to the 18th Seabees."

"Sea Gull," being a man of figures, also informed me that the famous "Toilet Paper Watch" kept on the officers' head at Tarawa had cost the Government $1473. "Tarawa was the only goddam place in the war," he said, "where they posted a guard to watch the officers' toilet paper."

The 18th had no doctor on Tarawa, and R. C. Miles (Pharmacist's Mate First, Mobridge, S. D.) carried on a lone battle against dengue and malaria. When the men got back to the island of Hawaii, Miles had a big argument with the sanitation officer, who didn't want the men to come ashore because they had so much dengue. Miles sprayed the ship, confined many of the men to closed ambulances for the trip to the hospital, and got all the men ashore.

On Hawaii "the Marines rested and the Seabees worked." On the vast Parker Brothers ranch, the 18th built Camp Tarawa for the 2nd Marines. Dust was eight inches thick. Water was a problem, so the 18th sank the first real well on Hawaii. The well, 663 feet deep, was dug by W. B. Pugh (Boatswain's Mate First, Clifton, Tenn.), who has dug wells all over the Pacific. The 18th also built a small airfield while it "rested."

Just before the 2nd Marines—and the 18th—left for the Saipan assault, they were given a big barbecue with beer drinking at the ranch. Then there was a beer bust at Pearl Harbor and one day of "sightseeing" in Honolulu. Then on to Saipan.

In the Saipan landing, the 18th lost two men killed and 35 wounded. The dead were Noah E. Danley (Machinist's Mate Second, Centerville, Texas) and Claude Hepp (Seaman First, Compton, California).

From D-Day on until Saipan was secured, the 18th unloaded 10,000 tons of cargo a day. On the fifth day a Piper Cub carrying pilot and observer crashed into one of the 18th's ammunition dumps. Despite the imminent explosion, four Seabees rushed onto the dump in an effort to rescue the fliers. The pilot was pinned hopelessly, but the Seabees managed to pull the observer out and save his life. The four, awarded the Navy & Marine Corps Medal, were: J. T. Patterson (Machinist's Mate Second, Fayette, Ala.); Jim Golding (Chief Carpenter's Mate, Amarillo, Tex.); Donald P. King (Chief Shipfitter, Oakland, Cal.); and H. A. Cooper (Carpenter's Mate First).

Dan D. Everett (Pharmacist's Mate First, Mendenhal, Miss.) got the Navy & Marine Corps Medal for continuing to care for wounded Seabees and Marines after he himself had been painfully wounded.

Pop Niday killed nine Japs on Saipan. He got mad when a Jap threw a grenade that hit him in the chest. He threw the grenade into the water, then killed the Jap with a saber he took off a Jap officer on Guadalcanal. Then, Pop, who is a mustached Texan with the energy of a twenty-year-old, rode one of the landing ramps to Tinian.

L. O. Boyd (Machinist's Mate First, McCamey, Tex.) was in a cave salvaging a Jap truck when a Jap threw a grenade at him. Boyd threw the grenade back, killed the Jap, then meticulously "field stripped" the Jap for souvenirs.

The 18th's funniest story, however, is about Benjamin Franklin Dunn (Carpenter's Mate Second, Odessa, Tex.), who operated a still while he was in the brig on Guadalcanal.

Dunn was what the Seabees call an ace distiller. Apparently he was not entirely without prewar experience. On Guadal he had a fermenting apparatus hidden in the battered fuselage of a Jap plane. It was a double-boiler affair which Dunn charged with raisins, water, and sugar, and on which, in the tropical heat, he could run off a five-gallon batch about every four days. The standard price for this jungle juice was $60 a gallon.

When the Master-at-Arms, William E. Gillum (Chief Boatswain's Mate, Kingsport, Tenn.) was ordered to crusade against moonshining, he promptly tossed Dunn into the brig on suspicion, but he couldn't find Dunn's still. Was Dunn guilty or not?

After the first few days it appeared that Gillum had fingered the right man. The battalion's source of jungle juice seemed to have been dried up. The drunkenness graph took a nose dive.

Then, strangely, jungle juice appeared to become plentiful again, and Dunn had been in the brig alone for ten days. It was a formidable brig, too, a tent and a foxhole in the center of a barbed wire enclosure. A guard was on duty twenty-four hours a day.

Gillum became worried. Obviously, he had arrested an innocent man. Somebody still at large was the distiller, so Dunn was given his freedom. This suited Dunn, but hell, he said, he had got so used to sleeping in the brig that he'd like to continue sleeping there. Nobody could object to that.

Meanwhile, the supply of jungle juice seemed to remain constant, and Gillum searched relentlessly for the distiller. At last he became suspicious of the brig and searched it. Everything seemed to be in order. The foxhole, under one of the tent flaps, looked like all the other foxholes in camp. It had a roof to give protection from falling shrapnel, and palm leaves on the floor to lie on. Nothing wrong there.

Two nights later Gillum thought he had something. He saw a light in the foxhole after Dunn had gone to bed. He rushed over and found Dunn calmly cutting a niche in the foxhole wall for a candle. This wasn't unusual. Air raid alerts were often long on Guadal, and many a covered foxhole had a niche for a candle. The candles gave enough light so that Seabee poker games could go on uninterrupted by Jap bombs.

Of course Dunn didn't have anybody to play poker with, but he explained that he liked to read during raids.

The next night, however, Gillum spied the candle again, crept out to the foxhole, and caught Dunn red-handed. He was in the act of lighting a fire under his double-boiler brewing contraption. He had dug the foxhole three feet deeper, built a false floor, and someone had smuggled in his equipment. Even more amazing, he had devised a method to trap the odor of the fermenting fruit. It was a perfect job of camouflage.

When Dunn was put out of business, the 18th had to go back to buying the potent and sometimes lethal "torpedo juice" from the Army at $20 a canteenful.

That's the 18th Battalion, a rugged band of Seabees, mostly Southerners and most of them Texans. The 2nd Marine Division pulled off and left them on Tinian to work on the big strips and to build Camp Churo, the native center. They were the "18th Seabees" again.

When I saw them on Tinian they were expecting to celebrate their third year overseas before they saw the Golden Gate. They had Guadalcanal, Tarawa, Saipan, and Tinian behind them—three D-Days—plus time served in New Zealand, Hawaii, and Noumea. They had built airfields and camps everywhere they had been, and won every decoration the Navy and Marine Corps could give. By the time they reached home, they would have traveled 25,000 miles in the holds of Liberty ships and LSTs. But on Tinian they were still moving their share of dirt, still cussing and griping, still cooking off a few batches of cane squeezings, and still able to chuckle at all the fool things Americans can do.

The Presidential Unit Citation, for Tarawa, is among the 18th's souvenirs.

The 110th Seabees were the "lead battalion" on the big West Field runways at Tinian. They were a boisterous outfit of earth-moving specialists led by Lieutenant Commander

John A. McAllister (CEC, USNR, Hawkinsville, Ga.). The commander is a soft-voiced, diplomatic Georgian who has the knack of doing big jobs without racing his motor, and his battalion was one of the most efficient in the Pacific.

The 110th's stories are about Eniwetok and Tinian. Each member of the battalion wears the Bronze Star for "participation in the occupation of Eniwetok Atoll, Marshall Islands, February 17 to March 2, 1944," and he is quick to remind you that Eniwetok was "the first Japanese territory taken from the enemy by forces of the United Nations."

Eniwetok was one of our most important stepping stones. From March 1, 1944, to July 1, 1944, when we began operating planes from Saipan, Eniwetok was our advanced air base and fleet anchorage in the Central Pacific. It was the jumping-off base for our operations against the Marianas, and all of our units going to the Marianas "staged" at Eniwetok. It was the 110th Seabees which converted Eniwetok and Parry islets from cocoanut-covered coral wastes into a modern air and naval base.

Two disasters occurred while the 110th was developing Eniwetok. An LCT unloading bombs caught fire and went up in one big explosion which nearly sank the island. It was the day after St. Patrick's Day, and Henry L. McNamara (Machinist's Mate Second, Boston, Mass.) was still wearing the green vest which he had stripped off a Jap and worn in honor of the good saint. His foot was broken in the explosion.

Fortunately, when the LCT caught fire she was lying hulldown behind an escarpment. At first only her small arms ammunitions began to pop, and while this was happening, Frank Mahodil (Chief Shipfitter, Yorktown, N. Y.) cut her cable, and a Seabee bulldozer pushed her off the beach. Meanwhile, the 110th's fire department, led by James W. Stewart (Shipfitter Third, San Francisco, Cal.), was rushing to the scene.

Just as Stewart got to the beach, the fire licked into the LCT's bombload and she went up. Every tent on the island was knocked down. Five-hundred-pound unexploded bombs were hurled clear across the island. Eniwetok became a mass of bomb craters and fires. Stewart, of course, was killed. He was a veteran member of the San Francisco Fire Department, had four years to go for his pension, and had a wife and eight children at home.

By a miracle, and by Mahodil's having pushed the LCT off the beach, only five men were killed and 133 injured. Forty of the injured were Seabees.

Eniwetok's flies, during the first two weeks, were fabulous. Attracted by the Jap bodies, they came as big as roaches and went more persistent than an insurance salesman. You couldn't scare them off; you had to rake them off. A man carrying a tray of food was helpless. The flies would eat most of his food before he could set the tray down and fight.

A Jap body was lying on the reef. The surf, coming in, would wash over it. A blanket of flies smothered the body, and it was fascinating to watch that blanket rise in the air as the surf came in, then fall back on the body. All day that blanket rose and fell as relentlessly as the surf itself.

C. O. Price (Chief Carpenter's Mate, Springville, Ariz.), in charge of insect control, buried 889 Japs on Eniwetok. All water had to be distilled because of the island's low sea level, and because the dead Japs fouled what fresh or brackish water existed.

Price was also the 110th's "rabbit master." He brought nine rabbits to Eniwetok to produce meat for the battalion. But despite the shortage of fresh meat, Price never ate a rabbit. "I just couldn't make myself eat a $20 bill," he told me. He sold 295 rabbits to the Marines at $20 a rabbit.

Mike Morrissey (Shipfitter First, Worcester, Mass.) broke his glasses during the landing. He searched the Jap bodies until he found a pair he liked, and when I saw him on Tinian he was still wearing the Jap glasses. He said he liked them better than the ones he had broken.

Eniwetok Kickapoo Juice became famous all over the Pacific. Its original formula is the secret of G. A. Grey (Shipfitter First, Liberal, Kan.), but its chief ingredients were potato peelings, cocoanut shoots, and brake fluid.

A familiar sight to all Pacific travelers was the long, perfect row of carrier planes parked near an airstrip. Each plane had its wings folded vertically over its back, and the long row of vertical wings always reminded me of how, as a kid, I used to line up dominoes, then tip over the first one and watch the whole line collapse.

Something like this did happen in Eniwetok's second major disaster. A B-24, taking off, went out of control and went skimming over two lines of carrier planes. Amplified many times, it sounded like the noise a boy makes when he drags a stick along a paling fence. Fire and destruction were everywhere. More than a hundred planes were destroyed.

The Seabees battled heroically to control the fires and rescue pinned men. Many members of the 110th were decorated for their efforts, and many others would have been decorated had there been time to collect their names. Three of those who received the Navy & Marine Corps Medal were: Richard J. Lugo (Machinist's Mate First, Los Angeles, Cal.); E. R. Driggers (Chief Boatswain's Mate, Mt. Pleasant, Tex.); and E. W. Diegoli (Chief Shipfitter, Brockton, Mass.). These men removed unexploded bombs from the flames.

In this case no one could be blamed for having lined up the planes. Space was at such a premium on Eniwetok that the Seabees were dredging coral from the sea and enlarging the island.

When the 110th reached Tinian, its cane-country contingent looked at all that sugar cane and began smacking their lips. The chow on Eniwetok had been garbage; there had been little food on the island to procure. Now syrup and hot cakes were to be had by a little ingenious procuring. John S. Hendry (Carpenter's Mate First, Baton Rouge, La.) and John M. Taylor (Shipfitter First, Montgomery, Ala.) were old syrup makers, and so was Jack D. Ray (Storekeeper Second, Savannah, Ga.). The three formed the Little Rebel Syrup Company, and began to reconnoiter for equipment.

Elverne R. Parsons (Chief Storekeeper, Seattle, Wash.) lent a hand, since syrup would help relieve an imminent sugar shortage. The group was trying to improvise a cane press out of a variety of Jap junk when intelligence brought word of a Jap press on Saipan which was not wrecked, was not being used, and was not well guarded.

In a typical Seabee flanking movement, the four "procured" an LCVP and took off for Saipan. There, after a series of pincers movements which had best not be reported in detail, they got the press loaded into the VP and started back to Tinian. Out in open water, a sudden squall hit them and nearly liquidated the Little Rebel Syrup Company then and there. But they got through.

A few months later the three Rebels—Hendry, Taylor, and Ray—were the most powerful and influential entrepreneurs on the island. They had Japs cutting the cane and stoking the press, and they had rigged up a Jap truck to furnish the power. They were cooking off huge batches of syrup every week.

The fresh syrup—Hendry really knew his syrup-making—was a powerful barter item. By trading syrup to ships for flour, the Little Rebel Company provided all the syrup and hot cakes the battalion could eat. At first the damnyankees turned up their noses, but gradually they began to grab those cakes and drown them in the Little Rebel product.

Little Rebel reached out as its fame spread. If the General

91

wanted a gallon of syrup, what did he have to offer? Okay, they'd take a couple of cases of that plus a new jeep. If the Army wanted syrup, let them bring over a batch of choice souvenirs.

When I visited the Little Rebel Company and surveyed all its wealth and prosperity, I asked Hendry why he didn't trade some syrup for a battleship to go home on when the war was over.

"Hell, man, we don't want no battleship," he replied. "We already got three B-29's. It'll take me just thirty-six hours to get back to Louisiana the day the war's over."

The electricity for the huge lights which guided the B-29's back to Tinian's runways, as well as the power for most of the island, was furnished by courtesy of the Imperial Japanese Government. Five Seabees of the 110th Battalion built the largest power plant west of Pearl Harbor entirely out of Japanese equipment which they salvaged. Here is how they did it.

As soon as the 110th came ashore, a salvage party led by Warrant Officer Melville O. Bigley (CEC, USNR, Findlay, O.) began to comb the island. They collected nearly 200 tons of Jap power equipment, including three Diesel marine engines weighing fifteen tons apiece. Everything had been damaged by shellfire, sabotage, flame-throwers, or worst of all, by souvenir hunters. Valuable gauges and dials, because they had been labeled in Japanese, had been carried off or partially dismantled for their souvenir value.

But the Seabees repaired while they collected. They rebuilt the gauges, repainted the dials, restored Japanese directions. Vital parts still were missing. All the overhead transformers had been shot up beyond repair. The salvage crew, however, unearthed some underground transformers—

part of a Jap emergency system—and it was found that these could be substituted for the overhead type.

Where were the fuel injectors for the big Diesels? In their attempt at sabotage the Japs had removed all the fuel injectors, and not one could be found on Tinian. Then Bigley remembered that he had seen the wreckage of a similar engine on Saipan. Two salvage experts hurried there and returned with two sets of injectors. Meanwhile, a third set had been discovered in a beach cave on Tinian, along with a large cache of new spare parts. Other searchers uncovered a Jap Diesel fuel dump containing enough fuel to operate the engines for a year.

In the completed power plant the three big Ikegai Diesel-marine two-cycle engines were enclosed in a brick building 52 x 60 feet. The bricks came from the Jap sugar mill. A twenty-seven-foot panel control board glistened with Jap switches, meters, and gauges, but Seabee electricians seemed to read Japanese, too. The engines, which the Japs had used less than a year, were started with compressed air supplied by a Jap compressor.

The engines were designed to burn the Jap type of Diesel oil, but the Seabees could easily convert them to American oil when the supply of Jap oil ran out. Power service from this big plant was more even and dependable than from the small standard overseas generators which we used elsewhere west of Hawaii. Without this plant, eighty Seabee electricians on Tinian would have been working full time operating and servicing the small units which this plant made unnecessary. Three men operated the big plant.

The four men who worked with Bigley to build the plant are Gus E. Sandifer (Chief Electrician's Mate, Houston, Tex.), who installed the generators; Joseph H. Boquette (Chief Boatswain's Mate, Saginaw, Mich.), who led the searching party; Richard D. Collins (Carpenter's Mate Second, Tampa, Fla.), who was draftsman for the job, and Carl Isley (Chief Machinist's Mate, Bismarck, Ill.), who installed the Diesel equipment.

"We sort of made a game out of this plant," Boquette said. "We determined to build it out of 100 per cent Jap stuff, and that's what we did. This plant hasn't cost Uncle Sam a dime except for Seabee labor."

Four Seabee battalions have received the Presidential Unit Citation: the 6th for Guadalcanal, the 40th for Los Negros, the 18th for Tarawa, and the 121st for Saipan. After the Saipan assault, the 121st moved over to Tinian where it became the "lead battalion" on the North Field runways. The 121st, which has three D-Days to its credit, is led by Lieutenant Commander William G. Byrne (CEC, USNR, Butte, Mont.).

First D-Day for the 121st was February 1, 1944, when they landed on Kwajalein with the 4th Marine Division. O. L. Tanner (Chief Carpenter's Mate, Pensacola, Fla.), in the second wave, was the first Seabee to reach the beach. His detachment brought in a load of mortar shells.

Ben J. Blackburn (Machinist's Mate First, Lampasos, Tex.) was on the first cat which came in to drag the ammunition slides. Blackburn lived on borrowed time. While he was dragging grenades up to the forward Marines on the afternoon of D-Day, a Jap officer leaped on the cat, thrust a shiny automatic into Blackburn's face, and pulled the trigger. The pistol snapped and Blackburn, unarmed, slapped the Jap to the ground. The Jap jumped back on the cat, snapped the pistol again, and again Blackburn smacked him off.

By this time T. E. Williams (Seaman First, Marianna, Fla.) had run up and killed the Jap with a tommy gun.

Blackburn crawled off the cat, picked up the Jap's pistol, pointed it to the ground, and pulled the trigger. It fired. He pulled the trigger again. It fired again. Later, he asked a chief gunner's mate to examine the pistol and its ammunition. Both pistol and ammunition were in perfect shape.

Blackburn showed me the pistol, which is his most prized souvenir. "My good luck began when I was born in Texas," he said, "and I guess that luck just held. But I'll never forget the sound of that pistol snapping in my face."

On the night of D-Day, Ben Hathaway (Electrician's Mate First, Wareham, Mass.) was on guard at the beach. He was scanning the water for Japs, who frequently tried to swim around to our beachheads and sneak in behind us. Suddenly Hathaway was certain he saw a Jap in the water. He opened fire with his tommy gun. The Jap kept swimming and dodging down the beach, and the next guard opened up on him. But the Jap seemed indestructible. He swam the whole length of our beach and continued on around the island.

Next day a log washed ashore. It had been splintered by more than 500 forty-five caliber bullets. The incident is known as the "Battle of the Log."

During the fourteen days it spent at Kwajalein, the 121st also restored the airstrip on Roi islet, which is part of the Kwajalein Atoll. On the night of February 12th, the Japs hit the jackpot in a bombing raid on Roi. One of their bombs found our largest ammunition dump, and one more islet was almost blown into the ocean. Many Seabees were wounded. Explosion of the dump dug a crater 182 feet in diameter by actual measurement. The Seabees made a swimming hole out of the crater.

Floyd Dunn (Shipfitter First, Greybull, Wyo.) had captured a Jap duck which he was fattening for Sunday dinner.

A bomb hit that duck squarely amidships and scattered feathers all over the island.

Eugene E. Atkins (Pharmacist's Mate Second, Miami, Fla.) received the Navy & Marine Corps Medal for his handling of the wounded. While the bomb dump was going up, it appeared that all of Roi was burning.

Two of the 121st boys had a hair-raising experience the first night on Saipan: S. E. Ippolito (Carpenter's Mate First, Paterson, N. J.) and Sam Francesconi (Water Tender Second, Inglewood, N. J.). A pair of abandoned boats were lying about seventy-five yards off the beach, and Ippolito and Francesconi were ordered to spend the night out in the boats and watch for a Jap counter-invasion.*

When they got to the boats, the two Seabees found that the bottoms were out of the boats, and they were hanging on the reef. Ippolito and Francesconi had to stand in the water inside the boat shells and watch for Japs. One of them always had his head above the boat sides, peering out and listening.

Near midnight some Marines farther down the beach, not knowing that the off-shore guard had been placed, began yelling that Japs were out there in the boats. Forthwith and immediately the Marines opened fire.

Ippolito and Francesconi were helpless. They yelled. They fired into the air. They dived. It was ten minutes before the Marines could be given the word, and meanwhile Ippolito lost twenty pounds and Francesconi's hair turned white.

The 121st had two men killed and twenty-one wounded by mortar fire at Saipan. The fatalities: Ellis J. Hebert (Sea-

---

* The first night on Tarawa the Japs swam out and emplaced machine guns in our knocked-out and abandoned vehicles. Next morning they began shooting our men in the back. After this lesson it became standard practice to post guards in our wrecked vehicles off the beaches until the island was secured.

man First, New Orleans, La.) and George Avila (Seaman First, Seattle, Wash.). Besides the Presidential Unit Citation, the battalion has seventy Purple Hearts and twenty-four Bronze Stars.

D-Day at Saipan was June 15th. On June 18th the 121st reached Aslito airstrip and repaired the strip so that the first plane could land at four P.M. on the 19th. Working with the Army Engineers, the Seabees spent four days extending the airstrip 1500 feet to make it operational for bombers and transport planes.

The 121st also repaired and operated the "Saipan Velly Limited," a narrow-gauge railroad which hauled supplies to the front lines and gasoline to the airstrip.

On Tinian, while a 121st survey party was running a line through a cane field, the man who was handling the range pole, F. J. Chmielewicz was attacked by a Jap. Chmielewicz killed the Jap by using his sharp-pointed range pole as a spear.

The men of the 13th or "Black Cat" Battalion on Tinian were the only Seabees who "served with the Russians." They were another old Dutch Harbor outfit, and while they were at Dutch in 1942, a detachment from the battalion was sent to Akutan Island to build a supply base for Russian ships.

Throughout the war the number of Russian-flag ships plying the Bering Sea on runs between Siberia and our West Coast was considerable. These ships were of two types: the old Russian coal-burners and the new oil-burning Libertys, which we had given the Russians. The Russians didn't want to bring these ships for servicing into our fortified harbors in Alaska and the Aleutians, so the Seabees were sent to Akutan, which is in Akutan Pass, to install servicing facilities on an unfortified island. Akutan was closed to all American shipping except the ships which brought in the oil, coal, and other supplies. This arrangement apparently satisfied both the Russians and the Japanese.

Akutan is an old whaling station. The Seabees modernized it and developed the harbor so that it could handle thirty ships at a time. The Russians had been refueling their coal-burners by hand. A Seabee detail, directed by P. G. Conover (Chief Carpenter's Mate, Elizabeth, N. J.) installed a modern conveyor belt which delighted the Russian crews.

Seabee-Russian relations were cordial—and noisy. The big mess hall which the Seabees built was the scene of many experiments in internationalism. There the Seabees showed the Russians Walt Disney shorts—which the Russians prefer above all else American—and there the Russians invited the Seabees to dance.

The first time a brawny Russian sailor walked up to an equally brawny Seabee machinist's mate and asked for a dance, in sign language, American-Soviet relations almost came a cropper. But gradually the Seabees learned that all men who dance together are not perverted, and at least three Seabees became expert "Russian" dancers. When "Sheriff" Jim Elliott (Carpenter's Mate First, Birmingham, Ala.) did that leg business from the squatting position, the Russians roared so loud they could be heard back in Omsk.

John E. "Bulkhead" Stone (Boatswain's Mate First), an excop from Pittsburgh, had a "dagger dance" that wowed the comrades, and G. W. Riedell (Carpenter's Mate First, Deming, N. M.) demonstrated the finer points of the buck-and-wing.

The Russians gave the Seabees one demonstration in practical Communism. The water supply was inadequate for all of Akutan's new customers, so the Seabees had gone back in the hills and began building a dam. But there was no road to the dam site and part of the pathway was almost straight up, so getting lumber up to the site was a backache.

When several Russian ships were tied up in the harbor, the Seabees dropped the hint that they'd appreciate a little reverse lend-lease. The Russians got the idea. More than 200 of them, men and women, trooped out to the lumber-yard, loaded themselves with lumber, and "piss-anted" * every foot of the necessary lumber up the hill in a single afternoon.

Seabees are not easily awed, but they were awed at first by the women on the Russian ships. These buxom, broad-beamed gals could throw a bull over the fence by the tail, and when they whacked you between the shoulder blades to accentuate a joke, they knocked the breath out of you.

As one of the 13th's boys explained to me: "I goosed one of them big Russian broads, and she *decked* me!"

When I was in the Aleutians for the Attu show in 1943, the Russian skippers were reluctant to allow Americans aboard their ships, and the women had been none too generous with what the Seabees call "reverse lend-lease." When I saw the 13th on Tinian, however, the boys told me that later there was some amelioration on both these points.

On September 25, 1944, the 13th left Hawaii on a "cattle

* The scornful Seabee verb to "piss-ant" needs explanation. The Seabees, masters of the machine, loathe doing anything by hand which can be done by machine. They like to dig big ditches where they can use a ditch-digging machine, but it is almost impossible to persuade them to dig a tiny little ditch where they must use a shovel—an "idiot stick." Little ditches and "idiot sticks" are for "gooks"—colored natives—and seamen.

If a Seabee has 500 pounds of lumber to move 100 feet, there are two ways he can move it. He can go get a "cherrypicker"—a crane—and move all the lumber at once. Or, in less time, he can pick up fifty pounds of lumber himself, make ten trips, and the job is done. But if he chose this latter method, he would be "piss-anting the lumber"—it's a transitive verb—and self-respecting Seabees just don't do it. "Piss-anting," too, is for "gooks" and seamen.

boat" for the usual long grind to Eniwetok and the Marianas. All the fifty or more battalions in the West Pacific traveled this route, and they all tell the same stories of endless days on a crowded ship, of "sleeping so damn far down in the hold that we applied for submarine pay," of short rations and long chow lines (usually on these trips the men were fed only two meals a day), of a Monte Carlo of crap and poker games on every deck, and above all, of the constant trafficking with the Merchant Marine crews, trying to obtain extra rations.

These trips would take from thirty to ninety days. The ships would tie up at Eniwetok anywhere from two to forty days, "staging" and waiting for developments and convoys. The Seabees who would "chip paint" or do other work on the ship would be given an extra meal a day by the ship's crew.

On the 13th's trip, J. E. "Dutch" Lerch (Chief Shipfitter, Nazareth, Pa.) undertook the job of holding the ship together and providing proper rations for the men.

"I began with that galley crew," Lerch explained. "I made every goddam one of 'em a stainless steel bracelet. Then, when we had eaten up all them bracelets would get us, I started to making rings for the galley crew. I had run out of steel, so I had to use fence wire which I polished up and told 'em was steel. When the trip kept dragging out, I had to keep borrowing them rings back and polishing 'em, so that galley crew wouldn't find out that the rings wasn't made out of steel."

A doctor aboard—a commander—caused Lerch no end of grief.

"This doctor," Lerch said, "wanted his watch set in one of them steel bracelets. I didn't want to fool with the damn doctor; he couldn't give us nothing to eat; I wanted to work for that galley crew. But the doc kept after me, and I took his watch and put it in my pants pocket. Next morning I

100

looked around and my goddam pants had gone to the laundry. I rushed down, but I was too late. The doc's watch had already had a good bath in caustic soda, and the crystal was gone.

"Then I started sweatin'. It was one of them fancy watches with half-a-dozen hands. I had to tear it up and make a few new parts for it out of one of them stainless steel eatin' trays. The doc kept asking me about his watch, and I kept putting him off. At Eniwetok I got some glass out of a Jap Betty and made a new crystal. Then I set the watch in a steel bracelet and carried it up to this doc. He took it, pleased as a possum. He never knew what'd happened to that watch, at least not until I had got myself off that ship."

Lerch was the 13th's chief bargainer. He traded steel watch bands to the Army and the Air Force and to ship's crews for sheet iron, glass, whisky, and radios. He, too, traded for a B-29 in which to return home.

The only fountain Coca-Cola dispenser in the Western Pacific was made by Lerch out of a Jap searchlight and oxygen tanks. (See photo.) Two thousand cokes a day have been dispensed by the machine.

The 13th boys considered their number and their black cat, which adorned all their equipment, very lucky. But they had bad luck with their banjo players. They had three, and all three went crazy.

Their big black cat, in a fighting pose, adorned the B-29, The Black Cat which the 13th sponsored. The emblem was painted on the bomber by the battalion's ace painter, Peter J. Pietraszek (Painter First, Fall River, Mass.). To denote bombing missions on The Black Cat, Pietraszek painted not the customary bombs, but black kittens. (See photo.)

Jack Bauchman (Steward's Mate Second, Los Angeles, Cal.), the 13th's colored bartender for the officers' club, was a great morale booster. He not only knew his likker

101

and syrups, but he also had an infectious grin and a great batch of stories. In private life he tends bar for Hollywood personalities, and in the Seabees he has tended bar in that fabulous officers' club at Dutch, in the club at Mauna Loa Ridge on Hawaii, and at Tinian.

"We had a batch o' tekila I never could get 'em to drink," Jack related. "Then one month down on Mauna Loa we run kinda shawt, so I disguised that tekila with lemon, syrup, and a slice o' orange, called it a 'Beachhead Cocktail,' and worked ever' damn bit o' that tekila off."

When the battalion was refitting in California between its Dutch and Western Pacific tours, Bauchman took leave and got married. When he came in AWOL, the commander listened sympathetically to his story and dismissed him with only a reprimand.

"Thank you very much, Commander," he grinned, "and I'm sho my wife thanks you, too." (See photo.)

Speaking of that fabulous officers' club in Dutch—the one with the "Golden Stairway"—I always wondered who designed it. It was one fancy layout. On Tinian I found the man. He is Michael J. Crowley (Chief Carpenter's Mate, Allston, Mass.).

"Yeah, they seemed to like that place," Crowley reminisced. "The most talked about part of it, of course, was my Ladies' Powder Room. It must have been the first one in Alaska. I put indirect lighting in it, then painted all them peeping faces on the wall. All the gals who came through there autographed the toilet seat, so it became quite a showplace." (See photo.)

The 50th or "Gooney Bird" Battalion had the waterfront job on Tinian. They were another lucky "Honeymoon Outfit," having spent a year on Midway, which has the finest climate in the Pacific, no mosquitoes, no malaria, plenty of game fish, and gooney birds.

At one time, of course, Midway was our most advanced outpost in the Central Pacific, saved only by the great Battle of Midway. As our outpost, it was our most important sub base. The old Fifth Seabee Battalion was rushed there to build the early installations. The 50th relieved the 5th. The Seabee camp and most of the installations were on Eastern Island, which has about five square miles of area and is the largest of the two islands known as "Midway." Sand Island—about one and a half square miles—is the other island.

The 50th's luck began when they left the States. Instead of sailing on a "cattle boat," they were on the palatial *Matsonia,* with linen table cloths and a choice between chicken and steak for every meal. Many of the boys still have towels with the big "M" on them. Some of them slept on cots in the *Matsonia's* swimming pool. There were 200 women on the ship—telephone operators, etc., going to Honolulu—and they gave a hula show. One member of the 50th, R. N. Cousineau (Chief Shipfitter, Chicago, Ill.) later married one of these women.

About ninety per cent of the battalion were "Rabbit Chokers" from Minnesota. This rabbit-choking was explained to me by E. E. Baugher (Carpenter's Mate First, Kansas City, Mo.), a bearded Scot with a twinkle in his eyes.

"What ham is to a Virginian," he said, "rabbit is to these goddam Minnesotans."

On Midway the ubiquitous birds were the Seabees' best friends and biggest problem. It's a bird sanctuary, and the gooney birds, the moaning birds, the bosun birds, and the frigate birds are there by the millions. The young goonies are hatched on the ground, and details of Seabees did nothing else on Midway but remove goonies from in front of trucks and cats. Whenever a plane took off or landed, the dead goonies would have to be picked off the runway.

B. J. Scott (Carpenter's Mate First, Denver, Col.), a fierce-looking, bearded fellow, said to me: "By God, I joined the Seabees to go fight the Japs, then they put me to nursing goonies on Midway." Scott was head of the detail which walked in front of all our equipment to remove the baby goonies.

John Marshall (Chief Shipfitter, Decatur, Mich.) made a rare bird discovery. He found twin goonies, both hatched from a single egg.

It was on Midway that a well-known commodore received the Pacific's most famous riposte from a 50th Seabee. The commodore was addressing all the Navy personnel on the island.

"Boys," the commodore said, "I can't understand why morale should ever be bad on this island. We live in comfortable barracks; the climate is ideal, with bright sunshine and blue water to swim in; we've got fish, good movies, good chow, and plenty of beer."

He paused to see how the boys were taking it. Back in the crowd a Seabee got to his feet.

"There's just one thing wrong with all them things you mention, Commodore," the Seabee shouted.

"What's that, mate?" the commodore inquired.

"Ain't none of 'em got teats!"

The biggest day on Midway was December 5, 1943, when the 50th gave a barbecue to celebrate its first year overseas. O. B. McKee (Chief Machinist's Mate, Fort Worth, Tex.) was in charge of the barbecuing, and sub crews, air crews, everybody on the island was invited. The officers and chiefs served the food to the men.

Funniest event was the gooney dance contest. No bird

is more graceful in the air than the gooney; no bird is as awkward on the ground. You'll split your sides watching two goonies dance. They bob and weave crazily—that jitterbug routine known as "pecking" comes from the goonies— and the Seabees had several two-man teams who had spent a year becoming expert in the "gooney dance." Winners of the hilarious gooney dance contest were the team of C. A. Thorsen (Carpenter's Mate Third, Montrose, Minn.) and R. W. Carlson (Machinist's Mate First, Minneapolis, Minn.).

Baugher, the bearded Scot, told me about his Navy & Marine Corps Medal.

"It was nothing," he said. "I just happened to be out there in a boat when a couple of sub boys needed some help, and I give it to them. But getting that medal shore did give me a good laugh on the boys of the battalion. The admiral give me the medal when we got back there to Mauna Loa in Hawaii. It was hot as hell. The boys all had to dress up in them whites and come marching by me in that red dust. I just stood up there and chuckled. I could see every man cussing as he marched by me, thinking about how he'd have to scrub them whites, all because of me gettin' a goddam medal."

The 50th's luck held on its trip from Midway back to Pearl. It got another luxury ship, the *Haleakala*. But its luck ran out on that long crawl across the world's belly from Pearl to Tinian. It was twenty-seven days on the usual cattle boat with the usual stop-over at Eniwetok.

On Tinian the battalion came ashore at night and dug in in a sweet potato field. It was the war's only occasion where a man could lie in bed and eat sweet potatoes.

One of the saddest chores of the war was performed by the 50th's Ira M. "Pop" Palmer (Chief Carpenter's Mate, Chicago, Ill.). This particular "Pop" was called "Pop" for a better reason than the usual one of age. His two sons, John E. Palmer (Carpenter's Mate Second) and Ira M. Palmer, Jr. (Seaman First) were in the same battalion.

The two boys had worked for "Pop" in his construction business, and the three of them had enlisted together on a promise by the recruiting officer that they could stay together. It was probably the war's only case where a recruiting officer's promise was made good.

"Pop" was forty-nine and a skilled carpenter. On Tinian he, like many of these old-timers, was given the somber job of making the coffins for our fellows who died in the hospitals.

On March 7, 1945, it happened. A bomb dump went up without warning, and John Palmer was one of those who "bought it." "Pop" and Ira Jr. sat with John two days and nights in the hospital, but he died. Then "Pop," his shoulders bent low and looking very old, went back to his carpenter's shop and built one more coffin.

After the military funeral, "Pop" took his first emergency leave in two years, and a big NATS plane flew him back to Chicago. The Navy sent him to break the news to the fourth member of the family, the mother.

The 67th Battalion, which had a major role in building the great John Rodgers Airdrome between Honolulu and Pearl Harbor, was the first battalion to land its full equipment on Tinian. It was a member of the 67th—Eddie J. Schouest (Shipfitter Third, New Orleans, La.)—who first suggested that the Seabee battalions "adopt" B-29 crews.

The result was one of the finest morale-building arrangements I have seen anywhere. Each Seabee battalion selected a bomber and crew and formally adopted it. All members of the bomber's flying crew and ground crew visited the battalion several times a week, and the flying crew appeared at the battalion theater after each trip to Japan and explained what targets had been hit, what resistance was met, etc. The battalion painters painted the insigne on the airplane and kept the record of missions up to date. Whenever the battalion's airplane was to take off on a raid, a delegation of its Seabee sponsors was on hand to wish the crew luck.

The arrangement was ideal for everybody concerned. A B-29 crew adopted by a Seabee battalion was considered very, very lucky. For the Seabees know how to take care of their own. Nothing was too good for the men who flew or serviced a "Seabee-29." They ate steaks; they slept on soft Seabee-renovated mattresses; they had a flush toilet even if some Seabee plumber had to go to Saipan and "procure" it; they had unlimited quantities of Seabee beer made cold by unlimited quantities of Seabee ice; they could have a jeep any time for the asking.

The feeling of having their "own" bombers up there smacking the Japs was a tonic for the men working long hours on the big strips. They watched "their" bombers take off; waited anxiously for their return; were impatient for reports from the crew. Watching the planes take off, the Seabees could see tangible results of their labor, and they worked with new vigor because they felt that at last "we're getting somewhere."

There was dismal days back in the Solomons and the Aleutians when the Seabees, working in jungles and williwaws, wondered if their work really counted, if the job would ever be finished. But on Tinian there were no more doubts. The Seabees could watch their own planes—Lucky Lady, The Black Cat, The Gooney Bird, Coral Queen, and others—take off for Tokyo.

Fifty-year-old Roscoe Saunders (Painter First Class, Birmingham, Ala.) of the 67th was the busiest of the B-29 artists. All the B-29 crews were after him to decorate their airplanes with a name and, usually, with a luscious dame to suit the name. I found him working on a plane called "Big Boots." He already had painted the name in a challenging red, and now he was working on the ample breastworks of the gal who was to illustrate the name.

"Looks like you've found a pleasant way to fight the war," I said.

"Yeah," he laughed. "These boys have got to have girls on their airplanes. I get a kick outa drawing them one that they like."

"Where do you get your ideas?" I asked.

"Well," he explained, "the crew usually thinks up the name and decides on it. The name usually suggests a girl. Then we have to produce a girl who fits the name. Sometimes the boys find a girl in *Esquire* or on some calendar that they like, and I just reproduce the girl in a suitable size on the airplane. When the boys don't find a girl, I talk it over with 'em to see what they got in mind, then I try to give 'em a girl who fits the name. Sometimes the pilot has a picture of his own girl, and I sorta use her features as a guide.

"Now take 'Big Boots' here. She's gonna be a pirate gal with a pair of big-topped boots on—and not much else. I'll give her a wisp of loin cloth and cover her nipples with a dab o' lace, and she'll be ready to go to Tokyo."

I asked Mr. Saunders if his girls had any distinguishing characteristic, like long legs or tiny feet.

He thought a moment. "You've got to give 'em long legs and big breasts. That's the Petty and Varga influence. But I try to give my girls a little more daintiness. I usually give 'em a lot o' hair—that makes 'em more feminine. And in giving 'em leg length, I give 'em a lot o' length between hip and knee, and not so much between knee and ankle. The boys seem to like that."

Mr. Saunders showed me other planes nearby which he had decorated. "Tamerlane—The Mad Russian" was the only one on which he had not used a girl. "Indian Maid" was a beauty, but I thought that "Lucky Lady" had the prettiest of all the girls.

"She's a lucky lady, all right," Mr. Saunders said. "It isn't every girl who has eleven escorts to take her to Tokyo and back." (See photo.)

Reduction of the last Jap stronghold on Tinian proved to be a major project for the 135th Battalion.

One Sunday afternoon, weeks after the last Jap soldier had been declared officially dead, a group of the 135th's men were exploring a section of beach, looking for cat-eye shells. Two of the men, Charles A. Schroeder (Electrician's Mate First, Bayside, L. I.) and Homer W. Cameron (Chief Carpenter's Mate, Port Townsend, Wash.) discovered an interesting sea cave into which the surf pounded for a distance of several yards. The two were standing at the mouth of the cave when they were fired on without warning. Schroeder was killed instantly, and Cameron was badly wounded.

Edgar C. Ferguson (Carpenter's Mate First, Scott's Bluff, Neb.) scrambled down the cliff, grabbed Cameron, and attempted to carry him up the cliff; but the Japs came to the mouth of the cave and opened fire. Cameron was hit again, and Ferguson had to leave him and go for help.

Ferguson returned with two Marines, Privates First Class B. F. Keith and R. H. Barnett. They caught the Japs in the act of pulling Schroeder's body back into the cave, and Keith killed two Japs with his BAR. Then, with Keith covering the cave, Ferguson and Barnett managed to climb back down the cliff and rescue the still-conscious Cameron, but he died shortly thereafter.

The problem then was a new one. If the Japs did not have Schroeder's body, the cave mouth would have been blasted and the battle would have been over. But the Seabees were determined to recover Schroeder's body.

A drilling crew from the 135th undertook the job of sinking a shaft forty feet into the rear of the cave so that it could be blasted from the rear. Searchlights played on the mouth of the cave to prevent the Japs from escaping at night. Japanese prisoners had tried in vain to persuade the Japs to come out and surrender.

Shortly after midnight one of the Japs crawled to the mouth of the cave and attempted to shoot out the floodlights. He was killed. Then, about three A.M., five Nips rode a swell out of the cave and attempted to swim for it. They were easy targets.

Next day the cave was blasted from the rear with charge after charge. Drums of gasoline were poured in and ignited. Late that afternoon a white flag appeared, and a Jap civilian came out, stripped. He was sent back in to get the others, and eight Jap soldiers and one sailor filed out. They were all badly beaten up by concussion. They insisted that everybody else in the cave was dead.

Three 135th men * then pushed their way cautiously through the cave mouth. They found Schroeder's body and removed it. The rest of the cave was a mess of shattered Japs. When they came out they blasted the cave mouth, and the last act of the Battle of Tinian was over.

Here are the remaining entries in my Tinian notebook.

* The three: Lester A. Smith (Chief Carpenter's Mate, Seattle, Wash.); Harold Scheer (Electrician's Mate Second, Poughkeepsie, N. Y.); and Grover E. Brunk (Shipfitter Third, Santa Fe, N. M.).

TINIAN

The old 9th Battalion, which pioneered in Iceland, had a model camp on Tinian. (See photo.) An amazingly high percentage of "original men" were still with the battalion. They expected to move on to Okinawa during the summer. One member of the 9th was the only honest-to-god professional sailmaker in the service. He was twenty-nine-year-old John M. Henderson (Boatswain's Mate First, Wilmington, Cal.). In private life Henderson makes sails for Hollywood and for private yachtsmen. He told me about making sails for General Patton's *Arcturus,* and for such Hollywood productions as *Mutiny on the Bounty* and *Captains Courageous.* He used to attend all the yacht races in Hawaii, and has been around the world five times.

"I was the first apprentice sailmaker to be taken into the trade in twenty-five years," he said. "It took me six years to become a master sailmaker. But since I have been in the Navy, the only time I've picked up a palm was when I made the battalion's theater curtain." (See photo.)

Another thriving industry on Tinian is the Bunn Mattress Renovating Company. John C. Bunn (Carpenter's Mate First, Hot Springs, Ark.) found his "sack" getting very thin and very hard. He procured some Jap equipment and built a crude but effective mattress renovator. In Ruel F. "Red" Hiberd (Carpenter's Mate Second, Garland, Tex.) Bunn found a partner who had worked as a mattress finisher for ten years in Dallas. The two were taking twenty old beaten-out mattresses a day, tearing them up, and rebuilding them softer and fluffier than new. (See photo.) They, too, had already "acquired" a B-29 to ride home in.

Frederick B. Hirschman (Shipfitter First, Baltimore, Md., the 92nd Battalion) is the only Seabee who ever used his bare white bottom to save his life. Hirschman was cutting across a canebrake one day to rejoin his pipe-line crew when grenades began to explode all around him. He had run smack

111

into a Marine patrol which was flushing out some Japs. Hatless, wearing only shorts, and with his own body as sun-browned as any Jap's, Hirschman knew the Marines would grenade him on sight in that canebrake. Hastily he dropped his shorts to expose his lily-white rump, and began yelling: "Don't shoot, I'm an American!"

"Yeah, mate, we see your white rump," a Marine sergeant hollered. "Put on your pants and come on out." (See photo.)

On Tinian I revisited the veteran 38th Battalion which was working on the West Field runways. The 38th built the big naval installations at Andrews Lagoon, Adak, and was the "assault" battalion on that dry-run into Kiska. The 38th, now led by Commander George Rezac (CEC, USNR, Charleston, N. C.), was also preparing to move on to Oki-nawa during the summer. The last time I had seen Com-mander Rezac he had been with the 120th Battalion at Arzew, North Africa. I also spent an hour in the 38th's photolab, shooting the breeze with my old friend Harold Lee Reed Cooper (Photographer's Mate Second, Freeport, N. Y.). The first night on Kiska, Cooper and I worked all night to convert a Jap galley into a photolab. When I left Cooper on Tinian he gave me four wonderful, nude pin-ups.

Tinian's resemblance to Manhattan would not be complete without a LaGuardia, and the 107th Battalion provided one. He was the battalion fire chief, "Mayor" Thomas A. Colucci (Seaman First, New Rochelle, N. Y.). "Mayor" Colucci, tearing up and down Tinian's "Broadway" looking for fires, was a dead-ringer for the impetuous "Little Flower." (See photo.)

IV

SAIPAN

As OKINAWA will be remembered for its fleas and Eniwetok for its flies, Saipan will be remembered for its frogs. Those goddam frogs were everywhere. They hopped into your foxhole and down your neck. When you laid down at night they were under your blanket, and you squashed them. When you bounded out of your "sack" and ran for the "head" in your bare feet, you squashed another big toad with every step.

The Japs, being the world's most skillful gardeners, like frogs. Frogs were important in the Jap scheme for colonizing the Pacific islands. As soon as they had grabbed Saipan from the Germans after the last war, they began sending in frogs with every shipload of colonists. The frogs were to eat all the insects on the island.

Almost as numerous as the frogs were the snails. The snails, also imported, served double duty: the snails ate insects and the Japs ate the snails.

"But the snails lived to reverse this process," one Seabee philosopher told me. "The Japs had brought in the snails to eat, but the snails wound up eating the Japs."

Ten Seabee battalions had a part in our conquest and subsequent development of Saipan. I have mentioned the 18th and 121st which, as parts of the 2nd and 4th Marine Divisions, were the assault battalions. A detachment of the far-sailing 302nd Pontoon Battalion handled the causeways, barges, and piers. A detachment of the 301st "Harbor Stretcher" Battalion brought in the dredging equipment for expanding the harbor. The 31st Special (stevedore) Battalion moved in to handle cargo. Then five construction battalions—the 17th, 39th, 51st, 101st, and 117th—came in to build the naval installations and do general construction.

The reef was the complicating factor in the landing on Saipan. There is a fair natural harbor, but the channel leading through the reef into the harbor is quite narrow. Our main beach—Blue Beach—was inside the harbor; on the night after the D-Day landing, the 302nd Seabees were ordered to build a pontoon pier on Blue Beach. To do this, they had to work the 175-foot pontoon assemblies through the narrow channel in the darkness, and in the face of Jap artillery fire. The job was accomplished, however, with Harry A. Ringle (Boatswain's Mate First, San Angelo, Tex.) guiding the lead assembly through the channel. The pier was ready by daylight, and about seventy per cent of all the Saipan cargo rolled over this pier.

On Yellow Beach, which handled vehicular cargo only, there was no channel through the reef. The landing ships drove in toward the reef and grounded up to 150 feet short of the reef. Single causeway sections were used to get the tanks and trucks to the reef, where they either were able to run or were pulled through the three-foot water to the beach 100 yards away. As in many Pacific landings, this operation was supervised by Lieutenant Commander Jack McGaraghan (CEC, USNR, Eureka, Cal.).

The men who operated the fuel and ammunition barges had a particularly rough time of it at Saipan. These fellows lived in a never-ending drama of TNT and high octane. They operated between the Liberty ships anchored offshore and the beach. No ship, unless it were unloading on the barge, would allow them to tie up alongside, because even

114

when empty, the ponderous barge could stave in the side of a ship. Loaded with mortar shells, bombs, or gasoline, the barge was about as welcome in your area as a floating mine.

The result was that from the moment they dropped their 22 x 40-foot barges off the LSTs, the barge men became the "Bastards of the Beaches." No one offshore loved them; everyone avoided them. In sun, wind, and rain they had to live and sleep on the open barges. They begged food from ships, which would toss them a few cans of rations hastily to get them to go away. Of course they weren't supposed to have fires aboard the loaded barges, and that should mean no smoking, no cooking, and no coffee-making while the barges were loaded. But sometimes it took hours to get a load of high octane up to the beach and unloaded.

For a study in taciturn contemptuousness, I found nothing in the war to equal this picture:

A pontoon barge, loaded with many drums of 100-octane, crawls slowly toward the beach. Four begrimed and be-whiskered Seabees are on it. They've been living on it for a month. Long since, they have ceased to give a good god-dam. One of them is at the helm, smoking his pipe. The other three are sitting together, cross-legged, on top of the drums. They are making coffee with a blowtorch, smoking, cussing softly.

At any instant one of those pipes or that blowtorch may send the whole barge to Kingdom Come. But the barge keeps chugging toward the beach; the Seabees keep smoking, making their coffee. What the hell!

At Saipan the 302nd had twenty barge crews—one crew to the barge—which operated continuously for fifty-four days. The crews averaged three trips a day, and during the entire fifty-four days, they slept ashore three nights!

The general handyman for these barge men was an old-timer named G. W. Shaffer (Carpenter's Mate Second,

Florence, Mont.). "I'm as good as any nurse, but I'm not as good-looking," Shaffer described himself. He "procured," cooked, made coffee, and bound up mashed fingers. Sitting atop a case of TNT, he would roast a whole side of "procured" beef, feed his own crew, then cut off chunks and heave them over to other passing barges.

Shaffer's coffee became famous at Saipan. On a couple of previous beaches, his coffee had tasted a little flat, but at Saipan, after he acquired a parrot which perched on his shoulder and roosted on the coffee can, his product attained that full, rich blend of fine flavors which the radio announcers extol.

The 17th Battalion, which I visited on Saipan, was an old "Newfie" outfit. They were the first of three battalions sent to Newfoundland in 1942 to build our big base at Argentia; and they are still telling stories about the Newfie Express, Newfie Screech, and the Laundry Queens.

The Newfie Express was a train which negotiated at irregular intervals the eighty miles between Argentia and St. Johns. It was as informal as the Toonerville Trolley, as unpredictable as Judgment Day. At innumerable unscheduled stops the passengers had to repair it before it could proceed. At each scheduled stop it was boarded by howling kids hawking beer in buckets.

It is estimated that, to make their "liberties" in St. Johns and to enjoy the merchandise of New Gower Street, the Seabees repaired the Newfie Express no less than 1473 times. It is hoped that this item will be included in the final totting up of Lend-Lease.

Another item which must be added to the Lend-Lease tab is all those teeth which the Seabees supplied to Newfie women. Because of a dietary deficiency, few of these "Laundry Queens" had any teeth, so the Seabees, who re-

116

fuse to bear unsightliness, either made or ordered from Sears, Roebuck hundreds of sets of teeth.

Newfie Screech is an abomination with which the Newfoundlanders enriched themselves at the expense of lonely, cold, and thirsty Americans. It tastes like a mixture of vodka and Vitalis, further fortified with red pepper and sulphuric acid. Once, after a Seabee got drunk on it, he didn't speak to his hut-mates for a week. They assumed he was mad, so when he did begin talking again they asked him what the hell he had been sore about.

"Hell, I haven't been mad," he exclaimed. "I just got my voice back!"

The International Fleet Canteen was Newfie's noisiest spot. Jitterbug music blared from fourteen loudspeakers, and convoy sailors of many nationalities gathered there to beer up and commit a little friendly mayhem. After the Seabees arrived and demonstrated their zest for both the beer and the mayhem, the "word" was passed in five languages: STAY AWAY FROM THOSE YANK SAILORS WITH THE GI SHOES.

The only "Jap jeep" on Saipan was the property of A. J. Waisner (Chief Machinist's Mate, Minneapolis, Minn.), a big, efficient forty-four-year-old Swedish mechanic. While he was giving me a ride in the Jap jeep, Waisner explained that it was a two-cylindered, air-cooled, four-wheel-drive affair, something like a four-wheeled motorcycle. He said it lacked the power of our jeeps, and wouldn't take much abuse. He also told me about his dancing with Joan Blondell in Newfie. "God, she smelled good," he said.

The old 1012th Detachment, which rushed down to build some installations on Ecuador's Galapagos Islands in the days when the Panama Canal was in danger, later became a part of the 17th Battalion. Roy H. Larkins (Carpenter's Mate First, Oklahoma City) and Jack Dismore (Carpenter's

Mate Second, Smithland, Ky.) told me about the big turtles and about how lonely it was down there.

One night on Saipan the 17th was watching Miss Betty Grable dance in that technicolored musical about Argentina. The title escapes me, but Don Ameche, with a sticky accent, was also in it. Miss Grable had just reached that part of her dance where she stops suddenly, throws back her arms, throws out her chest, and shakes all up the front, when a Seabee guard cut his carbine loose about fifty yards from the crowd. He fired the whole clip, then could be heard shouting to the corporal of the guard that he had killed a Jap.

Not a man left his hillside movie seat. The only reaction was a little low, angry muttering about that "goddam guard" making so much noise.

The 39th was the first Seabee battalion on Maui in the Hawaiian Islands. They landed on Maui February 5, 1943, took over from the civilian contractors, and completed the naval air base.

The 39th's work schedule, however, was interrupted briefly but seriously by a deep and burning issue involving the battalion's sacred honor. Only swift and Solomon-like judgment by Admiral Nimitz prevented the 39th from postponing its war against the Japs and waging bloody civil war against the 99th Seabees.

The 39th, mostly Texans, had labeled themselves the Lone Star Battalion. But so had the 99th, and there was gusty argument over which battalion was first, which was most Texan, etc. It is hardly a matter which Texans can discuss philosophically. Fort Sumter was about to be fired upon when Admiral Nimitz, himself a Texan, rushed in to arbitrate.

The Admiral heard all the argument, deliberated while

118

he practiced with his own six-shooters, and reached a verdict which dripped with Texan diplomacy. The 99th, he ruled, would be the Lone Star Battalion, but the 39th would become the Longhorn Battalion. He flew over to Maui to explain his verdict personally to the 39th and congratulate them on their "victory."

"The longhorn is a fierce and noble animal," the Admiral declared, "which embodies the fighting spirit of all Texans. There are two sharp ends to those horns, and there's a helluva lot of bull in between!"

After this speech and after Governor "Pass-the-Biscuits-Pappy" O'Daniel had wired the battalions that Texas loved them both, the 39th accepted the Longhorn label and went back to work.

In the rich world souvenir market, all Seabee battalions followed the same performance curve. When they arrived on their first island, they were a "buying battalion," but by the time they reached their second island, they had become a "selling battalion." Because they operated along the beach, they were in an ideal trading position: they could buy from the Army and Marines who were up in the hills collecting the souvenirs, and they could sell to the "swabies" who, the Seabees insisted, would buy anything.

The Seabees were the middlemen of the souvenir market. They dealt in quantity lots, and to keep their supply varied and plentiful, they were constantly making souvenirs to order. Signs reading "Souvenirs Made To Order" hung over many a Seabee shop.

The 39th had become a "selling battalion" by the time it reached Saipan. It specialized in cat-eye rings. In Seabee selling parlance, the cat-eye is a "semiprecious stone." Actually, of course, it is a shell, but it will take an extraordinarily high polish. Some of these Seabee rings are real works of art.

Jap searchlights on Saipan were a silver mine for the

119

39th's cat-eye jewelers. One searchlight yielded enough pure silver to make fifty rings. Set with a brilliantly polished cat-eye, such a ring would bring $50 in U. S. currency. Stainless steel rings ran from $20 to $40. E. B. Johnson (Electrician's Mate Third, Mulga, Ala.) had sold $2100 worth of cat-eyes on Saipan; Julius Millet (Gunner's Mate First, New Orleans, La.) had sold $900 worth.

Hara-kiri knives and Jap generals' swords are the most profitable items turned out by the Seabee metalsmiths. I know of one sword, made by a Seabee but alleged to have been taken from the Jap commander of Saipan, which was raffled off for $600. Hara-kiri knives, which a skilled metalsmith can turn out in three evenings' work, went for $50.

The 39th had an inexhaustible stock of Jap flags priced from $20 up. An Army man would always sell his soul to a Seabee for a piece of plyboard, so the 39th swapped plyboard to the Army for parachutes, then cut up the parachutes and made Jap flags.

The first day the battalion was on the island some of the 39th's merchandisers salvaged a Jap steam engine, rigged up hot showers, and began swapping "luxurious hot showers" to the Army for souvenirs. Similarly, they rushed an ice machine into operation and put themselves into an even more powerful bargaining position. When they began making ice cream, they cornered the whole souvenir supply.

Here's how the Seabees manipulated the ice cream. They traded ice cream to the Army for souvenirs; they traded the souvenirs to the ships for more ice cream "mix," which gave them more ice cream to eat and trade for more souvenirs. There was a neat souvenir profit on each transaction.

All Seabee battalions had hobby shops and encouraged the men to spend their leisure making souvenirs for themselves and their families. Their extra output, plus the volume of Jap stuff acquired by machinations like the above, put the Seabees in a very firm position in the souvenir market. (See photo.)

There are a number of individual Seabees who left the service with a neat $3000 souvenir profit with which to start a business or build a home.

The 39th claimed the world's softball championship of both the Army and the Navy. Their team won all the tournaments it had a chance to enter, and won 101 of 104 games played. Their star pitcher, E. P. Jones (Electrician's Mate Second, Blytheville, Ark.) won 63 games and lost one.

The 51st Battalion was still another old Dutch Harbor outfit. They were led by Commander Gerald W. "Snuffy" Smith (CEC, USNR, Kirkwood, Mo.), a driving, fast-talking old construction stiff, known to his men as "Windy." Smith was especially vociferous when supporting his contention that the Aleutians were the only "romantic" construction job of the war, that the Aleutians were the best training ground for the Seabees, and that all the key battalions in the final phase of the Pacific war were Aleutian-trained outfits.

"My boys are a bunch of solid Joes," he told me, "who tackled old Ballyhoo Mountain when it was fifty below zero, and built those big gun positions when we thought the Japs were coming after us. Those were the days when men had to be men."

In the middle of a fierce winter at Dutch, twenty 51st men were living on remote Erskine Point, building some installations there. A mail boat brought them mail and supplies. But for ten days a williwaw had prevented the boat from making its rounds. The men, almost mad from the williwaw, needed mail badly. Finally, one rough night the mail boat came to within 200 yards of the Point. It could venture no nearer because of the heavy sea.

Three men—Warrant Officer R. A. Manner (CEC, USNR, Davenport, Iowa); A. H. Corden (Seaman First, Lansing, Mich.); and Carl Simpson (Seaman First, Covington, Ky.) —volunteered to attempt to reach the mail boat. They launched a small boat, risked their lives for an hour battling the sea, and managed to get back ashore with the precious mail. In the snow-banked dugout, the men grabbed the letters hungrily.

Manner, wet and exhausted, sat down to read his one letter, from his wife. She informed him that she had filed suit for divorce.

The biggest single laugh at Dutch was provided by the 51st's fancy drum major, E. W. Burkart (Carpenter's Mate Second, San Francisco, Cal.). In a formal reception for the admiral, Burkart, while swinging his baton and maneuvering the 51st's band, backed off the dock and fell fifteen feet into icy water. Right in the middle of "Anchors Aweigh," the band stopped playing, and all the bandsmen joined the admiral in a belly-laugh while poor Burkart was being fished out.

Modest, soft-voiced, little forty-six-year-old W. R. Petersen (Boatswain's Mate First, Skamokawa, Wash.) was the principal character in another little drama of the sea at Dutch. Petersen is a commercial fisherman on the Columbia River in private life, and he handles a boat like Willie Hoppe handles a billiard cue.

A seventy-mile gale was blowing at Dutch. All boats had been ordered ashore, but at Eider Point, fifteen miles across open water, J. J. Breckenridge (Shipfitter Third, Seattle, Wash.) had appendicitis. If he were to live, he had to have an operation. Petersen, recognized as the best boat man at Dutch, said he thought he could make it. Dr. A. B. Carson (Lieutenant, MC, USNR, San Francisco) went with him.

It took Petersen three hours to work the boat across the

roaring, churning water. His face froze, and he had to wear a mask and be treated for many days before he recovered from the trip.

R. K. "Gunner" Moore (Gunner's Mate Second, Dunlap, Iowa) was the ace procurer and distiller of the 51st. He told me that those big coats the men wore at Dutch were a great help in the matter of "procuring" extra beers, but that the Saipan climate was much more favorable for the fermentation of squeezins.

Moore's hut-mates still talk about the time he was put on Shore Patrol at Dutch. At the end of Moore's first day with the "bulls," he really brought home the bacon—two Hormel hams and seven cases of beer.

While the 51st was at Hueneme, Cal., resting from its Dutch job, it threw such a "beer bust" that the camp skipper decreed no-beer for the entire camp for two weeks. This made the 51st about as popular in camp as dengue. At the end of the two weeks, the battalion was embarking for its second assignment. The camp band came down to the dock, carrying a big sign which said: FAREWELL 51ST! WE'LL HAVE BEER TONITE!

On October 9, 1944, the 51st, together with half the 88th Battalion, landed at Ulithi to do one of the vital, hurry-up jobs of the war. Ulithi had been chosen as a fleet anchorage in the Western Pacific. It is an atoll 600 miles southwest of Guam, with a lagoon broad enough to shelter not only our fighting ships but also the service fleet.

Largest islet of the Ulithi Atoll is Falalop. There are 260 acres on Falalop, eighty acres of which were used for the airstrip. The strip was large enough for the transport planes which roared into Ulithi by the score when the fleet was in. Fighter planes were also based there to protect the anchorage, and there were a few bombers to neutralize the Jap base at Yap, which was only ninety miles away.

The Seabees built housing, storage, and a tank farm on the rest of Falalop, and converted Mogmog, a small islet, into a beer garden for the fleet.

A C-47 was in the water at the end of the runway at Falalop. John Alvee (Boatswain's Mate First, San Francisco) had rigged a sling under it and was lifting it out with a crane. A major, the pilot, approached him and said: "I don't like the way you are pulling that plane out."

Alvee eyed the major and replied: "Hell, I don't like the way you put it in here."

One of the 51st's Filipino members, L. F. Tolentino (Machinist's Mate First, Manila, P. I.) smiled broadly when he saw all the game chickens the Japs had left on Saipan. He quickly became the island's cockfighting impresario.

The 31st Special Seabees, stevedores, unloaded 250,000 tons of cargo during its first five months on Saipan. It was commended by the Air Force for its rapid and careful handling of B-29 engines.

On Christmas Eve, 1944, the battalion sent its fine choir to sing carols for the boys in the hospitals. The choir had just begun singing "Silent Night." The majestic words poured out: "Silent night, holy night, all is calm—" but just at this point Jap bombs began to fall—"all is bright—" and at this point the lights on the island went out.

"That's all. Let's hit the dirt," the leader said.

The 101st Battalion was the "Roosevelt" Battalion—the only Seabee battalion ever to be "inspected" by the late President. When the President visited Hawaii, the 101st was selected to receive the Commander-in-Chief's "word" to the Seabees. They turned out in dungarees. The President, accompanied by General MacArthur and Admiral Nimitz, drove through the camp, then spoke briefly.

"I just wanted to say howdy do," he said. "This is the first bunch of Seabees I have ever inspected overseas. The Seabees are known all over the world today. You have come forward more quickly than any branch of the service, and I want you to know that we are all mighty proud of you."

After the President spoke, General MacArthur shook hands and chatted with an old personal friend in the 101st: fifty-year-old William M. Tucker (Storekeeper First, Little Rock, Ark.).

The 101st was the best-insured unit in either the Army or Navy. It was the only unit in the armed services in which every man owned a $10,000 National Service Life Insurance Policy. The record was due to the efforts of Irwin G. Rakel (Yeoman First, Cincinnati, O.). Rakel was an insurance salesman in private life, and he just wanted to be sure he didn't go stale while in the service.

After the 101st arrived at Saipan, Maurice G. Ruby (Machinist's Mate Second, Boston, Mass.) received a notice from his draft board ordering him to appear for examination. Ruby did his damndest, but couldn't comply.

During an aid raid on Saipan, William L. Doyle (Machinist's Mate First, Quincy, Mass.) jerked on his pants and ran to the edge of his foxhole. There he stopped suddenly and went into a strip-tease routine that would have shamed Gypsy Rose Lee. His "bumps" were particularly vigorous.

It developed that a hornet had sacked up in the seat of Doyle's pants, and Doyle was executing those vigorous "bumps" each time the hornet made contact.

Percy J. Hallett (Shipfitter First, Chagrin Falls, O.) was really "chagrined" when he waked and saw the evidence before him. After gnawing a hole in Hallett's drawers, a mouse had keeled over stone dead. The battalion newspaper announced that thenceforth Hallett's drawers, instead of traps and "other poisons," would be used in the war against Saipan's rats.

No man ever thought he'd live to see it in the Navy, but it happened. The Navy was once a hairy-chested outfit, and the Seabees exuded more all-around he-ness than any branch of the Navy. That's why every man-jack of the 101st blinked in holy horror when he examined the dungarees issued him on Saipan.

The britches had been prerump-sprung. They flared enticingly around the beam. As sure as God made little apples, they were WAVES' britches!

Either in resignation or defiance—and because no more britches were available—the Seabees crawled into the WAVES' britches—and wore them. (See photo.)

Those droopy bottoms on a thousand good men were a juicy target for a spate of hilarious wisecracks. I wish I could report a few of the best ones, but unfortunately, like much of this war's wisdom, they are unprintable.

In *Can Do!* I told of how the Supply Corps had furnished the Seabees a bidet on Kiska. At the time I thought the bidet was a mistake. But now that I consider it in connection with the WAVES' britches on Saipan, I am convinced that the Supply Corps is waging a planned campaign to femininize the Seabees.*

It is no secret that the Seabees liked the Chamorros better than any other native people in the Pacific. The Chamorros are proud, clean, friendly, and intensely loyal to America.

* Supply Corps officers are the most ruthless poker players in the Pacific. They check locks, show no mercy. Reporting this incident is one of my efforts to get even with them for all the money they have lifted from me.

They come nearer doing a day's work than any other natives. Most of the Chamorros live on Guam and are Americans, but there is a colony of several hundred on Saipan. No people we have "liberated" in this war have welcomed us as sincerely as have the Chamorros, and they deserve all the best from America.

On Christmas, 1944, the 101st Seabees gave a party for 200 Chamorro children. A detail had searched the island for a suitable Christmas tree. The cooks and the metal-smiths collaborated to decorate the tree, and the entire battalion had a part in making the gifts. When the great day arrived, a convoy of trucks brought the children into the camp, where they were "adopted" by 200 Seabee "fathers." Walt Disney's wonderful gift to all children, Mr. Mickey Mouse, was first on the program. The children responded with carols in their native tongue, and then came Santa Claus.

Aaron J. Peterson (Chief Carpenter's Mate, Le Grand, Cal.) was Santa Claus, wearing a cotton beard provided by the pharmacist's mates. Finally, there was ice cream, great, heaping bowls of it, so that Christmas could end for the Chamorro kids—as it should for all kids—with a tummy-ache.

The 101st's party for the Chamorros, however, was not the most remarkable Christmas party on Saipan. The most remarkable was given by the 117th Battalion, which performed the same routine using Japanese children!

The 117th had debated the question for weeks. They wanted to give a kids' party on Christmas; Christmas without kids is a dull business. But the 101st already had arranged for the Chamorro children. If the 117th was going to entertain kids, there was only one place the kids could come from: Susupe, the Jap compound. But would it be right to entertain Jap kids? Could a man feel warm and friendly sitting by a Jap kid on Christmas?

Finally, the 117th agreed that "kids is kids," so on Christmas Day big Uncle Sam trucks were at Camp Susupe to pick up the Jap kids. The "fathers" adopted the kids; Mickey Mouse elicited the usual squeals of delight; Santa Claus delivered the handmade gifts; and United States Navy ice cream poured down Jap throats. The little slant eyes bulged and twinkled over it all, and everybody felt good about it when it was over.

Greatest tragedy for the 117th was the death of "Queenie." "Queenie" was a beautiful white German shepherd, a war dog. The boys of the 117th saw her and loved her down on Cat Island, off Gulfport, Miss., where they trained. When they moved on, they—well, they "procured" Queenie and took her with them. She had been bred to another white shepherd.

On the ship going to Hawaii, the time came for Queenie to be delivered. No millionaire's wife ever enjoyed more solicitous care, or had more expensive medical talent standing by to aid her, or more men pulling anxiously for her to come through. Every one of the 2000 men aboard knew that Queenie was about to have pups, and he waited for the loudspeakers to bring him the word. A microphone had been set up in the delivery room, and doctors, veterinarians, and pharmacist's mates were there, debating how best to help Queenie.

At seven-thirty A.M., birth of the first pup was announced. The ordeal had begun. All day long it went on, and God, how Queenie suffered. The pups kept coming, and each one seemed harder for Queenie. Down in the engine room, up on the bridge, everywhere on the ship, you could see anxiety in men's faces as they listened, hoped, waited. The poker games began, became listless, then folded up. Conversation seemed unnecessary. Up in the delivery room a famous obstetrician and a veterinary matched their skills, tried everything. The skipper cut down speed so the ship wouldn't roll so much.

By five P.M., sixteen pups had been born. The ordeal was over. Queenie and the pups were brought out on deck so everybody could file by and see them. The pups looked fine, but it was obvious that the price had been too high for Queenie. Her soft, beautiful eyes had death in them.

With all her medical assistance, Queenie lived until the battalion reached Red Hill on Hawaii. There she died. The boys gave her the sort of military funeral a war dog deserves. And they raised her pups.

Queenie's sons and daughters were scattered all over the Pacific. Wherever they went, they helped Americans to see it through. Their friendliness and devotion made the loneliness a little easier to bear.

Their mother was a lady.

All pictures on the following pages are Official Navy Photographs. Some of them were taken by the author; the others by various Seabee photographers who worked with the author. Navy regulations prohibit the crediting of pictures to individual cameramen, but the author is particularly indebted to two men who contributed to this collection: Thomas E. Gilham, of Woonsocket, R.I., and William H. Nichols, of Morristown, N. J.

Vice Admiral Ben Moreell, Chief of the Navy's Civil Engineer Corps and Chief
of the Bureau of Yards & Docks, is the creator and top boss of the Seabees.
Under his direction the Seabees have built the great sea-roads from Normandy
to Okinawa.

Second in command of the Seabees in Rear Admiral L. B. Combs, Civil Engineer Corps, United States Navy. He is assistant Chief of the Bureau of Yards & Docks.

Suribachi and the First Terrace at Iwo. The soft, volcanic sand stalled our vehicles. The picture was made at Red Beach-1 shortly after H-Hour.

Two views of the Iwo beach on D-Day plus 4. At top, looking south toward Suribachi; bottom, looking north toward the bluffs. The wrecked vehicles hindered the landing of supplies and reenforcements.

Before and after views of the Central Strip at Iwo. With the Seabees working night and day, the wrecked Jap "meat balls" soon made way for the sleek P-51 Mustangs. The Mustangs are the planes which escorted the B-29's to Japan.

Like prairie dogs, the Marines and Seabees dug into the volcanic sand at Iwo. The view here is of Red Beach on the sixth day.

Here is how the Japs lived on the northern end of Iwo Jima. Compare these animal-like warrens to the Seabee quonset hut camp shown elsewhere.

Could this be the roof of a Bronx tenement house? It's the weather deck of an LST carrying Marines and Seabees to Iwo Jima. Note the pontoon barges slung on both sides of the ship.

Much of the sulphurous dirt handled by the Seabees at Iwo was boiling hot. Top, work is progressing on the North Field at Iwo. Bottom, the 31st Battalion's big cats line up after completing the highway up Mt. Suribachi.

Dedication of the 5th Marine Cemetery at Iwo. Four thousand Marines and Seabees gave their lives for the dirty little eight square miles called Iwo Jima. Most of the Seabees killed at Iwo are buried in this cemetery.

The first flag atop Mt. Suribachi. The flag in the famous picture made by AP Photographer Joe Rosenthal was the second flag on the blood-soaked volcano.

A typical Seabee camp. The 9th Battalion, veterans of a year in Iceland, built and occupied this camp on Tinian before moving on to Okinawa. Note the theater, warehouses, and machine shops, as well as the quonset quarters of the men.

The Seabees celebrated the completion of each new 8500-foot runway for the B-29's at Tinian. The plane here is one of many sponsored by Seabee units. Below, the curious ramp, described in detail in the chapter on Tinian, which the Seabees used to scale the bluffs in the landing operation.

Above, left, Joseph J. Millet, Gonzales, La., examines his stock of "cat-eyes." The rings bring from $20 to $100. Above, right, Charles A. Hinish, Lake Geneva, Wis., 112th Bat., dives for cat-eyes. Below, left, John M. Henderson, Wilmington, Cal., 9th Bat., only professional sailmaker in the Navy, Below, right, W. B. Pugh, Clifton, Tenn., 18th Bat., champion well-driller of the Pacific.

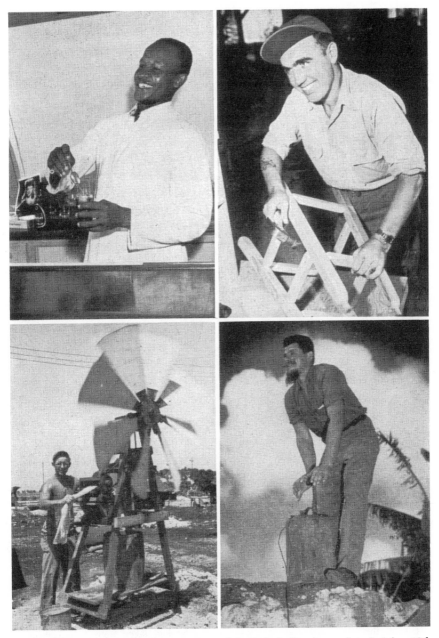

Four Seabee personalities on Tinian. Above, left, Jack A. Bauchman, Los Angeles, 13th Bat., bartender. Above, right, Michael J. Crowley, Allston, Mass., 13th Bat., builder of the fabulous "golden stairway" officers club at Dutch. Lower left, Thomas A. "Mush" Hennen, Pittsburgh, Pa., 107th Bat., demonstrates his windmill washing machine. Lower right, Milan Mihailov, Guy Mills, Pa., 92nd Bat., sets off a big blast.

H. D. "Pop" Niday, Houston, Tex., veteran of two world wars, is a colorful figure in the great 18th Bat. He was at Guadalcanal and made D-Day landings at Tarawa, Saipan and Tinian. When a Jap hit him in the chest with a grenade at Saipan, "Pop" struck off the Jap's head with that saber which he had taken from a Jap officer on Guadalcanal.

Above, left, Ben J. Blackburn, Lamgrasos, Tex., 121st Bat., holds the pistol which snapped three times when a Jap officer stuck it in his face at Kwajalein. He slapped the Jap down three times, finally got the pistol. Above, right, F. J. Chmielewicz, Camden, N.J., 121st Bat., holds the range pole with which he killed a Jap. Below, Edward N. Bittenbender, Wilkes-Barre, Pa., hefts a 225-pound tube from a Turnapull tire.

Carl S. Ball, San Francisco, Cal., 92nd Bat., is a "gook herder" on Tinian. Here Ball is giving a yo-yo to his Jap charge at left who has three children. At right is Frederick B. Hirschman, Baltimore, Md., 92nd Bat., who saved his life by exposing his white bottom. (See story.)

The 302nd Pontoon Battalion carries its barges slung alongside an LST in this manner. Below, men of the 302nd deliver mortar shells at Saipan.

Lieut. V. G. Martin, CEC, USNR, Long Beach, Cal., designed this ship-side elevator to facilitate the handling of wounded men in rough seas. Litters can be placed from small craft onto the elevator and then lifted to the deck of a ship.

The causeway pier erected by the 302nd Seabees at Chanon Kanoa, Saipan. Right, unloading ammunition over the causeways laid up to the reef at the other landing beach on Saipan.

Men going ashore inside the reef at Guam. Below, a 75-ton crane, mounted on a pontoon barge, is used to hoist a causeway section so that it can be slung alongside the LST. Inset, Alva Parker, Tampa, Fla., and Alfred Luna, Vertram, Tex., prepare to drop the causeway from the LST.

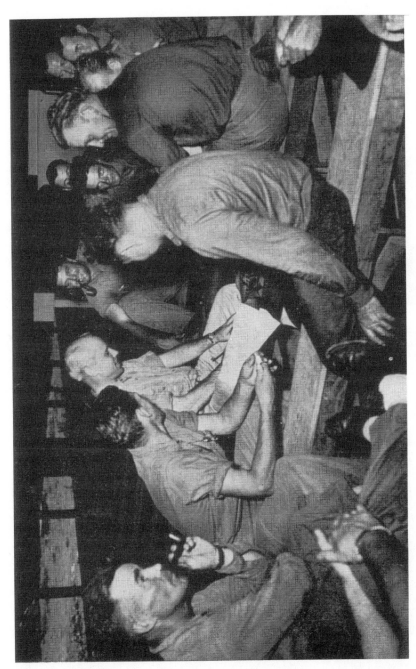

The author, War Correspondent William Bradford Huie, talking with a group of 48th Seabees on Guam.

The first experimental method by which we hoped to "bridge the water gap" at Normandy called for the construction of rubber roads which could be rolled up and transported. When unrolled and put under tension, the road could support heavy vehicles. This plan was tried out in Scotland and abandoned.

A second plan for "bridging the water gap" called for construction of 3300-foot-long stationary steel bridges and pierheads. This plan, also tried out at the experimental beach in Scotland, was abandoned because at low tide all cargo would have to be hoisted 20 feet to the pier level.

LST's were unloaded at Normandy by the Seabee-manned rhino ferries. Left, Seabees of the 111th Battalion are struggling to "marry" the big barge to an LST off Omaha Beach. Right, the first loaded rhino to start for Omaha Beach before H-Hour.

Above the rhino is married to the LST and taking on cargo off Omaha Beach on D-Day. Below, at the beach the rhino discharged its vehicles in about three feet of water.

Here are the first "phoenixes" sunk at Omaha Beach to form the sea wall. Each "phoenix" was fitted with an anti-aircraft gun manned by an Army crew.

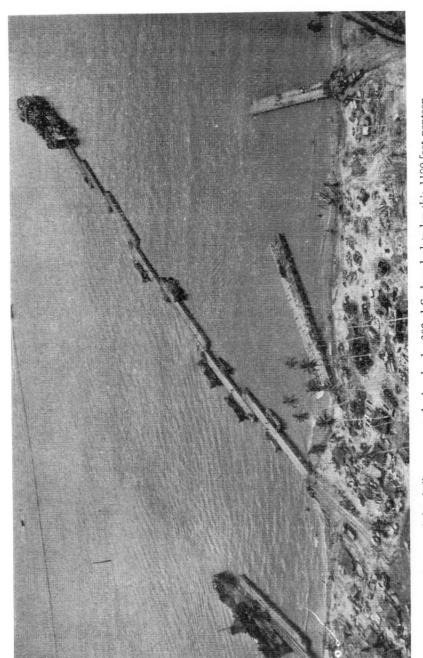

Because of the shallow water at the beach, the 302nd Seabees had to lay this 1100-foot pontoon causeway at Leyte to unload the LST's.

The Liberty ship docks at the great naval base at Samar in the Philippines were built by the rugged 75th Seabees, veterans of two years in the South Pacific.

The Filipinos aided the Seabees by providing entertainment and some labor. Above is a native band which played each day while the Seabees worked on the Samar airstrip. Below, a Filipino carabao crew is snaking pipe for the 75th Seabees. Three Filipinos operate one carabao; and the carabao will not work during the heat of the day.

A trio of dynamiters on the big strips at Tinian: Johnny W. Hartline, Palatka, Fla., 13th Bat.; John J. Burke, Scranton, Pa., 121st Bat.; and Elvin H. Vernon, Phillipsburg, N. J., 7th Bat. Below, heavy equipment repairmen: Roscoe H. Davis, Columbia, Tex., 121st Bat.; Chester W. Harris, New Orleans, La., 67th Bat.; and Frank Waski, Port Jefferson, Long Island, 13th Bat.

Commodore Halloran, designer of the intricate ramp used in the Tinian landing, is shown conferring with some of the men who built and operated the ramps. The commodore, a graduate of Dartmouth, was in charge of all Seabee operations on Tinian.

Signs such as this one are displayed at all Seabee camps. Here the mighty 61st Battalion advertises that it has served on Guadalcanal, Emirau, Banika, Leyte and Samar; that it has shot down four Jap planes, and killed 10 Jap paratroopers.

This picture, taken on Iwo Jima, gives some idea of the way the Japs build underground fortifications. The partially exposed concrete tube extends 30 feet downward to an ordnance room. Ladders and a crude elevator are inside the tube. Seabee earthmovers were constantly amazed at this sort of stuff on Iwo.

The Navy's fabulous Captain "Bill" Painter, Seattle, Wash., was in charge of raising the battleships *California* and *West Virginia* at Pearl Harbor. Here is the *West Virginia* as work was begun on her, January 5, 1942.

In rescuing the battleships the procedure was, first, to repair the torpedo damage so that the water could be pumped from the ships; then to bring the ships into drydock. The ships were made watertight by the construction of wooden coffer dams such as this one on the *California*.

The 2600-foot sunken pontoon causeway at Normandy functioned in the manner shown here. At any tidal stage, a craft drawing no more than five feet of water could reach a dry portion of the causeway with its ramp, and thus men and vehicles could go ashore "in the dry."

Top commander of the seven Seabee battalions which developed Iwo Jima was Commodore Bob Johnson, left, of Chicago. Right, the fabulous Captain Wil fred S. "Wild Bill" Painter, Seattle, Wash., leader of many scouting expeditions behind the Jap lines, in cluding the "Painter Expedition" into Jap-held China.

This is the way most of our tanks were landed in Normandy during the critical hours. The rhino ferries, like the one shown here approaching Omaha Beach on D-Day, took the vehicles from the LST's five miles offshore, then slowly chugged to the beaches.

Vice Admiral Ben Moreell, "King Bee" of the Seabees, inspected all of the landing devices on the eve of the invasion of Normandy. He is shown here with Lieutenant Harry Stevens, Salem, Ill., who was in charge of installing the floating bridges and pierheads at Omaha Beach.

Here is how the pierheads operated off the Normandy beaches. This line of piers, lying 4000 feet offshore from the high-tide mark at Arromanches — and parallel to the shore line — handled thousands of tons of cargo directly from the LST's and coastal vessels. The pierheads were connected to the shore by the floating bridges.

Here is the way a Jap surrendered if he chose to come out of a cave. One blast has been set off, and the Jap has come out. He has removed a'l of his clothes, and is here sending them up for minute examination. If no explosives are found in the clothing, they will be tossed back to the Jap and he will be allowed to surrender.

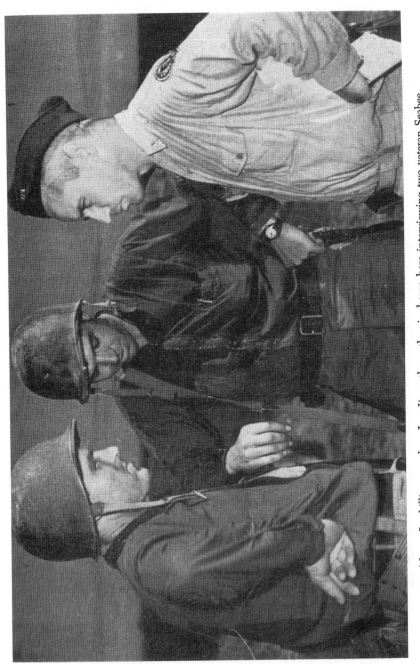

After a Jap-killing patrol on Iwo Jima, the author is shown here interviewing two veteran Seabee cave-blasters: George E. Barber, Lubbock, Tex., left, and Lincoln J. Byfield, El Paso, Tex. Both Barber and Byfield are potash miners, and both are demolition experts.

At Hollandia, New Guinea, the Seabees found it difficult to believe that there was a war on. Twenty-five hundred Wacs were there. Here is the 119th Battalion's fabled mountain-stream swimming hole, where Seabees and Wacs whiled the hours away.

V

GUAM

DESPITE their brutal fanaticism, the Japs were second-rate killers. They were reluctant, half-pint dragons hopped up with sake, *banzai,* and benzedrine. As in the final *banzai* on Iwo Jima, they often seemed more concerned with killing themselves than their adversaries.

In contrast, many Americans took to Jap slaughter with no visible reluctance. Tokyo Rose even insisted that we, not the Japs, were the barbarians of the war; that we relished killing Japs "just for souvenirs." She exaggerated, no doubt, but I'll admit that in Leslie L. Griggs (Carpenter's Mate First, 302nd Seabee Battalion) she may have had a case in point.

Griggs comes from hill country down in the Cordell Hull-Sergeant York section of East Tennessee. He was an "old man" for foxholes—forty-three, wind burned, with close-cropped hair and black eyes as cold as a rifle barrel on a frosty morning. Sitting in a jeep one moonlight night on Guam, he told me about the goddamndest mess of calculated killing I had heard of in four years of war rambling.

"The Japs got my lad," he began. "They killed him down in New Guinea. And my lad wasn't like me. Me, I'm a fightin' and a huntin' and a killin' man. I was born with a gun in my hand. When I was ten years old I could shoot a squirrel out of the highest hicker-nut tree, then shoot that squirrel again before he hit the ground. At night I was always oilin' my guns and a-monkeyin' with 'em to make 'em shoot straighter.

"But my lad wasn't like that. I never seen him with a gun in his hand. When he was a kid he begun workin' to be a doctor. I worked hard to help him. The Army let him finish medical school before it called him in. Then the Japs got him. He was Lieutenant Elmer E. Griggs, twenty-two, attached to the Air Force.

"I was in Sunday School when they called me out and give me the telegram. It hit me hard. I sat down and thought about what a shame it was. I made up my mind that I'd be rough on Japs when I got my chance."

Griggs paused to light his pipe. He wore a turned-up green cap and green shirt, and in the match glow his face took on the same greenish hue.

"Well, I had had a tough time a-tryin' to do any fightin' in this war. Lovin' guns like I do, natchly I was a National Guardsman. The Old Hickory Regiment. When we wuz sworn into the regular Army February 24, 1941, I had been everything from a buck-ass private to a top kick. At Camp Forrest I was a gunnery instructor.

"Then you know what the Army did to me? They told me I couldn't leave the country; I was too old. So I got out and joined the Seabees. That's how I got to Peleliu. I got in there on D-Day with a pontoon detachment of the 302nd. My trouble then was that I was supposed to stay on the beach. We had to bring in the stuff on those pontoon barges, and keep the causeways operating, and for the first four days we had to work night and day.

"But on the fifth day—September 20th—I got my first chance. My Chief knew about my lad, so along about noon he winked at me and I grabbed my carbine, hitched a ride on a duck, and headed for the hills.

131

"Up close to the lines I left the duck and was sneaking along a trail when a Marine sergeant saw me. 'Hey, you souvenir-huntin' Seabee sonuvabitch!' he yelled. 'Come here and get a load o' this ammo!'

"The sergeant loaded me down with three belts o' them big 50's, and me and the sergeant and two other Marines started up a ridge. We wuz almost to the top when a Jap machine gun raked us, and we plowed the dirt. We had been pinned down quite a spell when we spied some Japs sneaking out of a cave onto a ledge.

" 'Hold it,' the sergeant whispered. 'Let 'em all come out.' Then, when we had counted eight Japs, he said: "Let 'em have it.'

"I took the eighth and then the seventh Jap, and I'da got in more shots except that the shells from the sarge's BAR wuz fallin' down my neck and burnin' hell outa me. We got 'em all, and the eighth one couldn't be nobody else's but mine, since none of the Marines had fired at him.

" 'Say, this goddam Seabee can shoot,' the sarge said, and he credited me with the seventh Jap, too, and I felt pretty good. I took the eighth Jap's canteen and belt buckle and put him down as No. 1 in my book."

Griggs then showed me a greasy little book—his Huntin' Record—in which he had made many entries, complete with dates and brief, scrawled descriptions of his encounters.

"Well, from the time I got that first Jap until we left the island," he continued, "I made a total of thirty-seven huntin' trips. They are all there in the book. I'd work nights and do guard duty on the beach so I could have my afternoons free. Some days I wouldn't have no luck"—and the book showed several no-luck entries—"then other days I'd find 'em.

"It was iust like huntin' squirrels in Tennessee except the

Japs was in them caves instead of trees. I'd just go up there and still-hunt; just watch a cave until a Jap'd sneak out and then plug him. Most times I'd get a Marine to go with me so's we could 'turn' them Japs for each other. You know what a squirrel-turner is, don't you? When you're huntin' squirrels alone, the squirrel'll always try to keep the tree between you and him. So you take a 'squirrel-turner' with you—another guy who can ease around the tree and make the squirrel expose hisself to one or t'other of you.

"That Marine sergeant went with me several days, and we 'turned' Japs for each other. Didn't make no difference which way the Jap 'turned' around the rock, he got his ears shot off. A Jap sniper'd got me one day, sure, if it hadn't been for the sarge. The sniper fired at me before I seen him, and his bullet kicked coral dust in my eyes. I was blind as a bat for a minute, but the sarge picked off the Jap.

"My closest shave come one day when I wuz by myself and run into one o' them big Japs. Most Japs are little, but on Peleliu they had some o' them big bastards. Seven feet tall and weigh 300 pounds. One of these big 'uns jumped me one day and run at me with a bayonet. I opened up with my carbine, and I could tell I was hittin' him but I wasn't stoppin' him. He come on in on me, but he was nearly dead and I finished him off with my knife. I had hit that bastard fifteen times between his chin and his belly button and hadn't stopped him.

"That's the trouble with that little carbine. It's a sweet little gun, but the bullet's light. But from then on I used an old '03 I borrowed from my Chief. The bullet's heavier, and that old gun makes an affidavit ever' time she speaks.

"I learned something else the day I got my only 'wound.' A canteen'll explode if it's hit when it's too full of water. A Jap bullet hit right in the neck o' my canteen, and the damn thing blasted an acre o' skin offa my tail. The Marines guyed me and said I ought to get a Purple Heart for being shot in the tail by my own canteen.

"I had some luck trappin' Japs, too. We'd pick out a cave where we suspected Japs might be and rig up a trap in the mouth of it. I rigged up some fancy traps, and I found five dead Japs in one of 'em. Them blasted Japs were a pretty sight. But the still-huntin' was more fun."

I examined Griggs' Hunting Book carefully, then checked his story with his own and with Marine officers. All the officers agreed that his claim of fifteen "certain kills" and seventeen "probables" is modest. A Marine officer insisted that he should be credited with twenty-five Japs found dead in a cave after a Griggs-rigged explosion. Griggs, however, claims as "certain" only those Japs hit by his rifle fire alone and whose belt buckles he was able to get. The "probables" include the Japs found in his traps and Japs whom he believed he hit but whose bodies he could not examine because of other enemy fire.

His record is rendered more remarkable by the fact that Griggs killed most of his Japs after the island had been officially "secured." He enjoyed no lush, front-line opportunities for killing. No Japs rushed him in a death-inviting *banzai*. He hunted down every one of them.

"When I get home I'm gonna hang these Jap belt buckles under my lad's picture," he said. "I've got fifteen belt buckles now, and if the Navy don't kick me out for being too old, I may get a few more."

Guam is one of the most beautiful islands in the Pacific. Shaped like a peanut, lying north and south thirteen degrees above the equator, it is thirty-eight miles long, four to eight miles wide, and has an area of 225 square miles. The latitude is about the same as Nicaragua. The mean temperature is seventy-nine; the annual rainfall eighty-three to ninety inches. The north end of the island is a flat plateau, while the south end, where most of the development has been, is fairly mountainous. The vegetation is semitropical. There are few mosquitoes, little malaria. The climate, especially during the rainy season, is sticky, and your bed and clothes will mildew, but Guam, as Pacific islands go, is the best place west of Hawaii to live.

Guam is American, and you sense its American-ness the moment you arrive. Its 22,000 Chamorros, as I have stated, are proud to be Americans. They all speak English; they are all Christians, mostly Catholic; and many of them have visited the United States and are quite well educated. They suffered under the Japs, who stole from them and destroyed their schools; and, in the process of our returning, we demolished whatever was left.

Before the war the Chamorros were a happy and comparatively prosperous people. Our Navy was their principal source of income. Many Chamorro men were in the Navy—admirals prize them as mess attendants—and others were employed at the shore station. We maintained a company of Marines there, and the Navy was the best customer for the island's food production. The steamship companies, Pan-American Airways, and Standard Oil also were good friends, employers, and customers of the Chamorros.

Agana, a picturesque place with several modern homes, was Guam's principal city. Most of the commercial installations, however, were at the Apra harbor port of Sumay, which is on the Orote Peninsula and about six miles south of Agana. Civilian contractors were developing an airstrip on Orote for the Navy when the Japs moved in.

The Japs took the island virtually intact from us. Then, in the three years they had it, they stripped it and allowed it to deteriorate. The only piece of construction they added was a crude coral airstrip on the site of the Navy's present Agana Field. In the Battle of Guam, the island was leveled as though by a great hurricane. Not a house was left standing, and our development began with nothing but a bare, rubble-strewn island still infested with hundreds of Jap stragglers.

One year after the Battle of Guam, the island was second only to Oahu as the world's mightiest island fortress. It was the headquarters of both the Pacific Fleet and the 20th Bomber Command. It had the most finished appearance of any of the Pacific islands we developed. The housing was "advanced base type," but the planners planned for permanency. We didn't go back to Guam for any "duration"; we went back to Guam to stay. Guam will be our greatest permanent air and naval base in the Western Pacific.

In planning the development of Guam, the Army and Navy were not handicapped by political uncertainty. What happens to Saipan, Tinian, Iwo Jima, Okinawa, the Philippines, and all of our bases in the South Pacific is a matter for future political decision. But Guam was, is, and will continue to be ours, and this fact has worked to the advantage of both Guam and the Army and Navy.

Guam's B-29 story illustrates the difference between Guam and the other islands in our planning. Vast as were the B-29 fields on Saipan and Tinian, these fields were *operational fields only.* The key B-29 field—Depot Field— was on Guam. Depot Field was where every B-29 in the Pacific had to go for major overhauling. The great machine shops where a B-29 could be torn down and reassembled, the most expensive machinery, the permanent machinery —this was all on Guam. Now, in peacetime, Guam's installations will be sustaining our commercial and military aircraft.

Guam, too, had its purely operational B-29 fields. These

136

were the big North and Northwest Fields, each comparable to a field on Saipan or Tinian. Thus Guam had been given all the features of a temporary advance base *plus* the more permanent installations.

Similarly, with the Fleet. Harbor development on Saipan and Tinian was of the temporary type to promote the war. But on Guam, at no sacrifice in speed, the tremendous harbor development proceeded toward both short and long-range objectives. Guam's Apra Harbor will be one of the great ports of the Pacific.

Tinian and Saipan have no hard-surfaced roads. Guam has 103 miles of forty-four foot-wide black-topped highway with permanent concrete bridges, high fills, and wide vision ranges at all curves—the equal of any modern highway in the United States. In addition, there are 243 miles of first-class coral-surfaced roads on Guam.

On every other island west of Hawaii we came, conquered, and developed with the sole objective of speeding our march to Tokyo. But on Guam we came, conquered, and developed—to stay.

Fifteen Seabee construction battalions—the 25th, 53rd, 48th, 72nd, 59th, 23rd, 76th, 4th, 49th, 94th, 136th, 56th, 109th, 41st, and 103rd—had a part in the development of Guam. They were assisted by seven Army Air Force engineering battalions which worked under the overall Seabee command. The 301st "Harbor Stretcher" Battalion did the tremendous job of dredging; the 302nd Pontoon Battalion handled barges and causeways during the assault; and four Seabee stevedore battalions—the 2nd, 13th, 16th, and 29th Specials—moved all the cargo from "hold to dump." This makes a total of twenty-one Seabee battalions and seven Army battalions which did the Guam job.

In addition to the 302nd Pontoon Battalion, the 25th,

53rd, and 2nd Special Battalions had a part in the assault on Guam. D-Day was July 21, 1944, when the 3rd Marine Division and the 1st Provisional Marine Brigade began the Battle of Guam which lasted until August 13th. The 25th and 2nd Special Seabee Battalions were parts of the 3rd Marine Division, while the 53rd was a part of the 1st Provisional Marine Brigade.

After the assault, the Air Force battalions moved to the north, or B-29 end of the island and became the "lead battalions" on Depot and North Fields. The Seabees' contribution to Depot Field was the officers' quarters, the asphalt plant, and the refrigeration). Later, the 25th, 53rd, and 94th Seabees took over construction of the third, or Northwest B-29 Field.

The Orote Naval Air Station was built by the 23rd and 59th Battalions. The 23rd was an old Aleutian outfit, veterans of the assault on Attu. Agana Field, which handled more traffic than LaGuardia Field, was built by the 48th and 72nd Battalions, both of which had constructed airdromes in Hawaii.

CINCPAC—a separate community on Guam consisting of all the buildings which housed the headquarters of the Pacific Fleet—was built by the 49th and 94th Battalions. The 49th previously had spent a year in Bermuda building air installations. The 94th came from Hawaii.

Apra Harbor consists of an inner and an outer harbor. The inner harbor had never been accessible to merchant shipping. The 301st Battalion dredged open the inner harbor, and the 23rd Battalion built the now-famous breakwater. A storm destroyed the breakwater at one point during its construction, and the 23rd had to begin all over again. The finished harbor will have many big-ship berths in both the inner and outer harbors, and the outer harbor will be one of the finest anchorages in the Pacific.

The vast reefer (refrigeration) system at Guam was begun by the 25th Battalion, then finished by the 13th Special, in addition to its stevedoring. There were 500,000 cubic feet of electric refrigeration in the system, enough to support 500,000 men in American style for 30 days.

Every visitor to Guam marveled at the nine huge, wooden ration depots, each ninety-six feet wide by 540 feet long. Ration boxes were piled forty feet high inside them on their concrete floors. These depots were built by the 41st Battalion, an old Kodiak outfit which I visited in 1943.

All of Guam's hospitals—both Army and Navy, totaling 10,000 beds—were built by the Seabees. The Navy Base Hospital was built by the veteran 4th Battalion, first outfit to reach Dutch in the old days; two of the Fleet Hospitals were built by the 56th; another Fleet Hospital by the 48th; and the huge Army General Hospital was built by the 136th Battalion.

Water development on Guam was a difficult problem solved by the Seabees. The old water system brought water from Almagosa Springs, seven miles back in the hills, to Sumay and the harbor commercial installations on the Orote Peninsula. The water fed from Almagosa Springs down to Manoot Reservoir, thence to Orote. There was a ten-inch line from the reservoir to Sumay; and there was an eight-inch line extending around the harbor to Piti.

Miraculously, the Japs did not sabotage this water system, which had been built years ago by the Navy. The Seabees took up the ten-inch line, repaired it, and laid it back in place; then they took up the eight-inch line, repaired it, and used this pipe for new feeder lines on Orote. This Almagosa system supplied 1,500,000 gallons a day, enough for a city of 15,000 persons in the States.

Water for the Agana area came from Agana Springs, which are almost at sea level. The Seabees ripped out this system, overhauled it, installed tanks on high ground into which the water was pumped from the springs, and this system then furnished 3,000,000 gallons a day.

Yet 4,500,000 gallons a day was not enough water for Guam. The Seabees had to look farther. For years it had been supposed that the north end of Guam—the B-29 end —had little developable water. The land was flat and porous. The southern, mountainous end was thought to have the only water. The Seabees discovered, however, that the north end, because the rain water did not run off so fast, actually had more developable water than the south end. Deep-well pumps were needed to reach this water, and deep-well pumps were not included in our standard advance base equipment.

The pumps and pipe were rushed from the States. The Seabees' contingent of oil field veterans moved in their drilling equipment, and Guam soon had twenty wells averaging seventy-four to 500 feet in depth on the flat, coral plateau which is the north end. The pumps in each well had a capacity of forty to two hundred gallons a minute. Thus these wells gave the island an additional supply of more than 4,000,000 gallons a day, and in a pinch, Guam could pump 9,000,000 gallons of fresh water a day.

This water supply from the north end of Guam—which once was thought to have so little water—was actually more dependable than the supply from the south end. The south end is mountainous and impervious, and thus its water supply varies with rainfall, while the north end is flat and porous and is thus a natural storage basin with a constant supply.

The director of water development on Guam was Lieutenant H. P. Gulden (CEC, USNR, Carlisle, Pa.), a former mayor of his city.

The Seabees moved a total of 18,000,000 cubic yards of earth on Guam.

The 25th Battalion, led by Commander George Whelan (CEC, USNR, Atlantic City, N. J.), was another old "Marine" outfit. They left the States early in 1943 and went to New Zealand for advanced combat training with the 18th Regiment, 3rd Marine Division. Their memories of New Zealand are of Albert Park on a sunny Sunday afternoon, of a clean, powdered Seabee standing there with a poncho dangling from his arm, with Stateside cigarets and a package of Juicy Fruit bulging from his pocket, and of friendly women—hundreds of 'em—sidling by, ogling the Seabee, the cigarets and the gum, just asking to be picked up and taken to pick meadow flowers. All this and "stike-and-aigs-and-chips" for thirty-eight cents, too. It was Heaven!

After New Zealand the 25th spent nine months on Guadalcanal. Oscar J. Schenking (Chief Carpenter's Mate, Bellingham, Wash.) took a detachment to Vella La Vella and operated a sawmill just sixty miles from a Jap camp. The mill cut the lumber with which the Seabees built the hospitals to support the Bougainville operation.*

In August, 1943, three men of the 25th fought the first official enemy engagement of the 3rd Marine Division. An LST was running fuel up to the sawmill on Vella La Vella. To give the ship additional firepower against enemy aircraft, the Seabees placed trucks mounting 50-calibre machine guns on the weather deck of the LST. On the

---

* One reason for the time lag between invasions is that a complete new set of hospitals always had to be built at the jump-off point to support the new invasion. You couldn't begin an invasion before the new hospitals were finished.

141

morning of August 23, 1943, five Jap Zeros attacked the LST, and the Seabees shot down two of them. The three men were H. F. Alexander (Shipfitter Second, Macon, Ga.); W. E. Fales (Carpenter's Mate Second, Norfolk, Va.); and C. G. Sims (Boatswain's Mate Second, San Francisco).

On November 1, 1943, the 3rd Marines invaded Bougainville. It was the war's first amphibious landing in which the Marines and Seabees were fired on in the landing boats. We did not control the air, and strafing Jap planes gave the boats hell. Lafayette F. Farley (Carpenter's Mate Third, St. Helens, Ore.) was the first Seabee killed by these planes. After the first two waves had landed, our ships had to run from these planes, temporarily deserting the men on the beach. The Seabees got the first antiaircraft guns in operation. E. T. Willis (Machinist's Mate Third, Moorehead City, N. C.) engaged the Jap planes with the first 50-calibre, and shot down one of them. Sam Davis (Machinist's Mate First, Caldwell, O.), on a bulldozer, pulled the ammunition sleds from the beach up to the guns. Both Willis and Davis won Bronze Stars.

The jungle on Bougainville came down to the very edge of the water. The mud was deep, and mosquitoes were vicious. One of the first Seabee assignments was to bridge the Piva River, so that the Marines could get at the Japs on the other side. In placing logs for these bridges, the men had to work in mud which came up above their belts. They worked entirely naked.

Sidney Lishnoff (Carpenter's Mate Third, Bronx, N. Y.) described this situation for me. "We figured that if we had to work like horses we might as well look like horses," he said. "So we took off all of our clothes and just wallowed in that mud until we finished those bridges."

Marine-Seabee relations with the Army were disrupted on Bougainville when each group accused the other of

142

overcrowding its theater. Which sign went up first is a matter of dispute, but the Army theater had a sign reading: NO JAPS OR MARINES WANTED; SEABEES SHOT ON SIGHT. The Marine-Seabee theater had a sign which read: SEABEES AND MARINES WELCOME; DOGGIES APPROACH AT OWN RISK.

In landing on Guam, our strategy was to pinch off the Orote Peninsula and capture the Orote airstrip as quickly as possible. Thus, landing parties went ashore on both sides of the peninsula at its base. The third and largest landing party went ashore on Agana Beach, directly in front of the town of Agana. The 25th Seabees were in this third party; their commanding officer, Commander Whelan, and their executive officer, Lieutenant B. W. Walker (CEC, USNR, Jackson, Miss.), were beachmasters for the Agana landing. Both won Bronze Stars.

The complicating factor in the landing was the reef which lay 200 yards offshore at low tide. The Seabees had loaded five cranes on five pontoon barges, and at H-Hour —eight-twenty-nine A.M.—they rammed these barges aground on the reef. Ducks and amphtracks could cross the reef, so the cranes were in position to transfer ammunition and supplies from the boats and lighters to the ducks and amphtracks. The ducks and amphtracks could then go on to the beach and deliver the supplies.

These five cranes operating on the reef were choice targets for Jap mortar fire. All of them were spattered repeatedly with shrapnel, and one was knocked out entirely. The four crane operators, who spent three days and nights on the reef, and who were cited for bravery, were E. E. Archer (Chief Machinist's Mate, Stayton, Ore.); A. E. Bradley (Machinist's Mate First, Ashburn, Ga.); L. E. Bradley (Machinist's Mate First, Oregon City, Ore.); and H. S. Hatcher (Machinist's Mate First, Bedford, Va.). Hatcher is a fifty-two-year-old peacetime employee of the Virginia Forest Service.

The first Seabee on the beach was Harry F. Lee (Machinist's Mate First, Salinas, Cal.), a cat operator. When Lee was hit by shrapnel, his place was taken by W. W. Cox (Carpenter's Mate Third, Decatur, Ala.).

Three hundred yards back of Agana Beach was an escarpment which was much higher and more precipitous than the escarpment at Omaha Beach, Normandy. Bulldozers had to cut a tank road up through a break in this escarpment before tanks could reach the top. This road was built under fire by four of the 25th's bulldozermen: E. C. Beamer (Machinist's Mate First, Nettawaka, Kan.); A. H. Brown (Machinist's Mate First, Richmond, Va.); Elmer Vaughn (Carpenter's Mate Second, Hemingsford, Neb.); and S. A. Walter (Machinist's Mate First, Clanton, Ala.).

R. J. Hensley (Machinist's Mate Second, Ellenboro, N. C.), another bulldozerman, hit the sake jackpot. He plowed up a dump containing eighty cases of sake and many cans of tangerines and crabmeat. The canned tangerines were the choicest item in the Jap larder.

The 53rd Battalion also participated in the assault on Bougainville. Their A and C Companies were with the Marine Raiders in the first two waves. They had a large bunch of war dogs with them, and when our ships pulled out and ran from the Jap planes, the Marines and Seabees conferred on the beach as to the best way to cook dogs.

The first three men on the beach were Robert E. Mitchell (Chief Machinist's Mate, Shreveport, La.); E. A. Post (Machinist's Mate First, Portland, Ore.); and Fred Siegenthaler (Shipfitter First, McCamey, Tex.).

The jungle was so thick that a bulldozerman "couldn't see the front end of his cat." While H. S. Ballard (Car-

144

penter's Mate Second, Rockford, Ill.) was pushing his machine into this jungle, he spied a Jap sniper in a tree almost directly over him. Ballard slammed his big bull-dozer against the tree as the Jap fired frantically, flattened the tree, and crushed the Jap under his treads. The Jap, knocked to the ground, couldn't escape because he had tied himself to the tree so as to have both hands free to oper-ate his gun.

Randolph D. Nockovich (Machinist's Mate First, Burgettstown, Pa.) 'dozed over two "live" pillboxes. He told me he'd never forget the way those Japs screamed as he smothered them.

Fred Robertson (Chief Carpenter's Mate, Los Angeles) had strung his hammock between a carryall and a tree. When a strafing plane came over, the shortest distance between Robertson and his foxhole lay *through* the ham-mock. He couldn't take time to go around either the tree or the carryall; he busted right through the hammock.

E. T. Bass (Electrician's Mate Second, Tallahassee, Fla.) innovated the now standard hammock-over-foxhole system. He dug his foxhole between two trees, then strung his hammock over it. When enemy planes approached, he had only to roll out of his hammock to fall into his foxhole.

Monroe Ellis (Machinist's Mate First, Perry, Okla.) got seasick during the earthquake on Bougainville.

In the Guam assault, the 53rd landed with the Marines at the base of the Orote Peninsula near the village of Agat. Its H-Hour assignment was to reach the reef with a demoli-tion team and six cats, blast a pathway through the reef, and pull the tanks through. The two demolition men who led the way and set the charges at the reef were C. E. Scoville (Gunner's Mate First, Carson City, Nev.) and F. E. Long (Carpenter's Mate Second, Washington, D. C.).

R. T. Dean (Boatswain's Mate Second, Chicago) was the first man hit at the beach, and Albert Simar (Shipfitter Third, Orange, Tex.) was the first man killed.

During the second day on Agat Beach, the Seabees installed a record player and loudspeaker. Benny Goodman's clarinet could be heard for two miles. It was probably the only time Goodman has been accompanied by rifle and mortar fire, with 155s playing the bass.

The 53rd's "procurers" did all right on the beach. They found so much sake that they passed it out in their chow line; they hunted chickens with BARs; and they salvaged the old American doughmixer from the wrecked Marine barracks and began making bread with it.

The battalion's love life centered around three Chamorro charmers known as Silica Sue, Midnight Mary, and Anna from Agana. Silica Sue was so named because she preferred the coral-pit gang. Ralph J. Mobrak (Coxswain, St. Louis), the 53rd's Don Juan, introduced me to Silica Sue, but I didn't find favor in her warm brown eyes because I didn't work in the coral pit.

O. O. Winslow (Chief Shipfitter, Okmulgee, Okla.) told me a strange woman story. Winslow, who must be at least half Indian, is a sapper and Jap hunter. Once two Japs caught him under a shower and offered to surrender. "Wait till I get my forty-five," he told them; then he went and got his pistol and took them prisoner.

Exploring a cave cautiously with his tommy gun and searchlight, Winslow thought for a moment that he had found what everyone had been looking for in the Pacific: a caveful of geisha girls. Five young Japanese women, dressed in kimonos, were sitting on a ledge in the cave. But there was something ghostly about them. They were sitting up; no marks were on their bodies; and they were

146

stone dead. Apparently they had been dead for several days.

Winslow collected a few souvenirs, then backed out and blasted the cave.

"I thought I'd better close up that cave before the Marines found them women," Winslow said dryly.

In the wreckage of the old Marine barracks, the Seabees also found the bugle on which Marines had sounded "To the Colors" in the days before the war. The Chamorros had saved the flag the Marines had hauled down before surrendering to the Japs. In a ceremony to be remembered, 5000 Chamorros brought out the old flag and joined the 53rd Seabees in raising it again over Guam. Bernard Szaleniec (Carpenter's Mate Third, Chicago) blew "To the Colors" on the old Marine bugle, and the weeping Chamorros pledged allegiance and sang "God Bless America."

I have a particular sort of respect for the Seabee stevedore battalions. These boys have the most monotonous, back-bending job of the war. The construction battalions work with machines and have varied assignments, but when the stevedores empty one hatch all they can do is open up another one. This goes on three shifts a day, seven days a week, 365 days a year. The men in the stevedore battalions are construction men, too. All those in the early battalions had volunteered for the construction battalions. Less than five per cent of them had had any stevedoring experience, but when the unloading of ships became the Pacific's worst bottleneck, Seabees had to become stevedores to keep the stuff moving.

When the 2nd Special Battalion—the first stevedore outfit to go into action—reached Noumea in March, 1943, the harbor was cluttered with ships, some of which had been "riding the hook" for four months! In the war's most crucial period, when our shipping was shortest, these ships had been lying at anchor waiting to be unloaded for four solid months!

In an effort to relieve this bottleneck, the 20th Construction Battalion had been doing stevedoring at Noumea, and when the 2nd Special arrived, it took over from the 20th. Only forty men in the 2nd Special had previous stevedoring experience, but the entire battalion had some rapid instruction in cargo handling.

The battalion began unloading ships at the rate of better than one ship a day. Five meals a day were served on the docks, and the men were given twenty minutes to eat. At the end of one year at Noumea, the 2nd Special had unloaded 481 ships, handled 782,814 weight-tons of cargo, worked three shifts a day, built its camp in the time the men spent away from the docks, and its only time off was two hours on Christmas, 1943.

The battalion moved to Guadalcanal and spent six months handling another 150,886 tons at Koli Point, Tenaru, Tetere and Kukum. On D-Day at Guam, they were in there with the 3rd Marines, delivering the ammunition to within 100 yards of the front, and forming the "second line" against infiltration at night.

When I visited the 2nd Special on Guam, they were on their twenty-seventh month overseas; they were well into their "second million" tons of cargo; they had gotten a half-holiday on Christmas, 1944; they were still working three shifts a day, seven days a week; they had 745 "original men"; and they still had not killed a man in handling cargo.

In addition, these men had enjoyed no "boot" leave during their training in the States, no embarkation leave to see their families before they went overseas—the need for them was too desperate. There had been no "liberty" anywhere, and no athletic equipment had been issued them because they were too tired to use it. Their only recreation was movies which were shown afternoon and evening so that men on every shift could catch them.

Counting from the date these men entered the service as volunteers, their thirty-one-month record * of monotony and hard work exceeds anything I know of in the war in either the Army or Navy.

Two men of the 2nd Special were awarded the Soldier's Medal for heroism after an explosion on the docks at Noumea November 1, 1943. Five Army and Javanese stevedores were killed and ninety-five Army men, Seabees, and Javanese were injured. The battalion's commanding officer, Lieutenant Commander C. T. Barrett (CEC, USNR, Birmingham, Ala.) was knocked unconscious in his docks office, and Stilbern M. Kidd (Machinist's Mate First, St. Louis) went into the burning building and dragged him out. The other medal winner was Stanley E. Haverland (Chief Machinist's Mate, Everett, Wash.).

The battalion's Noumea stories are about that New Zealand "goat" which they had to eat, and about Mickey's Road House where you could purchase $22.50 whisky and $7 butterfly rum.

No item of "reverse lend-lease" was harder for Americans to take than that New Zealand mutton which everybody called "goat." Whether it was roasted, stewed, barbecued, or in cutlets, it still stank.

A. O. Pember (Chief Carpenter's Mate, New York City) commented on the chickens served at Noumea. "What chickens we got had been flown out from the States," he said. "They were that tough."

* The battalion was still at Guam, still adding to its record, as this was written.

Smallest member of the 2nd Special was a youngster named R. L. Armstrong (Machinist's Mate Third, Skelleytown, Tex.), who weighs ninety pounds when soaked in salt water. Armstrong was operating a "cherrypicker" on Guam when he spied a Jap. He jumped off the cherrypicker, grabbed a handful of rocks, began chunking at the Jap, and took him prisoner.

The 48th Battalion was a tough, sharp-witted gang of old construction stiffs—the kind of men you want on your side in a barroom brawl. (See photo XXXI.) Most of them came directly into the Seabees from Grand Coulee. They were a hard-cussing, hard-working, wisecracking outfit, and you had to be careful how you handled them.

Crossing to Hawaii in the old transport *Henderson*—she was a mule boat in the last war—they decided they weren't being treated with proper respect by the Merchant Marine crew. So William Philley (Seaman Second, Spokane, Wash.) beat up five Merchant Mariners in one day, and relations improved.

The battalion made its cooks out of one bartender, one sheepherder, and two professional wrestlers. After receiving one year's steady cussing, those four got to where they could make the finest soup in the Pacific.

The 48th went first to Maui and built the Kahalui Air Base. They also had a hand in building the Furnanay Base. But they were griped by all the stories of how Hawaiian landowners were charging the government $500 an acre for all the cane the Seabees had to knock down, and ten cents a yard for cinders. Finally, a group of the men cornered several of the local landowners and let them have it.

"How much would this goddam stuff have been worth if the Japs had come in?" O. W. Pollard (Gunner's Mate First, Helena, Mont.) demanded.

150

The answers were not satisfactory, so the Seabees took a brief workout and went away feeling better.

The battalion laughed longest and loudest at a story told by C. M. Smith (Shipfitter Third, Corpus Christi, Tex.) on their commanding officer. The commander was a stolid, sincere, but slightly maiden-auntish consulting engineer. He could have been the principal of the grammar school in a small town. The first morning on Maui, while the battalion was roughing it, he ventured into a warehouse to eat breakfast with the "mates." He sat down across a table from Smith.

Now you must know that the most famous of all Navy breakfast dishes is—what shall I call it here?—"stuff-on-a-shingle." It is chipped ham in a thick, mushy gravy poured over a piece of hard, dry toast. Navy enlisted men, from Boston to Bombay, have eaten tons of it.

"The commander eases in and sets down kinda uneasy like," Smith relates. "Of course he's used to them linen table cloths and them sunny-side-up eggs in the gold-braid's mess. Then one o' the mess cooks throws the *stuff* at him, only this morning there ain't no toast under it. It's just a straight bowlful of *stuff*.

"Well, naturally, the commander ain't never seen nothing like it. He looks around uneasy, sorta sniffs at it, then decides that it's cereal. He asks me to pass him the sugar, which I did. He dips out big spoonfuls of sugar and sugars the *stuff* good. Then he cautiously takes a bite. He makes a face, but he remembers old *can do* and he takes another bite. He's desperate by now, so he looks up at me sort of pleading like and says: 'Mate, what is this?'

"He'd asked for it, so I let him have it. I looked up at him and answered: 'Suh, that's *stuff*-on-the-shingle without the goddam shingle.'

"The commander just pushed that bowl helplessly out in front of him, got up, and eased hisself out."

John W. Carrick (Boatswain's Mate Second, New Or-

151

leans, La.), a lanky ex-Marine, carefully explained to me the role of the 48th Seabees in the assault on Guam.

"It was like this," he said. "The Navy was using the 48th Seabees and that old cattle boat as bait. Every night for ten straight nights Halsey sent us on a run up toward Tokyo, just hoping the Jap fleet would dart out and sink us; then Halsey could sink the Jap fleet. It made us feel noble as hell. Every day during the day Halsey sent us cruising leisurely around Orote, trying to make the Japs fire on us and expose their gun positions.

"This, of course, gave us a front seat for all the fighting, but we got kinda nervous 'long about the tenth day."

William J. Smith (Carpenter's Mate First, Chico, Cal.) is a husky, chuckling, moon-faced fellow who can do anything. He cooks, cuts hair, shoots craps, gardens, "procures," and doubles for the chaplain. The chaplain interceded with him, however, on the ship coming to Guam. Smith sang "The West Virginia Hills"—all about Nellie Brown and how she got "laid up in the mount-ings"—so long and so loud that the chaplain pleaded with Smith to stop.

Smith won all the battalion's money on the way to Guam, so he felt obligated to feed the boys. He salvaged a Jap field kitchen, "procured" forty gallons of hot cake batter from a ship, "rode a few Army trucks," and escaped with other delicacies, then set up a free grill. He began gardening and soon had twelve acres in cultivation, growing tomatoes, onions, lettuce, pepper, radishes, and corn.

When I visited Smitty's Garden, he had five or six Chamorros working for him. He told me that the soil was similar to that in the Sierra Nevada mountains, that he had to use a good deal of commercial fertilizer, but crops matured every six weeks. He had irrigated four of his twelve acres. At first, he said, he had used the old water buffaloes to do his plowing, but later he changed to a jeep and tractor.

In the early days on Guam, the Seabees took "rain baths" in the frequent showers. Whenever it began raining, the men would strip off and start soaping themselves. Invariably, however, at the moment they had themselves covered with a creamy layer of soap, the shower halted abruptly.

George E. Decker (Chief Gunner's Mate, Grand Coulee, Wash.) is wide open to a charge of trading with the enemy. He operated a shovel on the Pago River at Guam. He left his sandwich scraps lying around, and for several nights the Japs had been sneaking in and eating them. So Decker wrote a note and left it with the scraps. It read: YOU SONSA-BITCHES. I BEEN FEEDING YOU FOR A WEEK. EITHER YOU START LEAVING SOUVENIRS HERE OR YOUR RATIONS WILL BE CUT OFF.

The Japs got the idea. Next morning Decker found a hara-kiri knife waiting for him. But a Marine patrol broke up this profitable business arrangement.

Guam's famous Battle of the Cliff, fought by the 48th Seabees, began one afternoon after L. F. Aisenberry (Boatswain's Mate Second, Cincinnati, O.) had stepped on a camouflaged Jap. The Jap came boiling up, and Aisenberry "forgot all that judo I learned in boot and started swinging." Aisenberry beat that Jap to death, but other Japs in the party escaped into the cliff area near the 48th's camp. Aisenberry returned to camp with the report.

The 48th quit work. Patrols were organized under old ex-Marine Carrick. They headed for the cliff. All afternoon the battle raged. The whole island rocked repeatedly as the Seabees set off dynamite by the ton. Hundreds of rounds of ammunition were fired. The Marines took cover. Asked why they didn't go and help, one Marine sergeant explained:

"Listen, brother, those goddam Seabees are down there

153

huntin' a Jap. They're shootin' anything that moves. I wouldn't go down there for a million bucks."

When the Battle of the Cliff was over, the Marines claimed that the Seabees had killed only nine Japs. But this was slander. Carrick personally assured me that the number was *ninety*.

The 72nd Battalion also made the trip from California to Hawaii in the old *Henderson*. They landed at Barber's Point on the southwest corner of Oahu and took over the construction of air installations from the civilian contractors. O. C. Richardson (Carpenter's Mate Second, Denver, Col.) had been a foreman for the private contractors on the Barber's Point job. He had quit and gone home to join the Seabees; then, as luck would have it, he had been assigned to the 72nd and returned to Barber's Point to live in the same barracks he had left.

The 72nd spent thirteen months at Barber's Point building a giant "A & R" building—assembly and repair for aircraft. The all-steel building—about a twelve-million-dollar structure—was 420 by 610 feet and covered four acres.

On Guam the 72nd built the giant Agana Air Base. The Japs had worked on the field for a year, and the Seabees were amazed at the backwardness of the Jap construction methods. The only big piece of equipment on the field was an old Northwest crane which the Japs had seized from us. They were using caribou and a narrow-gauge track for pushcarts to haul coral, and natives were tamping the coral by hand.

The 72nd opened the first theater on Guam. It was named "Dengue Bowl," because it had been built by men who were too weak from dengue to return to their regular jobs. There was a section for Marines and a section for Chamorros. Betty Hutton gave the first show.

154

Forty-seven per cent of the 72nd's men had dengue on Guam, and dengue on C-rations is quite an experience.

The officer in charge of the 49th Seabee Battalion, Commander Marshall D. Barnett (CEC, USNR, Dallas, Tex.), was a remarkable fellow. In a profession and in a military organization hardly noted for piety, he neither drank nor swore. He was a sincere man of religion, and he worked at it.

There was nothing sanctimonious about him. About forty-five, he won his wings as a Navy flier in the last war, and when he found a little time off on Guam, he flew B-29's and Helldivers. He had one of the finest battalions in the Seabees, an outfit which built the big Naval Air Station at Bermuda, then was selected to build CINCPAC on Guam. He was just a blond, soft-spoken Texas construction man who, like General Montgomery, read his Bible and said his prayers at night, then got up in the morning ready to tackle any enemy or any job.

In private life Commander Barnett is a Sunday School superintendent at Gaston Avenue Baptist Church, Dallas, and chairman of that church's Board of Deacons. He is president of Barnett Construction Company.

As a gesture of respect to the Commander, the men of the 49th allowed no loud profanity or obscenity at their theater. No such order was issued by the Commander; it was a voluntary restriction imposed by the men themselves. I found no other similar instance in the war. Most chaplains did not enjoy such respect.

On Guam, in the general effort to help the Chamorros restore their Christian services, Commander Barnett volunteered to teach the adult Bible class at the Agana Baptist Mission. He had been teaching this class for several weeks when he was notified that his son, Lieutenant (jg) Marshall

D. Barnett, Jr., a Navy pilot operating from the ill-starred aircraft carrier *Franklin*, had lost his life while dive-bombing a Jap warship.

One Sunday, after he had learned of his son's death, I went with him to the Agana Mission. As we picked our way through the mud, he told me that he had had a nice letter from the chaplain on the *Franklin*. The chaplain had written that when he (the chaplain) had been sick for two weeks, young Barnett had substituted for him.

The Mission, ironically, was located on a hilltop within 200 yards of the stockade where we kept the Jap prisoners. The Mission was housed in a long tent furnished by the Army. I sat next to a Chamorro woman who looked fresh and clean in a well-pressed, red-flowered dress. During the preliminary part of the service, she and I sang "There's a Land That Is Fairer Than Day" off the same hymn book.

When it was time for the lesson, the congregation divided into three parts. The twenty or twenty-five adults went to the back of the tent to be taught by Commander Barnett; the teen-agers went to the center to be taught by the pastor, Waukine Sablan; and the children gathered up front to be taught by the Chamorro woman by whom I had sat.

The lesson was titled "Forgiveness." It was based on Scripture taken from the Sermon on the Mount. Commander Barnett said a prayer, then read the majestic words of Christ:

> "Ye have heard that it hath been said, 'Thou shalt love thy neighbour and hate thine enemy.' But I say unto you, 'Love your enemies, bless them that curse you, do good to them that hate you, and pray for them which despitefully use you, and persecute you; that ye may be the children of your Father which is in heaven.' . . . For if ye love them which love you, what reward have ye? do not even the publicans the same? And if ye salute your brethren only, what do ye more than others?"

156

An old Chamorro man had a question. "Does this mean, sir, that we are to forgive those?" he asked, pointing toward the stockade. "Those who murdered our children? Those who debased us? Those who ravished our women so that we'll have their kind with us always? Must we forgive those?"

I didn't envy the Commander his position. He hesitated a moment, then answered slowly.

"Yes," he said, "we'll have to forgive even those. We'll have to kill many of them, but some day the killing will cease. Then we'll have to forgive them, love them, and try to teach them the words of Christ. I haven't suffered like you people, but I know something about how hard it is to forgive those. But, you see, the way of forgiveness, the way of Christ, is the only way of hope for ourselves. If we are going to have faith in mankind's ultimate salvation, if we are going to have hope for the future, then we must go in the direction of forgiveness. To turn in another direction is to turn toward darkness. Yes, we must forgive even those."

There was more argument, and I'm not sure that all the Chamorros were convinced. But it was inspiring to watch a strong man who himself had suffered defend the ideal so vigorously in a mud-bottomed tent in the shadow of the Jap stockade.

Captain Wilfred L. "Wild Bill" Painter (CEC, USNR, Seattle, Wash.) was a truly fabulous figure. A movie could be made about his exploits. Until now, because so much of his work has been confidential, almost nothing has been written about him, and here I can give only a sort of preview of him.

If Painter had lived in the 16th Century, he would have been Captain Blood; if in the 19th, he would have been a mixture of Jeb Stuart, Buffalo Bill, and Jesse James. In his odd moments he would have built the Union Pacific. He is that kind of guy.

After Guadalcanal, Painter became one of the Navy's "advance scouts" in the Pacific. It was his job to pick landing sites, and particularly to pick the sites for airfields to support our operations. On every island in the Solomons on which we landed, Painter was there *before* the landing—surveying, taking soundings, determining whether and how fast an airfield could be built there. He had sneaked ashore from submarines and PT boats, hidden in caves, dodged Japs, ambushed Japs, made rendezvous with his subs and PT's, and returned with the information on which the decisions were made.

Painter is an engineer. To understand the importance of his work, you must understand the importance of engineering to the war's naval operations. Every landing we made in the Pacific was made with one principal aim in view: *to obtain an airfield.* If the Japs had an airfield on the island, was it on the best site? Could the Jap field be lengthened and enlarged for our use? If not, where was such a site? What about prevailing wind direction and its relation to proposed runways? Was there a coral deposit nearby? If not, what would be used for building material on the runways? What about supplying the airfield? Was there deep water nearby in which piers could be built and Liberty ships docked?

Some of our line admirals were slow in realizing their dependence on these engineering considerations, but Painter, with his brusque but efficient manner, was there to advise them. Admiral Halsey, no shrinking violet himself, quickly recognized Painter's value, and Painter became a captain at thirty-five—the youngest four-striper in the Navy.

The Japs know Painter well. They knew him in the "old days" when he was a hell-on-wheels civilian engineer in

China and Japan. After the war began they chased him, at one time or other, off most of Jap-held territory. Jap intelligence, I'm sure, expected to hear any day that a brawny, bearded figure wearing coveralls and carrying a tommy gun had been seen taking soundings in Tokyo Bay. They would know that it was Bill Painter.

Bill Painter is a product of the northwest woods. As a kid he worked around the lumber camps, then made his way through the University of Washington swabbing decks and driving taxicabs. The day he got out of school he left for China, working in the engine gang of a Dollar Line freighter. With ten bucks in his pocket, he jumped ship in Shanghai and went looking for a job. It was 1929. He barged into the Texas Company offices, and as a test question, the personnel director asked him what he knew about the growth of taxes on oil in China.

"I'm afraid I don't know anything about that, sir," Painter replied. "But, by God, I'll find out!"

Two days later Painter came back knowing more about Chinese oil taxes than the Chinese tax collector. The Texas Company hired him, soon sent him up to Dairen to build some distributing facilities. He plunged into the bizarre business and social life of Shanghai's International Settlement. He joined the Shanghai Volunteer Corps, a sort of international "National Guard" which was supposed to help protect business property from Chinese bandits, and which in peacetime was a rambunctious drinking and hunting club. Painter played on the American polo team. He has won thirty cups; he won the New Year's Hunt and thus became entitled to wear the "pink coat"; he rode in all the equestrian contests.

In 1931 he went "under fire" for the first time when the Volunteer Corps was called out to resist the maraudings of the Chinese 19th Route Army. Painter was sent to scout the

Chinese positions, and barely escaped death when Jap warships opened fire on the Chinese.

After the Volunteers had gone back to work, it developed that the Japs had camped on some of the Texas Company property and were slow in moving. Painter was detailed to get them off. He went to the American consul, and a young vice-consul was sent with him to the property to persuade the Japs to move. Painter listened to the vice-consul talk diplomatic verbiage to the Jap generals for an hour, then he moved forward.

"What this man is trying to say to you," he explained to the Japs, "is that you are to *get the goddam hell offa this property!*"

The Japs understood. Next day they were gone.

"I learned then that there is just one way to deal with Japs," Painter told me on Guam. "Whether it's in business or in war, you've got to use the direct approach with them."

In 1932 Painter left the Texas Company and set up his own construction company. He liked the Chinese. He helped them develop methods for distributing fuel, built storage facilities, and built some huge docks for the Chinese Government. He made a fortune, expanded his business, formed the partnership of Graham & Painter, Ltd., with John Graham, also of Seattle. The firm had offices in New York, Seattle, and Shanghai, and Painter "commuted" all over the world.

He has never married, and I asked him why not. "Life in Shanghai was not conducive to the marital state," he explained.

In only one effort was Painter a failure. He essayed the role of the Spartan warrior in the unexpurgated version of *Lysistrata* at the Shanghai Arts Theater. During a violent scene, the Spartan warrior lost his toga.

Painter was a second lieutenant in the Volunteer Corps in 1937 when war began in Shanghai. The Corps was on duty during all the fighting around Shanghai, and Painter made many excursions into Jap-held territory to rescue American families. He was shot at repeatedly by drunken young Jap officers who went about with cocked pistols shooting out windows. When the Japs clamped down on Manchuria, he knew that American business was through in the Orient, so he traveled leisurely across Russia and Europe and returned to his New York office. In 1940, he joined the Marines as a second lieutenant, but was induced to transfer to the Navy Civil Engineer Corps.

On Pearl Harbor Day he was building a dry dock at Long Beach. He was rushed to Pearl Harbor and placed in charge of raising the battleships *California* and *West Virginia*. He worked like a fiend. He dived with the divers, and was so covered with scum each night that he had to bathe in kerosene. A doctor was assigned to follow him throughout the dark, muddy bowels of the big ships to revive him when he collapsed from sulphur dioxide gas. He had both ships raised and in dry dock before anybody believed it was possible.

I discussed the South Pacific engineering in some detail in *Can Do!* The earliest Seabees had been rushed to Efate and Espiritu Santo, and they completed an emergency airstrip at Santo—our first jump-off base—just ten days before D-Day at Guadalcanal. Painter was in this area as engineering officer on the staff of Vice-Admiral McCain, commander of naval aircraft in the South Pacific. In effect, he became all-around engineering handy man for Admirals McCain, Turner, and Halsey throughout the South Pacific campaign. In effect, also, many of the engineering decisions were Painter's, as evidenced by the fact that he was jumped from lieutenant, to lieutenant commander, to commander, and then to captain in rapid order. He was thirty-five when he put on his four stripes.

Rank meant nothing to Painter, however. Like most of the Seabee officers, he was essentially a civilian, and wanted only to get the job done and get out. He hates red tape, and his adventures in cutting it are Pacific legends. He would "tell off" an admiral as quickly as he would a seaman second class, and only his sheer ability as recognized by broad-gauged men like Admirals Moreell, Halsey, and Nimitz kept him from being canned.

Painter tore around the South Pacific on all sorts of missions. Two days after the Marines had taken Henderson Field, he landed there in Admiral McCain's flag plane and began surveying sites for fighter strips Nos. 1 & 2. The Japs came over, Painter's plane had to run off, and he was left on Guadalcanal for twelve days without a razor. When the old destroyer *McFarland* was hit, Painter patched her up and saved her. When we were ready to move northward "up the slot," Painter was sent to New Georgia to pick the landing and airfield sites. He sneaked ashore there and found a British colonial official who was hiding from the Japs with a small party of natives.

The Britisher provided Painter with a canoe, a guide, and some bearers, and the party started on the water trip across Viro Harbor, which was held by the Japs. A storm almost swamped the canoe before it could reach shore. Painter spent the night in a cave. Next day, as the wind became even stronger, he abandoned the canoe and set out to explore all the land around Viro Harbor by foot. With his native guides, he waded swamp for two days, traversed thirty miles, and concluded that a landing was not feasible at Viro. There was no site where an airfield could be built quickly.

Painter left the Viro area, went to Segi Point, and found the spot he was looking for. Disguised as a native and in a captured Jap landing craft, Painter took soundings off Segi in full view of Jap land parties. Later, Painter returned to

Segi with a survey party and actually began work on the airstrip. The 47th Seabee Battalion landed there on June 30, 1943—D-Day in the Munda operation—and completed the airfield in ten days.

This was only the beginning of Painter's scouting experiences. He dressed like Davey Crockett. He flew thousands of miles, traveled in PT's and subs. He was fired on by Japs and Americans alike. He was on northern Luzon looking for airfield sites long before the Japs realized that they had lost the Philippines. He has been other places, too, but the full story will have to wait.

I am afraid that the religious revival which many have believed would come from this war is a forlorn hope. I searched hopefully for it. I talked to scores of chaplains, but I can't honestly report that I found anything very promising.

I remember the afternoon of June 4, 1944. We were lying in the harbor at Portland, England, ready to pull out that night for the D-Day landing in Normandy. I was on the first LST which was to go to Omaha Beach. There were about 600 men on the ship, Army and Navy. We had no chaplain. This was the Big Show; every man had a right to fear that he might not come back. An announcement came over the loudspeakers to the effect that because we had no chaplain aboard all the men who wished to attend a service or to consult a chaplain would present themselves at the port rail amidships, and they would be transported by small boat to another ship where services were being held.

I was intensely interested in the reaction to the announcement. I walked all over the ship, watching to see what happened. The poker and crap games, with the players using the new invasion franc notes for the first time, went on unabated. I couldn't find even a ripple of discussion regarding the announcement.

I stood at the port rail and listened to two coxswains argue about how large a craft would be needed to transport the "crowd." One of them thought that an LCM might be necessary—they can carry fifty men—but the other insisted that he could carry on his back all those who would want to go.

Only *five* men availed themselves of the transportation offer—less than one man out of a hundred. I asked each one his name and religion. But I didn't need to ask. They were all swarthy little Latin-extraction boys from around Boston and New York—all Catholics.

I believe that the true, dramatic story about chaplains in this war is how some of them have carried on in the face of such heart-chilling apathy.

My good friend Sam Franklin (Lieutenant, ChC, USNR, Maryville, Tenn.) was one of the most interesting of the Seabee chaplains. Sam is forty-two, a Presbyterian, educated at Edinburgh. He spent five years in Japan as a Presbyterian missionary. He has an earnest, finely-chiseled face, friendly brown eyes, a heart big enough to encompass all mankind. There is nothing effeminate about him. He speaks well, has many interesting stories to tell. He has a real passion to help men—all men—to decency and dignity.

Sam was chaplain of the 25th Seabee Battalion. He was the spiritual adviser to a thousand men. On Guam he had a cool, friendly chapel built almost at the water's edge. But he wasn't content with a comfortable routine; he also tried to work among the Japs. Carrying a megaphone, he went with Marine patrols and tried to persuade the Japs to surrender. He'd crawl up in front of a cave and shout his lungs out, trying to get the Japs to come out. When they didn't come, the Marines would use dynamite and flame-throwers.

Occasionally, a dying Jap would hear the chaplain speaking Japanese and would appeal to him. Sam never failed to hear. He'd sit down by the Jap, take his hand, tell him not to be afraid, that there was a God of all men who loved us all.

"Once I sat down by a boy who was from Kyoto," Sam told me. "I lived in Kyoto for four years; it's the old cultural capital of Japan, a beautiful place. I asked this boy if he had ever climbed up Mt. Hiei when the cherry trees were blooming, and of course he had. We talked of old Kyoto, and tears came in his eyes and he choked up. He died in a few minutes."

After the active fighting was over on Guam, Sam went to the stockade and began a Bible class among the Jap prisoners. He was hooted at by the people in charge of the stockade. After every visit to the stockade, he found himself covered with fleas. But, doggedly, he went back every Friday night. He taught the Japs practical English phrases.

I went with him on one of these visits—and got the fleas, too. It was amusing to hear a hundred Japs in unison trying to repeat after Sam: "May I go to the latrine?"

One Jap came up after the Bible lesson and asked what "go to hell" meant. Sam tried to tell him, but he explained to me that American profanity and obscenity—which, of course, the Japs contact first—have little or no meaning in Japanese. Our bad words just aren't bad in Japanese.

Another Jap told Sam that he couldn't see where it made any difference whether he lived or died.

"You are wrong, son," Sam replied. "You have a responsibility to God and to your people. You must go back to your country and help us build a new kind of Japan. You must help save what you and I both love in Japan."

From all the prisoners, Sam brought news of his great friend, Toyohiko Kagawa, the Japanese Christian leader. I tried to tell him that Kagawa had turned sour on us and betrayed his American friends, but Sam wouldn't believe it.

"It's absolutely impossible," he insisted. "Kagawa baptized my daughter. He has lived out the Christian Gospel as few men have ever done. The last thing I did before I left Japan was to have a long talk with him. He gave me a copy of his book, *Christ in Japan*. His last words to me were: 'Tell America to join us in building a Christian co-operative society.' I'll never believe that Kagawa has turned on American Christians."

A Jap officer in the stockade gave Sam great hope. He told us that Kagawa had been imprisoned immediately after Pearl Harbor.

There are several hundred Japs on the island of Rota in the Marianas. For a while we had plans to move in and take the island. Sam went to the Marine command at Guam with a suggestion. Since to assault Rota would cost the lives of many Americans, why not send him—Chaplain Sam Franklin—to Rota first to see if he couldn't persuade the Japs to surrender?

"We can't let you try it, chaplain," he was told. "It'd be just one more dead chaplain."

"But chaplains should be expendable where there is the slightest possibility of saving the lives of so many men," Sam argued. He lost the argument. Soon afterwards, the plans to assault Rota were postponed.

After Guam had been "secured" and the remaining Japs were holed up on the north end of the island, Sam persisted in his efforts to persuade Japs to surrender. The Marines co-operated, provided him a sound truck, and took him out to the cave area. In a voice that could be heard for miles, he pleaded with the Japs to come out. He made them an offer. He was going to turn loose a prisoner—a member of his Bible class—and the prisoner would stay in the area all night. The Marines would withdraw, and during the night the Japs could consult the prisoner as to how he had been treated. Next morning, all those wishing to surrender could be at an appointed place with the prisoner.

It didn't work. Either the prisoner decided not to return, or else the other Japs killed him. Sam got a lot of I-told-you-so's, then tried the same thing again with the same result. He told the Japs about the cherry blossoms on the hills outside Kyoto, about the New Japan, about God's love for us all. But the Japs didn't buy.

In the Philippines I was shown what appeared to be incontestable evidence that Kagawa had ratted on his American Christian friends, that he had come to the Philippines and done his best to turn the Philippine Christians against America. A speech, reliably ascribed to him, sounded about like any Jap jingoist.

VI

OMAHA AND UTAH

HERE I am going to swing halfway around the world from the Marianas and discuss how the landing was made in Normandy. Not how German resistance was overcome; that was a job done by the Air Force and the Army, assisted for a few hours by the battle fleet. The story here is how the *natural obstacles* were overcome.

To land in Normandy, we had to defeat two formidable enemies: the Germans and the sea. The sea was a strong and faithful ally of the Germans; and the Germans had counted heavily on the sea's aid. In the landing process, the Army battled the Germans; the Navy battled the sea, and in this sea battle, the Seabees played a brave and mighty role.

In *Can Do!* and in preceding chapters of this book, I have tried to convey some idea of the problems of amphibious landing. Remember how the LSTs grounded 300 feet offshore at Sicily, and how the Seabees used the floating causeways to bridge that 300-foot water gap in seven minutes? Remember those reefs in the Pacific, how the Seabees rammed cranes up on the reef and used them to transfer cargo from the pontoon barges over to amphtracks which could then go on to the beach? Remember how we tried to cross the reef with boats at Tarawa, and the disaster that resulted when the water proved too shallow? Remember how the swells and battering surf almost defeated us at Iwo Jima?

168

In planning a landing on the Channel coast of France, we had to confront all of these difficulties multiplied by a hundred.

The English Channel is one of the world's most awesome and unpredictable bodies of water. It is characterized by fierce wave action, sudden gales, vicious crosscurrents, and incredible tidal ranges. The crosscurrents can create new sand bars in a day, so charts always must be doubted. Remember all the characters of fiction who dreaded a routine Channel crossing? The Channel wrecked the Spanish Armada; and both Napoleon and Hitler stuck booted toes into its forbidding waters, shuddered, and preferred the snows of Russia.

The effect of the unbelievable tidal range is difficult to describe even to Americans who live by the sea. In the harbor at Cherbourg the water is twenty feet deeper at high tide than it is at low tide. This means that all of France's big Channel ports are and must be *lock* ports. The *Queen Mary* can dock in New York Harbor at any tidal stage. In no big American harbor is the tide a problem. But when a large ship goes into Cherbourg or Le Havre, she must go in when the tide is high; she must enter a lock alongside her dock and be locked in. Otherwise, when the tide went out, she would bury herself in the mud and keel over.

In scores of little French "tidal ports" along the Channel Coast, there is no water at all in the ports at low tide. The small craft, mostly fishing boats, simply sit high and dry in the mud when the tide is out.

On a flat Channel open beach, when the tide goes out, it goes out about half a mile from the high tide mark! This means that twice a day the water thunders in, then recedes, across 2600 feet of flat beach!

Now add squalls and storms and swells to this tidal action

169

and you have a seamanship nightmare. You can begin to understand how the all-conquering Nazis never quite got up the courage—and the equipment—to sail against England.

Only American guts and ingenuity, coupled with Britain's ancient knowledge of the sea, ever would have dared land an army across open, stormswept Channel beaches to attack so formidable a machine as the Wehrmacht. Let us never forget this!

In our early thinking about a Channel crossing—and Mr. Churchill began thinking about it even while the BEF was standing in the water at Dunkirk—we were ready to concede that the landing would have to be made at a port. To dare an open beach would be inviting disaster.

The Germans, too, believed this. It was inconceivable to them that a large-scale Allied landing would ever be attempted *except at or very near a port city,* so they concentrated their defenses in and around the ports.

Here's where the famous Dieppe Raid figures in our planning. We had conceded that the landing would have to be made at a port, and the Dieppe Raid was staged to determine whether a port could be assaulted successfully, how long the assault waves could hold the port, how long it would take the Germans to assemble and hurl preponderant strength against the invaders, and much other similar information.

The Dieppe Raid was an experiment—a costly experiment —in our planning for the ultimate invasion. From it our planners learned that *we could not invade at a port.* We would have to strike across an open beach.

The results of the Dieppe Raid were most disheartening. Allied confidence was badly strained. Dr. Goebbels exploited it masterfully. The most effective propaganda stroke of the war was the brochure depicting the Allied disaster at

170

Dieppe, which the Germans scattered all over Britain and Europe. The photography and press work were brilliant. Long lines of dirty, dejected Allied prisoners. The three thousand dead. The wrecked equipment on the beach.

Allied intelligence brought back to England the bitter story which since has come out in Marshal Pétain's trial. Europe's collaborationists shouted we-told-you-so; the fence-sitters fell over into Hitler's embrace; and the Underground Movements lost many supporters. Indeed, there were Allied planners who had despair written all over their faces.

But Dieppe forced us to accept the open beaches, and from that point, all planning was directed toward an open beach landing. This was in the Fall of 1942, almost two years before D-Day.

The open beaches were then selected: three beaches on the Normandy Coast between the mouth of the Seine and Cherbourg. I shall call the three beaches Arromanches, Omaha, and Utah. Arromanches, nearest the mouth of the Seine, was to be the principal British beach; Omaha, nine miles to the west, would be the principal American beach; and Utah, ten miles west of Omaha and on the Cotentin Peninsula, would be the secondary American beach.

Now you must envision Omaha Beach. It is a flat stretch of white sand four miles long running up into bluffs at both ends. From the high-tide mark the sand rises slowly back for about 300 feet, and there an escarpment rises precipitously to a height of perhaps 150 feet. But there are several draws in this escarpment along its four-mile length.

Now let's go back to the high-tide mark. The tide is in, so let's note the water depths. One hundred feet offshore the water is one foot deep! One thousand feet offshore the water is ten feet deep! Twenty-two hundred feet offshore—almost half a mile—the water is twenty feet deep! And don't forget, these are high-tide depths.

171

Now let's watch the tide go out. When the tide goes out, it recedes at almost the normal walking pace of a man. It goes out the entire distance of 2200 feet, leaving almost half a mile of sand between the high-tide mark and the low-tide mark. Of course this outgoing tide reduces the water depths even farther offshore. Forty-five hundred feet off-shore from the high-tide mark—almost a mile—the low-tide depth is only about thirty feet.

The first difficulty is readily apparent. We could not bring Liberty ships closer to the shore—closer to the high-water mark—than one mile! No matter what we did to Omaha, every Liberty ship would have to stand off there one mile in rough water, and every pound of Liberty-ship cargo would have to be brought up one mile through that surf by some sort of extremely shallow-draft lighter.

But Omaha Beach was where we were going to land. The other two beaches were similar to it. The problems had to be solved.

We began to study Omaha. Engineers went over there at night in submarines, got out on that flat beach at low tide, crawled over every foot of it. They found that the bottom was sandy, not muddy, and they smiled, for this meant that our trucks could pour out of the landing craft and drive to the shore with no steel matting under their wheels.

The problem then was to find a beach in England which matched Omaha, had the same tidal range, the same gradient, the same wave action. Three places in England suggested themselves. The Bristol Channel has a forty-six-foot tide range; at the mouth of the Mersey, Liverpool, there is a thirty-foot range; on the Solway in Scotland there is a twenty-three-foot range. This last area seemed best. At Cairn Head on Wigtown Bay, the British Royal Engineers began building a camp in December, 1942, and there, early in

1943, were begun the experiments from which came our methods for defeating the sea at Normandy.

The man who directed this experimentation at Cairn Head was Lieutenant Colonel John G. Carline, of the Royal Engineers, to whom I am indebted for much of this explanation.

The first problem was to *bridge the water gap* between ship and shore. I have already explained that the gap for Liberty ships would be 4500 feet. The British have a smaller cargo carrier, called a "coaster," which they believed could approach safely within 3000 feet of the high-tide mark at Arromanches. But what about our principal landing craft, the LST? How wide would the LST gap be?

A loaded LST draws six and a half feet of water at the bow and eleven and a half feet near the stern. Remembering those high-tide water depths at Omaha, if an LST drove toward the shore at high-tide where would she ground? She would ground *at the stern* about 1100 feet from the edge of the water, and the water would be eleven feet deep at her bow ramp. It would be impossible to unload her from this position with floating causeways. We had used 300-foot floating causeways at Sicily, but 1100-foot floating causeways—in Channel surf—were impossible.

Thus it was decided that some sort of pier or unloading platform would have to be erected 3100 feet offshore from the high-tide mark. At this distance the water would be deep enough, at both high and low tides, for coasters and LSTs.

But what sort of pier could it be? If it were a stationary pier, built with steel and concrete, it would have to be built at the high-water level. Yet at high-water level the ships, at low tide, would be twenty feet below the level of the pier! You might hoist cargo from the coasters up to the pier, but LSTs carry vehicular cargo and they unload at the bow.

Furthermore, what about the bridge connecting the pier with the shore? If the pier was stationary and above the high-water level, you might have a 3100-foot-long stationary bridge, under which the water would rise and fall.

Such a plan as this—called the Hughes Scheme—was the first one tried at Cairn Head. (See photo.) It called for stationary piers resting on the ocean bottom, 3100-foot stationary steel bridges, and hoisting equipment to lift vehicles and cargo to the pier level. Some of this equipment was built—at tremendous expense—and tried out, but the plan was discarded because of the twenty-foot lift.

Thinking then centered on some sort of floating pier; a pier which would rise and fall with the water level, just as the ship alongside it would. From this thinking came the Loebnitz Pier, which was adopted. It was a huge barge with a towering, concrete-filled steel leg at each corner. These four legs were called "spuds." Afloat, crossing the Channel, these "spuds" stuck high in the air, but when the pier was maneuvered into position, the "spuds" were dropped to the ocean bottom, and the pier moved up and down on its spuds with the tides. The spuds did not support the pier; they only held it in place. Water buoyancy supported the pier.

If the pier was to float and go up and down, the bridge also had to float and go up and down. Colonel Carline experimented with a "Swiss Roll"—a rubber mat—a rubber roadway that could be rolled up, then unrolled across the water gap. After you unrolled it, you put strong tension on the offshore end—pulled it as tight as possible—and it actually would support trucks. (See photo.)

A 100-yard length of this "rubber roadway" was built, with thirty-five tons of precious rubber, before the plan was abandoned.

Then steel bridge sections, to be supported at eighty-foot

174

intervals by boats, were tried. These boats had to be very strong since 2200 feet of the bridge, with its ponderous traffic, would be resting on hard sand at low tide, so sturdy, steel, boatlike pontoons, called "whales," were substituted for the boats, and this plan was adopted.

The plan for the Loebnitz piers, to be installed 3100 feet offshore, and for the floating bridge to connect the piers with the shore was ready for presentation to Messrs. Churchill and Roosevelt and their Joint Chiefs of Staff at Quebec in September, 1943. The plan was adopted, and the vast construction job, which had to be completed within less than six months, was set in motion.

But *bridging the water gap* was only one of the two major problems of an open beach landing. The second problem was how to calm the water, how to create a harbor in which the intricate pier and bridge arrangement could be set up and operated.

The most fantastic scheme was the "Bubble Harbor." A group of British engineers suggested that compressed air could substitute for masonry as a breakwater. They proposed that a row of pipe, with holes at six-inch intervals, be laid on the ocean bottom all the way around the proposed harbor at Omaha, that a wall of compressed air be forced constantly from the holes in this pipe up through the water. They believed that this air would break the incoming waves and result in a smooth-water harbor.

Yes, it was fantastic, but so was almost everything else about our invasion plans, so it was tried out. At tremendous effort and expense, divers and welders rigged up such an apparatus at Cairn Head. The air compressors began to puff, and a line of bubbles appeared all around an acre of water. Amazingly, the air did break the waves, but it had no effect on the swells. For this failing, as well as for other difficulties, the plan was discarded.

The next plan tried out at Cairn Head—the one adopted—called for the construction of a sectional, re-enforced-concrete breakwater. In effect, this was to be a pre-fabricated sea wall, built in hollow sections which would float.

The standard section of this sea wall was called a "phoenix." The "phoenix" was a huge hollow cube of re-enforced concrete. Each standard "phoenix" was 200 feet long, fifty-eight feet wide, sixty feet high, and weighed 7000 tons! The "phoenixes" were to be towed across the Channel, floated into place, then sunk by opening their sea cocks and flooding their ten water compartments.

The "phoenixes," the Loebnitz piers, and the floating bridge were all tried out in miniature aboard ship in Mr. Churchill's bathtub while he was en route to the Quebec Conference.

Meanwhile, the Royal Navy was not to be left out of the planning. The Navy planners claimed that we had to have a method for calming water out to sixty-foot depths, so that the ships would not have to be taken so close in to shore, and so that we could have a wider choice of landing spots.

The first Navy idea was suggested by those floating, rubber-based platforms you see around all bathing beaches. The British call these things "lie-lows." Some engineer was sunning himself on a "lie-low" one day when he happened to notice that the water was calmer on the landward side of the "lie-low" than on the seaward side. He leaped up and rushed to the Admiralty with an idea he was sure would make possible the Second Front.

Why couldn't huge concrete cylinders be suspended in the water off a beach by rubber bags, and why wouldn't these massive structures break wave and swell action and create calm water behind them?

The "lie-low" experiments were approved at a technical conference in Washington, and the British built three very strange contraptions. The wave-breaking part of a "lie-low" was a pencil-like concrete cylinder 200 feet long and eight feet in diameter. It weighed 750 tons.

Now how was this 750-ton concrete pencil to be suspended in the water? A huge, four-layered rubber bag, with four separate air compartments—and requiring twenty tons of precious natural rubber—was made to fit over this concrete pencil. Then the rubber bag would be inflated, and the huge concrete "pencil" would hang in the water "suspended" by the floating rubber bag.

When completed and in the water, the "lie-low" looked like a great whale. The round, 200-foot-long rubber bag extended above the surface of the water, and the dangling 750 tons of concrete hung to a depth of nineteen feet below the surface.

British seamen, ordered to tow the three "lie-lows" out of Portsmouth Harbor and experiment with them, were certain that their superiors had gone nuts. The damn things were unmanageable. The towing staple was fourteen feet under the water. Once you started moving them in the water, how were they to be stopped? When the first two "lie-lows" kissed each other, they exploded their outer bags, but continued to float. One of them got loose and had to be sunk with gunfire when it threatened to tear up some of the harbor defenses.

The other two "lie-lows" were towed to the Isle of Wight and sunk, whereupon the seamen handling them sighed with relief.

Nothing daunted, however, the Royal Navy stuck to its guns. It still was going to suspend something in the water off Normandy and break up the waves.

The next idea—the one adopted—was for a cuneiform

steel structure, called a "bombardon." It was a riveted, steel-plate contraption, looking something like an Indian arrowhead in cross-section. It weighed 2000 tons, was 150 feet long, and drew nineteen feet of water. When it was floating, all you could see of it was the 150-foot-long steel "wall" projecting up three feet above the waves.

The Navy built several of these "bombardons," installed them off the coast at Newhaven, and began studying their effect on wave action with all sorts of intricate instruments. I visited a shack on a bleak section of coast where two British officers had been doing nothing else for months but watching graph-making instruments which compared the wave action on the seaward side of the bombardons with the action on the landward side. They concluded that one row of "bombardons"—set twenty-four to the mile—would reduce wave action one-third, and that two rows would reduce it two-thirds.

At Quebec, the following "harbor equipment" was ordered built:

> 95 2000-ton bombardons.
> 24 Loebnitz pierheads.
> 146 7000-ton phoenixes.
> 10 *miles* of steel floating bridge.

This vast amount of never-before-used equipment was to be built within six months, and personnel to handle and install it was to be trained. It was to be used to create two artificial harbors: one British harbor at Arromanches and one American harbor at Omaha.

Rapid construction of all this stuff in an England in its fifth year of war was "the father and mother of a job." Both the bombardons and the phoenixes were supposed to be built in dry docks. Because the bombardons were a Navy idea, the Royal Navy grabbed the big *George V* dock at

Southampton— the best dock in England—and monopolized it with bombardons. The Royal Engineers then had to improvise dock space along the Thames. To build the phoenixes, they scooped out huge holes near the Thames, built the bases in there, then opened channels between the holes and the rivers, floated out the partially completed phoenixes, and completed them as they floated on the Thames.

Most of the floating bridge was built on the River Stour, near Richboro, in Kent, by the Royal Engineers and the Seabees. Somehow the job was done, and all the stuff was assembled in England's Channel ports.

All of this artificial harbor planning, however, was only a part of our strategy for the battle against the sea at Normandy. The artificial harbors—with their intricate floating piers and bridges—were not to be ready for operation until twelve days after D-Day. The most critical days on the beach would be past before the artificial harbors could be completed. How, then, were we going to unload the LSTs and Liberties on D-Day and on the eleven most critical days to follow?

The United States Navy Civil Engineer Corps had been developing a method by which a pontoon barge could be "married" to the bow of an LST in open water. The "marriage" could be made secure enough so that vehicles could run out of the LST and onto the barge even in a fairly rough sea. The 81st and 111th Seabee Pontoon Battalions had been perfecting this technique.

The barges, called "rhino ferries," were the largest pontoon assemblies the Seabees had employed. Each barge was six pontoons wide by thirty pontoons long, or forty-one feet wide by 176 feet long. It was propelled by two huge outboard engines. To give the ponderous barge more maneuverability and power in heavy water, each barge was

179

accompanied by a small "rhino tug" which was powered by two more of the engines. Thus, after the rhino ferry took on its load, it employed four of the engines to drive it toward the beach.

The rhino could carry as many as eighty trucks and jeeps; it could carry ten Sherman tanks. Two rhinos could carry the entire load of an LST. The rhino drew only forty-two inches of water when loaded, which meant that it could ram its ponderous nose into the sand at Normandy and unload its vehicles in only about three feet of water.

The rhino was adopted for both British and American beaches. The Seabees assembled sixty-four rhinos—thirty-two each for the Americans and the British—using 11,500 steel pontoons and 256 outboard engines.

When the first thirty-two American LSTs left port for France on June 4th, each ship had a long and strange tow. Two hundred feet behind the LST rode a great, flat barge, with a bulldozer chained down in the center of it, and with a tent flopping in the wind on the back of it. The ubiquitous Seabees bargemen, wet, phlegmatic, and cussing, were back there on the barge, decks awash, going to France, too. A hundred feet back of the barge came the rhino tug with more Seabees.

After it became so dark you couldn't see the barge from the stern of the LST, you occasionally would see a flash of light in the tent on the rhino. It would be that inevitable blowtorch heating the coffee.

As we approached the beaches in the dark morning hours of June 6th, the LSTs halted about 10,000 yards offshore. There, about four A.M., the Seabees on the rhinos dropped the towing lines, cranked up their outboard engines, and began maneuvering to get in front of the LSTs and get "married up." The water was much rougher than had been expected. Four-foot waves broke over the rhinos.

While the beach was lighted with flares and our bombers unloaded in relentless procession, the Seabees fought those waves. Men were washed overboard. As the sterns of the rhinos were drawn close to the LST ramps, there was imminent danger that the men working the lines would be crushed. Time and again I saw men washed overboard, and each time it seemed inevitable that they would be caught by the churning screws of those outboards.

Every one of the thirty-two rhinos was successfully married to an LST before H-Hour. The 81st Battalion took twelve of the rhinos to Utah Beach, and the 111th Battalion took the other twenty to Omaha. They averaged at least fifty vehicles a rhino, so they delivered a total of 1500 vehicles to the beach on their first trip in.

This is how most of our vehicles were landed in Normandy during the crucial days. The Seabees brought them in. Eighty-five per cent of all the vehicular cargo landed on the beaches during the first three days was brought in by the Seabees. After the third day, their percentage fell because of a great stroke of luck which I shall explain here.

I mentioned earlier that if an LST * drove toward Omaha Beach at high tide, the ship would ground about 1100 feet from the high-tide mark. Then, when the tide went out

* Perhaps the reader wonders why I seem continually concerned with the LST and seldom mention the other landing craft—the LCIs, LCMs, etc. The answer is that, in the European theater, only the LST and the much smaller LCT carried *vehicular cargo* to the beaches. All the other craft were designed to carry personnel and non-vehicular cargo to the beaches. In the Pacific we used another vehicle-carrying craft called the LSM—larger than an LCT but smaller than an LST— but the LSM was never used in the Atlantic. The LST, most valuable and most successful of all our landing craft, was the big slugger which vomited our tanks and trucks on the African and European beaches.

2200 feet, the ship would be high and dry with the water 1000 feet astern.

Why, you may ask, didn't we plan to do just that? Why didn't we plan to unload all LSTs by driving them aground at high tide, letting them "dry out," and unloading on the dry sand?

We couldn't plan to operate LSTs in this manner for several reasons. First, if the LSTs had gone in there in the early hours, they would have been wrecked by German gunfire, and second, we expected the Luftwaffe. Despite all the brilliant work of the Air Force, the Germans still had hundreds of first-rate planes which they could have thrown at the beaches in the first days. Why the Luftwaffe didn't fight still remains a mystery to me.

But by the second day, when we had partially cleared the beach of obstacles, and when we had realized that the Luftwaffe was not going to fight, we began to experiment with the "drying out" method for unloading LSTs. One LST was sent in. She grounded successfully, "dried out," and unloaded in two hours. The ambulances drove up into her tank deck and deposited their wounded; then the ship closed her bow and "retracted" at high tide.

It was wonderful! Three LSTs were sent in on the next tide, six on the next, and at one time I counted fifty-one LSTs "dried out" on Omaha Beach, unloading trucks and loading wounded, all on one tide.

This was the American way of turning what was expected to be a great tidal disadvantage to our own advantage. Nothing contributed more to our victory in the Battle of the Build-Up than this "drying out" of LSTs.

As soon as we began "drying out" the LSTs, the Seabees diverted the rhino ferries to the Liberty ships, and the big rhinos became, in effect, floating docks on which the Libertys could unload. Then the docks moved to the shore.

About three P.M. on July 7th, Rhino Ferry No. 4 was unloading on the section of Omaha Beach called "Fox Red." Fifty yards to the left of the barge was a section of water still not cleared of obstacles and mines. Four ducks drifted into this section, hit mines, and were wrecked. Apparently all of the personnel except one driver were killed. But this driver, badly wounded, was alive and clinging to wreckage.

The officer in charge of that sector of the beach could issue but one order: no man and no vehicle would be allowed to go in after the wounded man. He was in a mine field; it was certain death to go in there, so the risk would not be allowed.

Two Seabees dived off the back of the rhino, swam the fifty yards into the mine field, and brought the wounded man out. The two were R. G. Dare (Machinist's Mate Third, Cape Girardeau, Mo.) and Thomas Newman (Carpenter's Mate Third, Bronx, N. Y.), both of the 11th Battalion.

In addition to the artificial harbor and the rhino ferries, the Seabees also employed the pontoon causeways in Normandy. But the causeway method was entirely new. The causeways are designed to float, to bridge the water gap between the bow of an LST and dry land. But in Normandy the rhinos handled the LST cargo until we began beaching the LSTs, so the causeways were turned to new purpose.

There were only three types of craft which landed vehicles directly on the Norman beaches: the rhino ferry, the LST, and the LCT. I have explained the use of the rhino and the LST; the causeways were used to help the LCT.

The LCT—landing craft, tanks—is the barge-like, one-deck craft which is even older than the LST. An LCT, which carries a relatively small number of vehicles, draws about fifty-four inches of water at her stern when loaded. Many LCTs crossed the Channel under their own power with tank loads. But note this! Every vehicle unloaded from an LCT directly onto the beach had to go through three and a half feet of salt water to reach the shore. It was the same with the rhinos.

Our planners had anticipated this three-foot salt water bath, and all of the vehicles which were to land in Normandy during the first few days had been waterproofed.

This waterproofing was a handicap. Not only was it a big job to waterproof the vehicle in England, but the vehicle had to be de-waterproofed soon after it reached France, so it was extremely desirable, if not imperative, that we devise some system whereby the LCTs and the rhino ferries could unload their vehicles "in the dry" instead of dunking them in brine.

To solve this problem was the task assigned the famous Ten-o-Six Pontoon Detachment, veterans of Sicily and Salerno. Back in England *two miles* of pontoon causeway had been assembled. It was in the usual two-pontoon-wide, 175-foot-long sections. LSTs which were not towing rhinos to the beaches were towing these causeway sections.

At high tide on D-Day plus 1, Ten-o-Six rammed one of these causeway sections high and dry on Omaha. Then, quickly, they connected other sections until they had a single-lane floating causeway extending 2450 feet out to sea. Then they opened the cocks and flooded the pontoons, and the entire causeway sank to the bottom.

Since the pontoon is five feet high, this meant that a five-foot-high steel roadway was lying on the contour of the beach to a length of 2450 feet. Only a few feet of this roadway was exposed at high tide, but when the tide went out 2200 feet, virtually the entire length of the causeway was gradually exposed. The incoming tide covered it in a similar manner.

At 500-foot intervals along the length of this raised steel

184

roadway, there were pontoon platforms called "blisters." The "blisters" were the same height as the causeway and were connected to it.

Now notice what would happen as an LCT approached the beach. If the tide were high, the LCT, instead of driving aground and unloading in forty inches of water, would approach the causeway "blister" which was 500 feet out from the high-tide mark. This "blister," five feet high, would be protruding out of the water at high tide. The LCT would berth alongside the causeway, drop her ramp on the "blister," the vehicles would run out onto the "blister," over onto the causeway, and thence to the beach without even wetting its tires. Rhinos could use the causeway in the same manner.

If the tide was halfway out, then the LCT would use the "blister" which was 1500 feet from high-tide mark; if the tide was all the way out, then the LCT would stop at the "blister" which was 2400 feet from high-tide mark. Whatever the tidal stage, there was always a dry "blister" waiting for the LCT ramp.

A Ten-o-Six detail commanded by Lieutenant Alexander M. Zak (CEC, USNR, Franklin, N. H.) laid the sunken causeways at Omaha, and a detail under Lieutenant W. C. Pietz (CEC, USNR, Pittsburgh, Pa.) did a similar job at Utah.

Towing and installation of the vast artificial harbor equipment was handled by the 108th Seabee Battalion. The men had trained with the British at Cairn Head, then had set up a practice harbor at the Isle of Wight.

Towing began on D-minus-1 and the first equipment arrived at Omaha on D-plus-1. It was easily the largest towing job in history, and tugs flying a dozen different United Nations' flags participated. Six-man Seabee towing crews rode each of the phoenixes going to Omaha; ten-man crews were on the Loebnitz pierheads; and six-man crews handled the bridge sections. The 10,000 feet of floating bridge assigned to Omaha was towed in 480-foot sections.

Of all the seasick Americans arriving in France, the sickest, I think, were the Seabees who rode those bridge sections. The long, articulated bridge sections, riding on seven pontoon-like "whales," crawled like 480-foot serpents across the Channel.

Directed by Lieutenant Harry Stevens (CEC, USNR, Salem, Ill.), the Seabees assembled three 3300-foot floating bridges and connected them with a line of ten Loebnitz pierheads. The phoenixes were sunk in a great arc; and the bombardons were moored out beyond the phoenixes. The harbor was completed on June 17th, one day ahead of schedule.

Then the storm struck. For three days a Channel storm, the like of which had never been seen in June, beat at our beaches. At both the British and American beaches, those 2000-ton bombardons broke loose and struck fear into the heart of every skipper. In that sea they could stave in the side of a battleship. Gunfire sank most of them, and they wrecked only a few ships.

The sea wall, created with the phoenixes, was supposed to extend ten feet above the highest water line. But the storm-driven waves crashed over the wall at Omaha, broke the back of the massive phoenixes. Knots were tied in those 3300-foot floating bridges at Omaha, and LCTs and bombardons were piled high on top of the knots. The sunken causeways were covered with sand; the rhino ferries were driven high and dry on the beach. Two hundred and fifty-six craft, ranging from LCTs down to LCVPs, were piled on the beach at Omaha and wrecked.

On the morning of June 20th, Omaha Beach was a solid,

four-mile-long mass of twisted steel. To view that wreckage was a heartbreaking experience. The Germans had counted on something like this, and there were many Allied leaders who believed that the storm would prevent our breaking out of the beachhead until the Spring of 1945. Had the storm come eight days earlier, there seems little doubt that it would have converted our invasion into the most terrible military disaster in history.

Almost miraculously, the British artificial harbor at Arromanches survived the storm with the loss of only the bombardons. The storm had not struck Arromanches at the same angle it had struck Omaha. Also, Arromanches had been protected to some degree by a reef, called the Calvados Reef. It was decided, therefore, to transfer what equipment could be salvaged from the Omaha harbor to Arromanches, and to strengthen the Arromanches harbor with new and large phoenixes.

What saved the day for us after the storm was the beaching of LSTs, and the rapid manner in which the beaches were cleared.

A second disaster followed close on the heels of the storm. When we got into Cherbourg we found that the Germans, after practicing on Bizerte and Naples, had really learned how to wreck a harbor. Under our original plans, the open beaches were to be used only a short time. As soon as we had moved into Cherbourg, then into Brest, St. Nazaire, and other Brittany ports, we would abandon the open beaches. We had minutely detailed plans for the development of each of these ports.

But the Germans changed these plans. Cherbourg was a liability for many weeks; Brest was hopeless; we still had nothing but the open beaches. What saved us was the audacity of the Army leadership, coupled with the fact that, in the years of amphibious warfare, we had become masters of open beach operation. We actually could unload more tonnage over an open beach than we could in a harbor.

The Germans inflicted a disaster on us at Dieppe, crowed long and loud about it, and thus drove us to an open-beach landing. Then, using open beaches, we landed enough men and material to win the Battle of France.

VII

THE PHILIPPINES

IF YOU can chuckle instead of sneer at human frailty, you can get a lot of good, solid enjoyment out of wars. They are so human.

Take the Great, Stupendous, and Colossal Battle of the Typewriters and the Cameras which raged unabated among the branches and sub-branches of the armed services. Here is a rich field for the postwar satirist. Well-publicized face, it appears, is more important to a military branch than it is to the Ladies' Uplift Society in Sauk Center. Battles have been held up, waiting for the *Life* cameraman to get into position. The Marines, I understand, finally used a thirteen-man instead of the old twelve-man squad; the thirteenth man was the photographer. Sixteen Coast Guard caption writers cracked under the strain after writing "Coast-Guard-manned" in front of the word "transport" 1,672,399 times.

The Seabees, who of course have enjoyed no such high-octane publicity, are phlegmatic fellows who liked to chuckle at it all—especially at the Army. On no less than three occasions, Seabees have been driven off the beaches by Army MPs so that the newsreel cameras could catch the doggies "charging a Jap-held shore" with fixed bayonets.

In the old days in the Solomons, Army prestige was about as high as a grasshopper's chops. The Marines and Seabees had been making all the landings; the Marines had been getting all the publicity. Whenever the doggies reached a beach, sharp-tongued Marines and Seabees were always waiting to chide them for "landing just behind the USO." The Army publicists determined to show the folks at home that the Army got there first, too.

After the Seabees had been working at Koli Point, Guadalcanal, for several weeks, an Army "invasion armada" approached. The MPs and cameramen came ashore and "asked" the Seabees to abandon their equipment and quit work for a while. The Seabees obliged, went back into the jungle, perched in trees, and cheered lustily as the doggies "stormed ashore" with fixed bayonets—and with the cameras grinding. Then the doggies used the Seabee bulldozers to show how they "ripped out the jungle" as soon as they had landed.

On Bougainville the same act was repeated except that a group of Seabees were in swimming on the sector of the beach which the Army wished to "storm." The swimmers obligingly walked back into the jungle, but unfortunately, the Army cameras caught two swimmers who were far down the beach and who were thought to be out of camera range. The entire film was ruined, so next day the doggies had to "storm the beach" again.

By the time this Army "beach-storming" act played Emirau Island in the St. Mathias Group, the Seabees had become veteran spectators and prop boys. They cheered mightily from their trees, and threw rocks into the water in front of the charging doggies so the folks at home could see "wicked Jap mortar fire."

Our principal naval base in the Philippines was built on the southeastern tip of the island of Samar. We had nothing there before the war; it was a completely new development. The site is by no means ideal for a naval base. There are serious weather and water handicaps, and the site was decided upon after long argument and much wrangling.

Several powerful officers in the Navy had long held that our principal base in the Philippines should be on the Pacific side of the archipelago, not on the South China Sea side, where the Fleet might possibly be bottled up. Also, the water was shallow in Manila Bay, MacArthur was in Manila, and Filipino politicians didn't want the Navy back in Manila. All of these considerations were debated before it was finally decided to put the base at Samar.

The one thing in the site's favor is that about the only large coral deposits in the Philippines are there, and coral is important in the building of roads, causeways, and airfields.

In fact, coral has never seemed quite so important as it seemed to the Seabees and Army Engineers after the first three wet, dismal, muddy, and disastrous weeks on Leyte. The Leyte mud was bottomless; the rain was merciless; drainage seemed impossible. Planes cracked up on the soft airstrips, and at least one strip had to be abandoned. Samar's coral looked like a godsend after that Leyte mud.

Among the many Seabees in the Samar area, the "lead battalions" were rugged veterans of the South and Southwest Pacific campaigns. They had served with "MacArthur's" Seventh Fleet, and their stories were of Gamadota on Milne Bay, of Finsch and Hollandia and Biak, of mud and Japs and jungle.

Which battalion landed first in the Philippines is a matter for dispute. The 61st, veterans of Guadalcanal, New Zealand, and Emirau, landed at Dulag, Leyte, with the Army and went to work on the San Pablo airstrip, while the 105th, veterans of Gamadodo and Hollandia, landed at Tacloban on Leyte.

When it was decided to divert part of the invasion fleet—and virtually all of the Navy activity—from Leyte to Samar, the 93rd Seabees, who had made the D-Day landing on

Greene Island with the New Zealanders, led the way into Samar. Indeed, the 93rd's seventy-five-man survey party were the first Americans to land on Samar, and they attended the first liberation party given by the natives.

The 75th Battalion, which has made six major moves in the Pacific, was first to land on Calicoan, the small island which forms the southeasternmost tip of Samar, and which is most important to the vast base development.

The 61st Seabees were another Southern outfit, composed mostly of boys from Florida and Georgia. They made the rounds from Guadal to New Zealand, to Emirau, to Banika, to Leyte and to Samar.

While the battalion was at Emirau, Charles T. "Beachhead" MacDouglass (Chief Carpenter's Mate, New Orleans, La.) often visited a nearby island. He taught the natives there to sing "Dixie," "Old Black Joe," and "Oh, Susannah!" The natives insisted that "Beachhead" preach to them, so at a big festival he preached for a solid hour about the pearly gates and the streets of gold.

Several days later, while the battalion was at work on the airstrip, a big party of native canoes beached on Emirau. The natives, all decked out in their most colorful hairdresses and breechclouts, had come to repay "Beachhead's" visit. Wishing to reciprocate fully, the native chief wanted to preach to the Seabees.

The battalion could do nothing else but halt work for an hour while the men repaired to the theater to applaud the native show—and the sermon.

After spending ten months on Guadalcanal, the 61st went to New Zealand for a rest. They threw a big dance party in Auckland, after which the men were given fourteen-day leaves. While they were scattered all over the two islands, the leave was canceled suddenly. Every radio in New Zealand began broadcasting orders for "the 61st Seabees" to return at once to their headquarters. For a week, thereafter, New Zealanders did little else but track down Seabees and give them the news, which needless to say interrupted many promising friendships.

The 61st boys soon learned *not* to ask for napkins in the New Zealand cafes. The first waitress who was asked for a napkin was so astonished that she dropped her tray. In New Zealand, it seems, the word *napkin* has only one meaning: Kotex.

Emirau is a beautiful little island just one degree south of the equator in the St. Mathias group. It lies between New Britain and the Admiralty Islands, and was important for two reasons: it "put the stopper in Rabaul," and its development was the last step toward the invasion of Manus, which was to become our greatest base in the Southwest Pacific.

The 22nd and 61st Seabees landed with the Marines at Emirau on March 22, 1944. The 88th, 27th, 63rd, and 77th Battalions then moved in, because Admiral Halsey had ordered the island developed in forty-four days. The 61st and 88th Battalions built the airfield, and had it ready for large-scale operation only thirty-three days after the landing. The island is four miles wide by eight miles long.

After staging sixty days at Banika, the 61st joined the Leyte invasion convoy. They landed near Dulag and pushed eight miles inland to three adjoining airstrips which had been abandoned by the Japs. The Japs had never been able to drain the strips sufficiently to use them during rainy weather. The surface on the strips was too thin for American planes.

Despite the many air alerts, the 61st went to work trying to condition the boggy strips. They had orders to continue working until Jap planes were actually over them, then to dive under their equipment. They were proceeding in this manner when, at six-thirty-seven P.M. on December 6, 1944, they became the first American unit to be attacked by Jap paratroopers.

The Japs were dropping over the fields from their transports before any alert was sounded. There were about 200 of them. Some of the Seabees, like James A. Stewart (Shipfitter First, Elmwood, Ill.), were in the shower when they saw the Japs landing in the camp. They bolted, buck naked, for their guns. The Japs began throwing grenades even before they hit the ground.

Franklin R. Bednar (Machinist's Mate First, Fort Bragg, Calif.) tommy-gunned the first Jap paratrooper to hit the ground. James T. Nalls, Jr. (Machinist's Mate First, Hilliard, Fla.), killed two more. In all, seventy-five Japs were killed by crossfire in or near the camp. The Japs made little attempt to fight; they seemed interested only in reaching the dumps. They managed to blow up a huge fuel storage dump which contained hundreds of barrels of fuel oil. But they were all wiped out before they could reach a cache of fifty-one tons of dynamite.

After the rainiest November in Leyte history, the 61st was forced to abandon the San Pablo airstrips. With no coral available, it was impossible to build a surface hard enough for our planes. The battalion transferred to Guiuan, on Samar, and with the 93rd Battalion, began trying to build a field on marshland which looked almost as hopeless as San Pablo.

The ancient Church of the Immaculate Conception at Guiuan had fallen into disrepair under Jap rule, and the liberated natives were anxious to repair the church in time to celebrate Christmas Mass. Two of the 61st's electricians salvaged a Jap generator, wired the old church with Jap wire, and had it lighted for Christmas. A clever painter,

P. B. Blankenship (Painter First, Lynchburg, Va.), repainted the holy pictures.

The citizens of Guiuan also were anxious to reopen their schools, but they had no English texts. The editor of the 61st newspaper, Davis B. Webb (Carpenter's Mate Second, Miami, Fla.), ran off enough extra copies so that the schools could use the paper for their English classes.

The 61st immediately hired 3000 Filipino natives to help with the clearing on Samar, and the first pay day came just before Christmas. The natives, ranging in age from eight to seventy, lined up happily to receive their pesos and rice. The pay scale, set by the Filipino Government, was sixty-two and a half cents a day for the average unskilled labor (most everybody), eighty-seven and a half cents a day for semiskilled, and $1.12½ for skilled.

Payment of the natives was handled by Robert W. Holmes (Storekeeper First, Lexington, N. C.).

When the Filipinos celebrated Christmas Mass in their Seabee-painted and lighted church, the boys of the 61st donated $508 to the church—a fortune to the poor peasant natives of Samar.

This illustrates the difference between a Japanese occupation and an American occupation. The Japs pillage; the Americans give.

One other member of the 61st deserves mention in any book of mine. John Lino (Ship's Service Man's Tailor, First Class, East Boston, Mass.) was making a skirt for a Filipino girl when I saw him. He interrupted this important work to make a baseball cap for me.

Milne Bay was our first great concentration point in New Guinea. Most of the "Seventh Fleet" Seabee battalions —all of which later were to congregate in the Philippines—

either worked or staged at Milne. The 105th Battalion specialized in warehouses at Milne. Put together, all the warehouses they built would make a shelter forty feet wide by fifteen miles long. The two men who supervised most of this warehouse building were O. E. Pearson (Chief Carpenter's Mate, Brandon, S. D.) and Donald E. Champagne (Chief Carpenter's Mate, Ballston Spa, N. Y.).

At Tacloban, on Leyte, where they worked on roads and the airfield, the battalion experienced 182 raids in thirty-three days. Only one man was killed, however: Richard J. Agnew (Carpenter's Mate Third, Maynard, Mass.).

Now you must understand that Seabees have a standard ritual for air raids. When a Jap plane comes over, the men lie in their foxholes and watch that Jap like a thousand hungry tomcats eyeing one canary. The moment the Jap plane is hit, everybody gets set to leap and run, and just as soon as the plane goes into a dive, every Seabee jumps out of his hole and races toward the spot where he thinks the Jap will fall.

A plane, falling out of control, is tricky; it's hard to judge where it will land. Often the plane will reverse itself in mid-air. But there are Seabee veterans who can tell within eight inches where a plane will hit, even though it starts falling from 10,000 feet. They'll be standing there waiting for the plane to crash, then they'll proceed to "field strip" the plane. These old wiseacres are rich with souvenirs.

There has been repeated, raucous demand for clarification of the rules governing this type of "salvage." The pilots who shoot down some of these planes have insisted that they should have the right of salvage, that the wrecked plane should be guarded until they can land and have first chance at "field stripping." Army antiaircraft gun crews have protested angrily that they should have the right to salvage the planes they shoot down, that at least the Seabees should be forced to stay in their foxholes until the raid is over and the gun crews can get an even start in the race for the prizes.

But none of these arguments have shaken the firm Seabee conviction that the sovereign right to "field strip" belongs to the first man who can reach the Jap plane.

At Tacloban, however, where the prizes fell thick and fast, two enterprising boys of the 105th precipitated a bitter intra-Seabee row when they introduced a new technique. These two, L. B. Williamson (Machinist's Mate First, Hutchinson, Kan.) and H. M. Fair (Machinist's Mate Third, Odessa, Tex.), decided that they could reach a fallen prize faster if they remained mobile during a raid. So when a Jap came over, instead of getting in a foxhole, these two got in a jeep and began circling, trying to anticipate where the Jap would fall even before he was hit. Then, when the Jap was hit, Williamson and Fair had the further advantage of a running start.

In this manner, the two men grabbed off one of the sweetest prizes of the campaign. A Betty crashed in a nearby swamp—without even catching fire—and the two were standing there in mud waist-deep, just waiting for the plane. They hit the jackpot, with binoculars, pistols, and enough flags to celebrate a Japanese Fourth of July.

The howls of protest were so loud after this that a Seabee law had to be laid down: the "running start" was outlawed; everybody had to start, flatfooted, from a foxhole.

At one point during the Tacloban fighting, the Seabees suspected that a conspiracy existed between a P-38 squadron and certain Army ground units. It seemed apparent that the fighter pilots were trying to shoot down Japs only over Army-held territory, and thus the Seabees were being "robbed" of prizes. One night when Jap planes were all over the Seabees, but no P-38's were around, H. Ellis (Machinist's Mate Second, New York City) called General Mac-

Arthur's headquarters and asked to speak with the General. When an aide insisted that the General was in bed, Ellis demanded to know why-the-hell no P-38's were over the Tacloban strip.

"Why, the P-38's are shooting down Japs as fast as they can," the aide insisted.

"Yeah, that's the hell of it," Ellis shot back. "They ain't shooting down any *over us!*"

The happiest day for the 105th at Tacloban was the day one of its bulldozers uncovered a cache of Jap torpedo juice. There were seven fifty-five-gallon drums of drinking alcohol!

Later, a calamity developed when two of these drums were buried, and a night crew built a road fill over the burial place. The calamity was not that the alcohol was lost, but that the fill had to be moved.

When the 122nd Battalion arrived at Gamadota on Milne, there was a shortage of stevedores, so the boys were put to unloading ships with the pontoon barges. When they were unloading the beer cargoes, they would be forced to work twenty-four hours a day: eight hours a day unloading, and the other sixteen diving surreptitiously for the cases they had thrown overboard in shallow water.

Later, the 122nd moved up to Hollandia with the 102nd, 113th, and 119th Battalions. There they encountered a Navy captain who objected furiously to what the Seabees were doing to the South Pacific islands. Bulldozers offended him.

"Nature made these islands beautiful," he declared, "and now the Seabees are ripping them up with no regard to the preservation of their beauty!"

The 122nd dubbed him "the Ferdinand of the Navy," sent him word that they heartily concurred in his judgment, and that if he could arrange it with General MacArthur they'd be glad to quit "spoiling nature" and go home.

198

At three A.M. on September 18, 1944, all of Hollandia erupted into a celebration. Four thousand Seabees turned out, yelled their heads off, fired their pieces, got drunk, and serenaded the Wacs. Some drunken pilot, returning from a routine flight, had originated a radio report that the war in Germany was over.

Hollandia, to the Seabees, meant just one thing: Wacs. The first big contingent of Wacs sent to the Pacific—2500 of them—went to Hollandia, and 4500 Seabee wolves were baying on the beaches when they arrived. What really happened is for the postwar novelist; certainly I can't tell the story here.

By New Guinea standards, every Wac looked like Betty Grable. She might be low and wide—"three ax handles across the beam"—she might have buck teeth, bad breath, and B. O., but there was a Seabee who loved her. The four battalions vied to see which one could do the most for the Wacs.

Of course the Wacs had no footlockers. The Army scorns such refinements. The 102nd boys made Wac footlockers. So much furniture was made in the 102nd's carpentry shop that a stern sign was put up: NO MORE (censored) FURNITURE MADE IN HERE!

The Wacs had no mattresses; the Army scorns these, too. The 122nd Seabees came bearing mattresses. I can't say that the storekeepers of the 122nd *provided* the mattresses. To do so would put those men in the shadow of the Navy prison at Portsmouth. I can only report that the Wacs in Hollandia enjoyed Seabee mattresses, and that a Seabee storekeeper around a bunch of Wacs was like Frank Sinatra at the Paramount.

The 113th Seabees built its famous Club Tropicano for Wacs and enlisted men. The club was far back in the jungle, and only one narrow, guarded path led to it. No officers were allowed: only Wacs and Seabees. The 119th Battalion countered with a beautiful, secluded mountain swimming pool, where the Wacs could drape themselves over the rocks. (See photo, XLII.) The 102nd Battalion built a dance hall for the Wacs, and it, too, had a gem of a "head." In fact, this "head" was equipped with the only flush toilet in New Guinea—except MacArthur's—and Seabees don't give away flush toilets lightly.

This dance hall, incidentally, was the point at which the serpent entered the Garden of Eden. It seems there were two kinds of Wacs at Hollandia. Most all of them were attached to Army Services of Supply, and SOS demanded that its Wacs wear pants: *absolutely no skirts*. But a few of the Wacs were flying Wacs, attached to the Air Force, and the more radical Air Force allowed its Wacs to switch to skirts on occasion.

You can see that this situation exudes dynamite. At the big Seabee dances, the SOS Wacs would appear in their inevitable pants. Then the few flying Wacs would come sashaying in, also wearing pants, but carrying overnight valises. The flying Wacs would step into the "head," and appear shortly thereafter *sans* pants and *sans* valises. They'd be wearing trim skirts, and the wolf lines would form on the right.

Of course the pants-wearing SOS Wacs weren't going to take it long. After the dance one night, when the flying Wacs went back to the "head" to change into their pants, they found that liberal quantities of beer had been poured into their valises; their clothes were saturated.

After that lesson the flying Wacs never dared shed their pants at the dance hall. Everybody kept her pants on.

The Wacs had no laundry equipment either, so they adopted a love-me-love-my-laundry technique, and when they appeared for the supper dances each night, they'd come bringing their laundry for the Seabees to get done.

Each Seabee got an allotment of beer chits each week. The Wacs got beer chits, too, so it was customary for a Seabee and his Wac to pool their chits. Needless to say, the Seabees got the worst of this pooling arrangement.

The Seabee pharmacist's mates, who handled the "medicinal alcohol," were great favorites with the Wacs, and the cooks, who handled those magic Seabee ice cream machines, had more influence with the Wacs than Colonel Hobby.

The chiefs of the 113th Battalion have a good Wac story. They were having a hot campaign for the presidency of the Chiefs' Club at Hollandia. C. E. "Casey" Jones, of Dayton, O., was managing the campaign for Ralph Wesner, of Pottstown, Pa., a little, short guy. The campaign slogan: "A Wac for every Chief and a Pony for Wesner."

When Wesner won the election, Jones had to throw a party and produce the pony—and the Wacs. The pony was easy; Wesner came charging into the chow hall on a native cayuse with a banner: BUCK WESNER RIDES AGAIN! But there was a catch to the Wacs. Jones could get them all right, but to do so he was sort of obligated to invite a tough sergeant Wac who always had to sign the girls' liberty cards. The battalion had to curry favor with the sergeant Wac, and this meant that somebody had to be a goat.

And I do mean a goat. For this sergeant Wac was a formidable creature. She was a good three ax handles across the beam, with a face that would frighten Tojo. She had no footlocker; whoever took her to the party would have to make her one. She had no mattress; whoever took her would have to get her one even if he had to give her his own. She was a sink-hole for beer; she was sure to drink up a month's allowance of beer chits in one evening.

But the "goat" whom the lot fell on proceeded bravely to

his task. He made the footlocker; he "procured" a mattress at the risk of his life; he gaily watched the sarge drink up his whole month's allowance of beer; and he gave that old gal an evening she'll never forget.

From then on, the 113th could get Wacs when nobody else could. The door opened more easily for the 113th.

And what of the "goat"? I won't identify him here, because he is a family man. But his fellow chiefs tendered him suitable honors. They gave him a special Distinguished Service Cross for courage, and awarded him the Purple Heart for "wounds received in action."

Just what the *quid pro quo* was for all this work the Seabees did for the Wacs, I am not prepared to say. But I can report that in the Philippines when a Seabee who had never been stationed in Hollandia met one of the Hollandia veterans, the non-Hollandia Seabee always asked:

"Say, mate! Back there in Hollandia, how the hell couldya tell there was a war on?"

One of the oldest practices in armed services everywhere is never to give a rookie a break. The Seabees are merciless. When the 93rd Battalion landed at Banika, fresh from the States, they came ashore at midnight. You could tell they were rookies. They wore head nets and impregnated clothing, and they clutched their pieces as though they expected to be ambushed.

The old-timers knew what to do. They brought out the coconuts and spent the rest of the night selling coconuts for a dollar a piece. They showed the rookies the coral pits, told them they were bomb craters.

Next day every member of the 93rd had the Tropical Trots from the coconuts, and he could see that coconuts could be had by the thousands for the picking up.

The 93rd, however, soon developed into a highly capable

outfit. They built a big hospital on Banika, which is forty miles north of Guadalcanal and more healthful. Then, with the 33rd, 37th, and 15th Battalions, they made the D-Day landing on tiny Greene Island, which is at the extreme north end of the Solomons "slot." Greene had to be developed very rapidly so that fighter planes could roam over the big Jap base at Rabaul and neutralize it for our subsequent operations at Emirau and Manus.

On Samar the 93rd joined the 61st Battalion in building our first successful bomber field in the Philippines. There were grave doubts that the field could be built. Water was up to the floor boards of the big cats as the clearing began. But we had been forced to abandon the Leyte fields because of the rains, and the Jap air attacks were extremely serious, so the Samar field simply had to be built. Seabee determination, round-the-clock work, and the abundance of coral combined to save the day.

Two waterfalls, both higher than Niagara, helped the 75th Seabees solve the water problem at the Samar base. The falls feed the short, tempestuous Balusao River on Calicoan Island. Men of the 75th hacked their way, foot by foot, through the jungle for 3600 feet, then laid pipe lines from the river to the docks which the 75th was building at Calicoan.

The terrain was so soft and difficult that bulldozers could not be used, so the Seabees used the native carabao to snake the pipe into position. (See photo.) This meant that little work could be done between ten A.M. and four P.M., since not even the Seabees could find a way to make the carabao work in the hot sun.

The pipe lines, when completed, could deliver 3,000,000 gallons of water a day to thirsty ships at the docks.

The 75th Battalion boasted the finest record for maintaining its equipment in the Seabees. When it landed at

Samar, the battalion had been overseas for two years. They had made six major moves, handled many tremendous jobs. Yet they began work on Calicoan with every one of the original bulldozers which they had brought from the States! They still had forty per cent of their trucks.

Much of the credit for this amazing record is given to Warrant Officer J. R. Smith (CEC, USNR, Cumberland, Md.), a former shop foreman for the Baltimore & Ohio Railroad. Officer in charge of the 75th was Lieutenant Commander D. H. Gottwals (CEC, USNR, Washington, D. C.), who was construction engineer on many of Washington's buildings, including the Kennedy-Warren Apartments.

One day while I was at the Naval Base on Samar, I traveled thirty-five miles westward along the coast to visit a sawmill where a detachment of Seabees was cutting lumber for the base. I went in an LCVP which was operated by young C. W. Jefferson (Electrician's Mate First, Warrior, Ala.). Jefferson had never been to the mill, but we knew it was located on the Balingiga River. By shouting "Balingiga?" to the native fishermen and getting them to point, we eventually found the mouth of the small stream and reached the mill.

Lieutenant J. N. Owens (CEC, USNR, Dallas, Tex.) was in charge of logging operations. In private life Owens is an office-sitter—a consulting mechanical engineer—but in the Seabees he spent two years tramping the backwoods as a boss logger. He logged at Koli and Lunga Point on Guadalcanal before coming to Samar.

The Balingiga mill was guarded by a platoon of the First Filipino Infantry Regiment of the U. S. Army. Lt. J. D. Davidson (USA, Amarillo, Tex.) was in command. Davidson told me that he and his Filipinos patrolled the area and killed an occasional Jap sailor who had reached the Samar shore after the big naval battle.

Owens and I walked back into the hills where the trees were being felled. It was a hot, humid day, and we had to stop occasionally to let me catch my breath.

"You have to be careful in this tropical climate," he told me. "You can strain your heart before you realize it."

The timber was completely virgin. Native fallers were cutting the trees. Barefooted, they would erect precarious little bamboo platforms at the base of the trees to get up above the "knees." Then they'd stand on these platforms and saw.

The logs were being snaked to the mill by cats under the direction of D. R. Reed (Chief Electrician's Mate, Ardmore, Okla.), formerly with the Oklahoma Gas & Electric Company. Reed is now known as "Carabao" Reed, because he first attempted to snake his logs with the big water buffaloes.

"It takes three natives to operate one carabao," he explained. "One native pulls, another twists the old buffalo's tail, and a third must walk along and hiss 's-e-e-e, s-e-e-e' in his ear. Then when the sun gets hot, the carabao quits entirely. I thought of rigging up some sort of portable sprinkler system to try to persuade the carabao to work in the sun, but I finally gave up and brought in the cats."

D. P. Pangle (Chief Shipfitter, Grand Falls, Tex.) was the sawyer at the mill. He said he expected to saw 3,000,000 board feet at that location, that most of the timber was mahogany. He explained that he had a lot less "saw trouble" on Samar than he had on Guadalcanal, because there was no shrapnel in the Samar timber to tear up his saw teeth. Because there had been so much fighting, bombing, and shelling on Guadal, hardly a day passed that a saw didn't rip into a buried shell fragment.

205

That afternoon, just before I left the mill, hot and exhausted, Lieutenant Owens and I went into the rough but efficient chow hall to get a drink of ice water. There, believe it or not, H. F. Strickland (Ship's Cook Second, Selma, Ala.) offered us heaping bowlfuls of that precious Navy ice cream. He had no spoons, however, so Owens and I ate the ice cream with huge kitchen spoons fully two feet long.

"This is America for you, isn't it?" Owens remarked. "Here in a virgin jungle 10,000 miles from home, we have this ice cream two days a week."

The first Seabee casualties from the *Kamikaze* (suicide pilot) attacks were suffered by the 113th Battalion which made the D-Day landing at Mindoro. At nine A.M. on December 15, 1944, during a furious air attack by the Japs just off Mindoro, a *Kamikaze* dived onto the deck of LST 472. Five Seabees were killed; seven were wounded seriously.*

The surviving Seabees and crew members of the LST were rescued by the destroyer *O'Brien*, which then sank the burning and exploding LST with gunfire.

A second LST carrying men and equipment of the 113th barely escaped a similar fate. A *Kamikaze* dived at the ship, but when it was fifty feet away, it was shot down by M. A. Peppo (Motor Machinist's Mate Third, New Orleans, La.) of the 113th. Peppo, who had replaced a wounded gunner

* The dead: William L. Wilkinson, MM2c, Springfield, Ill.; Morris W. Mewton, CM1c, Chanutte, Kan.; Joseph A. Roy, MoMM3c, Pontiac, Mich.; Irno Tozzini, GM2c, Bronx, N. Y.; and William V. Womack, EM1c, Toledo, O.

The wounded: Henry Wolf, F1c, Philadelphia, Pa.; Edward C. Ahlberg, S1c, Long Beach, Cal.; Eugene F. Carter, CM2c, Los Angeles, Cal.; James W. Frost, S1c, Columbus, O.; Carl E. Gaddis, CM1c, Portland, Ore.; Donald A. MacDonald, SF2c, Neeham Falls, Mass.; and James A. Priam, S1c, Stelton, N. J.

of the ship's crew, was awarded the Silver Star. He was burned severely when the plane exploded virtually in his face.

For two weeks after D-Day—December 15th—the Mindoro operation was rough. On the night of December 26th the Japs very nearly re-invaded the island. The Seabees were defending a point where they were building a PT base. Jap destroyers moved in, lighted up the point with star shells, and began shelling the area. Our planes and PTs had been attacking the approaching Japs for an hour, and only at the last moment did they succeed in driving them off.

Three thirty-one-foot-long Jap torpedoes ran high and dry up on the beach in the 113th's camp. One of them barely missed the fuel dump. The torpedoes, properly disarmed, became part of the battalion's collection of souvenirs.

The 113th was closely associated with the PTs ever since it arrived in the Southwest Pacific. A detachment of its men, commanded by Lieutenant H. F. Liberty (CEC, USNR, Stamford, Conn.) traveled exclusively with the PTs and built PT bases at Biak, Cape Sansapor, Morotai, Leyte, Mindoro, Zamboanga (Mindanao) and at Port Sual in Lingayen Gulf.

The 102nd Battalion, aforementioned veterans of Finsch and Hollandia, were at Subic Bay when I visited them. Together with the 115th Seabees, they were salvaging some of our old naval equipment at Olongapo and building the required new installations.

Most exciting experience of the 102nd was the attempt made by their patrols to rescue the Army personnel who had bailed out of a burning C-47. From the 102nd's camp area, the plane was seen to explode over the almost inaccessible country around Zigzag Pass on Telegraph Trail in northern Bataan. Three parachutes were seen to blossom under the plane, and some observers thought that a fourth parachute opened near the ground.

A searching party, led by Joseph P. Greelish (Chief Machinist's Mate, Medford, Mass.), headed for the scene. It was slow going. The party had to cut its way with axes and machetes. After ten hours of steady hacking, the party found three Air Force personnel and brought them out. The fliers were not seriously injured, and they, too, thought that a fourth man had escaped from the plane.

Next day three Seabee patrols went back up the mountain and attempted to fan out. All three patrols ran into Japs who apparently had seen the plane explode and then had prepared to ambush the expected rescuers. In the first patrol Fred D. Sanders (Chief Machinist's Mate, Deniston, Tex.) fought a gun duel with a Jap captain. The captain fired first from behind a rock and winged Sanders; then Sanders shot it out with the Jap and killed him.

The second patrol was ambushed, and two Seabees lost their lives: John E. Krantz (Machinist's Mate Second, Kalispell, Mont.) and Sam C. Amato (Carpenter's Mate Third, Chicago, Ill.). The third patrol was also ambushed and two were killed: Riley C. Thurmond (Carpenter's Mate Second, Rabuen Gap, Ga.) and Gerald L. Crittenden (Shipfitter Second, Henderson, Ill.). Both patrols accounted for a number of Japs in the ensuing fights.

Several Seabees were wounded,* and it was an almost impossible job to extricate the wounded from the dense

* The wounded: Robert A. Hopkins, MM2c, Fitchburg, Mass.; Orvel Luker, MM3c, West Point, Ga.; Edward J. Oliver, SF2c, Washington, D. C.; Harry E. Seeley, MM1c, Newburgh, N. Y.; and James H. Neal, CM2c, Fernwood, Pa.

thickets. Thomas Manion (Hospital Apprentice First, Los Angeles) stayed all night at the side of one of the dying men who could not be moved, and tried to save his life, but the man died before morning. It was late the next day before enough trails could be cut to get out all the wounded.

Additional searching parties, including natives, then fought their way through the wild area, but the fourth airman was never found. It is probable that he never got out of the plane, and if he got out, his parachute may not have opened enough to break his fall.

One of the Navy's problems throughout the world in this war was how to prevent the men from giving or trading away their white mattress covers. From North Africa to the Philippines these white, sack-like sheets were coveted by the natives. Every man was supposed to have his name stenciled on his mattress cover. At a Captain's Mast at Subic I saw a 102nd Seabee arraigned on a charge of giving his mattress cover to a Filipino girl. The Seabee pleaded not guilty. The girl was called in, told to pull up her dress and turn the hem over, and there, for all to see, was the accused man's name.

The accused flushed, grinned sheepishly, and changed his plea to guilty.

While the 115th Seabees were at Milne Bay, their electricians were ordered to lay a communications line from Gamadota, twelve miles around the bay, to Ladava, where other installations were located. The route lay through one of the worst swamps in New Guinea. In man-killing heat, the men worked in slime up to their armpits. It was so muddy the electricians couldn't distinguish between the tools in their belts. One man was always on watch to kill the big snakes and alligators.

The first plan was to string the line through the swamp

on poles. The poles were floated part of the way in, then dragged through the swamp by the men themselves. When the line was almost completed, a storm knocked out sixty-four poles. The Seabees had to go back into the swamp, clear out the poles, and lay a submarine cable.

F. J. Delmore (Electrician's Mate First, Bagley, Wis.) was in charge of the job. John F. O'Sullivan (Boatswain's Mate First, Brooklyn, N. Y.) died in the swamp of heat and exhaustion while working on the job. In private life he was in charge of sound equipment in the New York City school system.

At Subic the 115th boys were sitting at their theater one night when a Jap fired from the woods into the crowd. Two men were wounded and given Purple Hearts: J. E. Van Auken (Seaman First, Lancaster, O.) and A. Bobrick (Seaman First, New York City). The picture they were seeing was *Kiss the Boys Goodbye.*

The 63rd, 119th, and 24th Special Battalions built the 7th Fleet's installations at Manila. One of the 119th's favorite stories is the one about their famous Thanksgiving feast at Hollandia.

The turkeys had not arrived, and the battalion was doomed to a Spam Thanksgiving unless something could be done. Two mighty hunters—Ignatius Burnette (Gunner's Mate Third, South Good Year, Ariz.), an Indian, and Allen O. "Dead-eye" Bryan (Shipfitter Second, Coweta, Okla.)—formed a party and headed into the jungle with full equipment. They were gone for two days, and they really brought back the "bacon"—enough deer and boar to feed the whole battalion.

The hunters became heroes. The meat was carefully re-frigerated, and the cooks began planning the mighty feast. Then, at midnight before Thanksgiving, when half the battalion was asleep and dreaming of mountains of tender venison, the blow fell. Dr. Edward L. "Simon Legree" Loughlin (Lieut. Comdr., MC, USNR, Los Angeles, Cal.) examined the meat and pronounced it spoiled. Great was the howling in Hollandia.

Next day the battalion lined up for the feast, and ate the inevitable Spam. When you're gonna get it, you're gonna get it!

The 119th's first job in the Manila area was to repair the 2,100,000-gallon water tanks which formerly had serviced our fleet at Cavite. The Navy had not sabotaged these tanks in 1942, and neither had the Japs. But shrapnel from our bombs had knocked holes in them. The Seabees quickly patched these holes, and the old tanks were ready for new business.

In Manila the 119th used a two-chow-line plan which was employed, with variations, by all the Seabees in the Philippines. All Seabees eat out of the standard Navy metal tray. The tray is partitioned, and has places for six different courses. After they have finished eating, the men usually dump their trays in garbage cans, then jiggle them in a barrel of hot disinfectant, and toss them to a mess cook on a washing table.

But in the Philippines the men took the trouble to scrape their uneaten food into several separate containers, so that all the uneaten corn would be in one can, the beans in another, etc. Then the Filipino chow line formed at these scrap cans, and the Filipinos ate every last scrap that the Seabees had left on their trays. It was a most popular practice with the hungry natives.

The Filipino farmers utterly confounded the Seabees by

211

their willingness to trade fresh vegetables, including corn, cucumbers, and tomatoes, for Spam and bully beef! The 119th's chief commissary steward, L. H. "Bully Beef" Machemer, Buffalo, N. Y., was able to obtain truckloads of vegetables in this manner.

Manila, of course, was the biggest venereal headache in the Pacific for the Army and Navy. The Filipino Government insisted on allowing the brothels to remain open, and besides this, the nonprofessional sisterhood—the Laundry Queens—swarmed around the camps with ever-ready "pompom."

The 119th met this problem boldly. They built a complete shower room and medical dispensary at the entrance to their camp area, and placed medical corpsmen on duty there twenty-four hours a day. The use of prophylactics was not left to the discretion of the individual; every man who came back into the camp from a liberty was "processed" through the showers, and the prophylactic was administered by a medic.

When I visited the 119th, they had the cleanest venereal record in Manila. They didn't have a man off duty from "v.d.," and their plan had been recommended for general adoption by all Army and Navy Units.

VIII

OKINAWA

IN DISCUSSING the Seabees at Okinawa at the moment this is written, I am under several severe handicaps. The Japanese are in the process of surrendering, yet our occupation of Japan is still to be implemented. Since Okinawa is our most advanced position, censorship regarding it must still be strict. The Jap surrender came at a time when development of the great base was proceeding furiously, and the decisions as to how the surrender is to affect the planned development of the base have not yet been made. Thus I cannot report on the individual Seabee battalions and their specific assignments, and any discussion of the base must be in general terms.

Still another handicap is the fact that I have run out of adjectives. I am like a toastmaster who has winded himself introducing all the lesser personalities, then turns up speechless when it's time to introduce the Speaker of the Evening. As an earthmoving project, I have compared Tinian to the Panama Canal. I have compared Guam to six Boulder Dams, and Saipan to the building of the pyramids. For Okinawa, all I can say is that it was planned to be bigger than Guam, Saipan, and Tinian all put together.

As a base for military operations, nothing like Okinawa had ever been envisioned. It was to be a construction *Gotterdammerung;* the last act in an incredible construction war. It was the final projection of America's apparently unlimited mechanical might.

213

Before this war we thought of Singapore as a "bastion"; a "vast base" from which Britain controlled much of the world for a century. Singapore *was* a "vast base," but the Singapore installations would have been lost on Okinawa.

I have described how 10,000 Seabees labored on Tinian, with acres of heavy equipment, to build two great airdromes. But, as this is written, *twenty-two* airdromes on Okinawa are either completed or in process of construction.

I have told of Guam's road miracle: 103 miles of black-topped highway and 243 miles of coral-surfaced road. But Okinawa was to have *fourteen hundred miles* of first-class road, much of it four-laned.

Since Okinawa is only 60 miles long and averages about 10 miles wide, this 1400 miles of road is enough to give it 20 highways running the entire length of the island. If all this road is completed, the island virtually will be cut into city blocks.

I have described "vast" harbor development at Guam. Okinawa was to be much more vast. Okinawa has at least one very fine natural harbor, and in August, 1945, its ports were handling more cargo than the Port of New York handles in peacetime. I have pointed out that 4000 Seabee stevedores handled all the cargo at Guam. Several times this number of Army and Navy stevedores were employed at Okinawa.

Handling of the native populations on Guam, Saipan, and Tinian was a problem requiring much temporary housing, food, and supervision. Yet there were only 12,000 Japanese on Tinian; there were 250,000 on Okinawa. Eight Seabee battalions were required to handle civilian housing alone on Okinawa.

One Seabee battalion is a big organization, capable of developing a fair-sized island. In the old days, many big jobs were handled in the Aleutians by less than a battalion.

Dutch Harbor was built by four battalions; Guadalcanal by eight. Yet *forty* Seabee battalions were assigned to Okinawa in the original plans, and most of these were at work when peace came. This didn't include the many Army Engineer battalions and the Marine Pioneers.

Can you conceive of the amount of fuel storage required to service twenty-two airdromes, a tremendous port, and thousands of trucks, jeeps, tanks, and bulldozers? Of the amount of refrigeration and warehousing demanded? Of the water lines, sewer lines, power lines, communications lines?

The State of Rhode Island has an area of 1067 square miles; a population of 687,000. Our development of Okinawa was to be comparable to the total development of Rhode Island from virgin forest land.

If everything in the State of Rhode Island—its cities, railroads, great buildings, highways, everything down to the rings on its people's fingers—was sold for what it cost, the amount of money derived would not pay for what Okinawa cost the American people in dollars and cents!

Okinawa is another one of those pieces of Pacific real estate so incredibly expensive that we did not dare to count the cost.

Curiously, while the Fleet suffered the heaviest casualties in its history at Okinawa and the Army and Marines divisions took frightful losses, the Seabee battalions had only slight casualties. Nor was the development of the island impeded by the furious Jap resistance. This was because of the unusual nature of the fighting. Okinawa was not another Iwo Jima; the "second echelons" were bombed and shelled, but the work proceeded on schedule.

The landing at Okinawa was what the British call "a piece of cake." The Japs didn't choose to fight on the beaches. The men in the assault waves walked ashore on Easter morning, pinching themselves to make sure it was true. We were landing on ancient Japanese soil, and the Japs were doing nothing about it.

The landing was made about two-thirds of the way down the long island, and the plan was to cut across it and form a line facing south. It was expected that the principal resistance would be on the southern end. The population centers of Naha and Yonabaru, as well as the Jap naval base and biggest airdrome, were on the southern one-third of the island. While the Army divisions held the southern line, the Marine divisions were to clear the northern two-thirds of the island as quickly as possible, so that the construction program could get under way.

This part of the plan was carried out speedily. The Marines found surprisingly little resistance along 40 miles of the island's length—400 square miles of area—and the construction program ran ahead of schedule. It's important to understand this, because of the criticism voiced in Washington over the conduct of the Okinawa campaign.

It's true that the Okinawa campaign was long and bitter, and that the price was high. But the campaign proceeded almost exactly according to plan despite the *Kamikazes* and the fanatical resistance of the Japs around Shuri and Naha. The war's timetable was not affected by either the *Kamikazes* or the bitter land resistance. What determined the speed of the war in the Pacific was the construction program. The war moved at the speed of a bulldozer, not at the speed of a Mustang. The Army and Marines presented the construction gangs 400 square miles to work on within five days after the landing.

During the three months that our ships were battling the

Kamikazes offshore and the Army and Marines were broiling Japs on the south end, the Okinawa construction program was proceeding according to plan with comparatively little interruption from the Jap air force.

Suppose three months *were* required for our ground forces to capture Naha? According to the original plans for the development of Okinawa, Naha was to be taken on D-Day plus 90. Even if the fighting forces could take the port before then, the construction forces could not begin its development before that time. Naha was captured on D-Day plus 93.

The most spectacular attempt by the Japs to interrupt the construction program was the landing made on Yontan airstrip by *Kamikaze* airborne troops. The crack 87th Seabees, veterans of two years in the South Pacific, were building Yontan at the time, and they helped to wipe out the grenade-throwing Japs.

The Japs made their landing at night. An air raid was in progress at Yontan, and a Nip bomber had just been shot down after dropping a string of bombs in a fuel dump. The Seabee fire wagons were rushing out to fight the fire, when suddenly a green-colored Jap "Sally" came roaring in from the east with one engine burning. The plane hit the runway in a belly skid and screeched and crunched for a hundred yards. Jap infantrymen poured out and raced toward a line of our transport planes, hurling grenades and phosphorous bombs.

A second "Sally" dropped down and landed near the operations tower, but it exploded on landing and only two Japs got out of it. A third "Sally" missed the runway and landed among some tents, causing a few casualties, but no Japs escaped alive from this plane.

Meanwhile, the Seabees had grabbed their guns and begun firing at the Japs who, by then, were silhouetted around the burning planes. All the Japs were dead within a few minutes, but they did manage to burn up several transports.

The landing at Okinawa was complicated by the reef which lies about 300 feet offshore, but at high tide the water in most spots was deep enough over the reef for pontoon causeways to float clear. This enabled the Seabee pontoon specialists to push the causeways all the way up to the beach, lay them over the reef, and then extend them far enough beyond the reef to reach the LST's and LSM's.

Handling of the causeways was directed by veterans of Sicily, Salerno, and Normandy, men of the old Ten-o-Six Pontoon Detachment, now incorporated into the 128th Pontoon Battalion. About 600 officers and men of the 128th handled the causeways and piers.

The longest floating causeway of the war was installed on what was called Red Beach-1. The single-lane causeway was 1428 feet long, with a T across the end of it for LST's. It floated in over the reef at high tide, and a hole was blasted in the reef under it so that it would also float at low water. By the fourth day, the 128th had eight piers and causeways operating at all tidal stages.

In no Pacific operation have the causeways worked to such advantage as at Okinawa. More than 64,000 troops and 110,000 tons of cargo were handled over them within the first few days of the operation. Not a single ship was damaged in the unloading process.

The pontoon barges, which served as lighters for the Liberty ships, were handled by the 70th Pontoon Battalion, which fought the game but loosing battle at Iwo Jima. At Okinawa the barges were very successful. The 70th carried more than a hundred barges into the area, and kept an average of 90 of them operating 24 hours a day.

The assault construction battalions were the 145th, attached to the 1st Marine Division; the 58th, attached to the 6th Marine Division; and the 71st, attached to the Amphibious Corps.

Road-building was the biggest headache from the beginning. The Marines were moving nor⁺hward very fast, and the few primitive roads were bogs with all bridges blasted. For the first time in the Pacific, the Seabees used the Bailey Bridge, the miraculous British-invented "mechano set" with which so many chasms were crossed in France and Germany.

Okinawa does not have the abundance of coral which Guam, Saipan and Tinian have, and for this reason getting out of the mud was a slower process than usual. The 145th Seabees were the principal road-building battalion during the first crucial days.

Upon completion of one of the airfields on Okinawa, the Marine commander of the field addressed a letter of commendation to a Seabee unit which was led by Lieutenant Harlow H. Lippincott (CEC, USNR, Detroit, Mich.). The letter read, in part:

"Sirs: You have seen this field grow from a wrecked mudhole to a good all-weather airfield. You have enjoyed much company, mostly Japs. You have been shelled, bombed, rain-soaked, wind-blown, dusted, disgusted, overworked, underfed, cussed at, and praised.

"You have been given the dirtiest details; you have slept in mud and filth if and when you got a chance. You worked on your own camp only after you had completed everyone else's. You worked all night on the airstrip so that the Group could take off on its first flight against the Japs, and you got the hell bombed out of you for your pains.

"You have handled every drop of gasoline that has been used on this airfield, and much of this handling was done while enemy bombs and shells were falling. You have

219

helped with the ammunition, though this was not part of your duties. You repaired the field lighting when it was bombed or shelled out without waiting for the end of the attack. You put other people's galleys into operation when you should have been working on your own.

"This was my first time to be in close contact with the Seabees in the field. They told me you were a green or 'newly-activated' outfit. 'Newly-activated' may be appropriate, but never the word 'green.'

"Your unselfishness has been an inspiration on this island, and I shall consider it a privilege to buy any one of you a drink when we all get clean again and this thing is over."

APPENDIX

WHERE THE SEABEES WORKED AND FOUGHT

Here, for the first time since the organization of the Seabees, is published the complete record of where the 150 construction battalions and the 39 stevedore battalions were employed during the war. The record is as of September 1, 1945.

1ST BATTALION

Efate and Wallis Islands. Inactivated in 1943.

2ND BATTALION

Upolu, British Samoa; Wallis Island; Funafuti in the Ellice Islands; Tutuila, American Samoa. Inactivated in 1944.

3RD BATTALION

Bora Bora, Society Islands; Noumea, New Caledonia; Funafuti, Ellice Islands; Nandi, Fiji Islands; Kwajalein and Eniwetok, Marshall Islands. Inactivated in 1944.

4TH BATTALION

Dutch Harbor, Alaska; Adak and Amchitka Islands in the Aleutians; returned to States. Second tour: Oahu, Guam and Okinawa.

5TH BATTALION

Oahu, Midway, French Frigate Shoals, Palmyra, Johnston and Canton Islands; returned to States. Second tour: Samar in the Philippines.

6TH BATTALION

Espiritu Santo, New Hebrides Islands; Guadalcanal and Tulagi, Solomon Islands; New Zealand; returned to States. Second tour: Okinawa.

7TH BATTALION

Espiritu Santo, New Hebrides Islands; returned to States. Second tour: Oahu, Okinawa.

8TH BATTALION

Dutch Harbor, Alaska; Adak in the Aleutians; returned to States. Second tour: Oahu and Iwo Jima.

9TH BATTALION

Iceland; returned to States. Second tour: Oahu, Tinian, Okinawa.

10TH BATTALION

Oahu; Guam; Samar.

11th BATTALION

Tutuila, American Samoa; Noumea, New Caledonia; New Zealand; Banika in the Russell Islands; Los Negros, Admiralty Islands; Samar and Subic Bay in the Philippines.

12TH BATTALION

Kodiak and Dutch Harbor, Alaska; Adak and Attu, Aleutian Islands; returned to States. Inactivated in 1944.

13TH BATTALION

Dutch Harbor and Akutan Island, Alaska; returned to States. Second tour: Oahu, Tinian, Okinawa.

WHERE THE SEABEES WORKED AND FOUGHT

14TH BATTALION

Noumea, Espiritu Santo and Guadalcanal; returned to States. Second tour: Oahu and Okinawa.

15TH BATTALION

Espiritu Santo and New Zealand; Banika and Pavuvu Islands in the Russells; Green Island; returned to States. Second tour: Okinawa.

16TH BATTALION

Oahu; Funafuti, Nanomea and Nukefetau in the Ellice Islands; Apemama, Tarawa and Makin in the Gilbert Islands; returned to States. Inactivated in 1944.

17TH BATTALION

Argentia, Newfoundland; returned to States. Second tour: Saipan and Okinawa.

18TH BATTALION

Noumea; Guadalcanal; New Zealand; Tarawa, Hawaii, Saipan and Tinian; returned to States. Inactivated in 1945.

19TH BATTALION

Noumea; Australia; Goodenough Island and Oro Bay, New Guinea; Cape Gloucester, New Britain; Pavuvu Island in the Russells; returned to States. Second tour: Okinawa.

20TH BATTALION

Noumea; Woodlark Island; Oleana Bay; Vangunu Island; Viru Harbor, New Georgia; Milne Bay, New Guinea; Brisbane, Australia; Russell Islands; returned to States. Second tour: Okinawa.

223

FROM OMAHA TO OKINAWA

21ST BATTALION

Dutch Harbor, Alaska; Atka, Adak and Ogliaga, Aleutian Islands; returned to States. Second tour: Oahu and Okinawa.

22ND BATTALION

Sitka, Alaska; Attu; returned to States. Inactivated in 1944.

23RD BATTALION

Kodiak, Cold Bay, and Dutch Harbor, Alaska; Atka, Adak and Attu in the Aleutians; returned to States. Second tour: Oahu and Guam.

24TH BATTALION

Noumea and Guadalcanal; Rendova, Kokurana, Baribuna and New Georgia in the Solomons; New Zealand; Banika; returned to States. Second tour: Okinawa.

25TH BATTALION

New Zealand; Tutuila, American Samoa; Guadalcanal; Bougainville; Guam.

26TH BATTALION

Guadalcanal, Tulagi, Nugu, Munda and Malaita in the Solomons; returned to States. Second tour: Kodiak. Inactivated in 1945.

27TH BATTALION

Tulagi; Guadalcanal; New Zealand; Emirau Island; returned to States. Second tour: Okinawa.

28TH BATTALION

Iceland; returned to States. Second tour: Scotland and England; Cherbourg, Le Havre, Calais, and Paris, France; returned to States. Third tour: Okinawa.

WHERE THE SEABEES WORKED AND FOUGHT

29TH BATTALION

Scotland, Ireland and England; returned to States. Second tour: Leyte, Samar and Subic Bay in the Philippines.

30TH BATTALION

Trinidad, British West Indies; returned to States. Second tour: Oahu and Samar.

31ST BATTALION

Bermuda; returned to States. Second tour: Hawaii and Iwo Jima.

32ND BATTALION

Dutch Harbor and Adak; returned to States. Inactivated in 1944.

33RD BATTALION

Noumea; Guadalcanal; Russell Islands; New Zealand; Green Island; Pelelieu in the Palau Islands; returned to States. Inactivated in 1945.

34TH BATTALION

Halavo, Florida Islands; Guadalcanal; Russell Islands; Tulagi; returned to States. Second tour: Okinawa.

35TH BATTALION

Espiritu Santo; Russells; New Zealand; Manus, Admiralty Islands; returned to States. Second tour: Manus.

36TH BATTALION

Espiritu Santo; Banika, Russell Islands; Bougainville; returned to States. Second tour: Okinawa.

FROM OMAHA TO OKINAWA

37TH BATTALION

Noumea; Guadalcanal; New Georgia; Green Island; returned to States. Second tour: Okinawa.

38TH BATTALION

Kodiak and Adak; returned to States. Second tour: Oahu and Tinian.

39TH BATTALION

Oahu; Maui; and Saipan.

40TH BATTALION

Finschafen, New Guinea; Los Negros, Admiralties; Noumea; returned to States. Second tour: Okinawa.

41ST BATTALION

Kodiak; returned to States. Second tour: Guam.

42ND BATTALION

Dutch Harbor and Adak; returned to States. Second tour: Oahu and Samar.

43RD BATTALION

Kodiak and Sand Point, Alaska; returned to States. Second tour: Oahu and Saipan.

44TH BATTALION

Espiritu Santo; Manus; returned to States.

45TH BATTALION

Sitka and Kodiak, Alaska; Adak and Tanaga in the Aleutians; returned to States. Inactivated in 1944.

WHERE THE SEABEES WORKED AND FOUGHT

46TH BATTALION

Guadalcanal; Milne Bay and Finschafen, New Guinea; Los Negros.

47TH BATTALION

Guadalcanal; Russells; Segi Point, New Georgia; Noumea.

48TH BATTALION

Oahu; Maui; Guam.

49TH BATTALION

Bermuda; returned to States. Second tour: Guam.

50TH BATTALION

Midway; Oahu; and Tinian.

51ST BATTALION

Dutch Harbor; returned to States. Second tour: Ulithi in the Caroline Islands; Saipan; Marcus.

52ND BATTALION

Dutch Harbor and Sand Bay, Alaska; Adak; returned to States. Second tour: Oahu and Guam.

53RD BATTALION

Noumea; Guadalcanal; Bougainville; Vella La Vella; Guam.

54TH BATTALION

Bermuda; Algeria; Tunisia; returned to States. Second tour: Leyte, Samar and Cebu in the Philippines.

55TH BATTALION

Australia; Port Moresby, New Guinea; Hollandia and Mios

Woendi, Dutch New Guinea; returned to States. Inactivated in 1945.

56TH BATTALION

Oahu and Guam.

57TH BATTALION

Espiritu Santo; Manus; returned to States. Inactivated in 1945.

58TH BATTALION

Vella La Vella; New Zealand; Banika; Los Negros; Guadalcanal; Okinawa.

59TH BATTALION

Oahu and Guam.

60TH BATTALION

Australia; Woodlark Island; Finschafen; Owi, Noemfoor and Amsterdam Islands in the Netherlands East Indies; Leyte; returned to States. Inactivated in 1945.

61ST BATTALION

Guadalcanal; New Zealand; Emirau; Banika; Manus; Leyte; and Samar.

62ND BATTALION

Oahu and Iwo Jima.

63RD BATTALION

Guadalcanal; New Zealand; Emirau; Manus; Manila.

64TH BATTALION

Argentia, Newfoundland; returned to States. Second tour: Oahu and Samar.

WHERE THE SEABEES WORKED AND FOUGHT

65TH BATTALION

Freetown, Africa; returned to States. Inactivated in 1944.

66TH BATTALION

Adak and Attu in the Aleutians; returned to States. Second tour: Okinawa.

67TH BATTALION

Oahu; Tinian; and Eniwetok.

68TH BATTALION

Adak and Attu in the Aleutians; returned to States. Second tour: Okinawa.

69TH BATTALION

England; Omaha Beach, France; Bremen, Bremerhaven and Frankfort, Germany.

70TH BATTALION

Algeria, North Africa; returned to States. Second tour: Oahu and Guam.

71ST BATTALION

Guadalcanal; Bougainville; Manus; Los Negros; Okinawa.

72ND BATTALION

Oahu and Guam.

73RD BATTALION

Noumea; Guadalcanal; Munda; Banika; Pelelieu; returned to States. Inactivated in 1945.

FROM OMAHA TO OKINAWA

74TH BATTALION

Oahu; Tarawa; Kwajalein; Okinawa.

75TH BATTALION

Noumea; Guadalcanal; Bougainville; Banika; Milne Bay; Leyte; Samar.

76TH BATTALION

Oahu; Palmyra; Guam.

77TH BATTALION

Guadalcanal; Vella La Vella; Bougainville; Emirau; Brisbane, Australia; Manila.

78TH BATTALION

Noumea; Finschafen; Ponam, Manus and Los Negros in the Admiralty Islands; Okinawa.

79TH BATTALION

Kodiak and Cold Bay, Alaska; Adak and Amchitka in the Aleutians; returned to States. Second tour: Okinawa.

80TH BATTALION

Trinidad; returned to States. Second tour: Subic Bay in the Philippines.

81ST BATTALION

Scotland and England; Utah Beach, Normandy; Paris; returned to States. Second tour: Oahu; Guam; and Okinawa, Ie Shima and Aguni Shima in the Ryukyu Islands.

82ND BATTALION

Noumea; Guadalcanal; Vella La Vella; New Georgia; Treasury Islands; Okinawa.

WHERE THE SEABEES WORKED AND FOUGHT

83RD BATTALION

Trinidad; returned to States. Second tour: Oahu and Samar.

84TH BATTALION

Brisbane and Darwin, Australia; Milne Bay; Thursday Island; Biak; Morotai; and Palawan in the Philippines.

85TH BATTALION

Dutch Harbor and Adak; returned to States. Second tour: Espiritu Santo.

86TH BATTALION

Great Sitka, Adak, Amchitka and Tanaga in Alaska and the Aleutians; returned to States. Second tour: Okinawa.

87TH BATTALION

Noumea; Banika; the Treasury Islands; Okinawa.

88TH BATTALION

Noumea; Guadalcanal; Treasury; Emirau; Leyte and Samar.

89TH BATTALION

Replacement battalion; no overseas service.

90TH BATTALION

Oahu; Angaur and Pelelieu in the Palau Islands; Iwo Jima.

91ST BATTALION

Milne Bay; Palm Island, Australia; Madang and Finschafen, New Guinea; Leyte and Samar.

92ND BATTALION

Oahu; Saipan; and Tinian.

FROM OMAHA TO OKINAWA

93RD BATTALION

Russells; Green Island; Leyte and Samar.

94TH BATTALION

Oahu and Guam.

95TH BATTALION

Oahu; Apemama; Kwajalein; Iwo Jima.

96TH BATTALION

The Azores; returned to States. Second tour: Samar.

97TH BATTALION

England; Scotland; Wales.

98TH BATTALION

Oahu; Tarawa; Maui.

99TH BATTALION

Oahu; Hawaii; Johnston; Canton; Angaur; Samar.

100TH BATTALION

Oahu; Majuro Atoll, Marshall Islands; Angaur; Samar.

101ST BATTALION

Oahu; Saipan; Okinawa.

102ND BATTALION

Finschafen; Hollandia; Leyte; Subic Bay.

103RD BATTALION

Oahu and Guam.

WHERE THE SEABEES WORKED AND FOUGHT

104TH BATTALION
Milne Bay; Los Negros; Australia; Leyte.

105TH BATTALION
Milne Bay; Leyte and Samar.

106TH BATTALION
Oahu; Iwo Jima; Ie Shima.

107TH BATTALION
Oahu; Kwajalein; Tinian.

108TH BATTALION
Scotland; England; France; returned to States. Inactivated in 1944.

109TH BATTALION
Oahu; Kwajalein; Guam.

110TH BATTALION
Oahu; Eniwetok; Saipan; Tinian.

111TH BATTALION
England; Omaha Beach; returned to States. Second tour: Samar.

112TH BATTALION
Oahu; Tinian; Okinawa.

113TH BATTALION
Finschafen; Hollandia; Mios Woendi, Amsterdam and Soeme-soeme Islands; Leyte, Samar. Mindoro, and Manila in the Philippines.

FROM OMAHA TO OKINAWA

114TH BATTALION

Cherbourg, Nantes, St. Nazaire and Lorient, France; returned to States. Second tour: Attu.

115TH BATTALION

Milne Bay; Hollandia; Subic Bay.

116TH BATTALION

Oahu.

117TH BATTALION

Oahu; Saipan.

118TH BATTALION

Milne Bay; Zamboanga and Subic Bay in the Philippines.

119TH BATTALION

Milne Bay; Aitape; Wakde; Hollandia; Manila.

120TH BATTALION

Oran, Casablanca, Fedala and Safi, in North Africa; Palermo, Sicily; Salerno, Caserta and Naples, Italy; returned to States. Inactivated in 1945.

121ST BATTALION

Kwajalein; Maui; Saipan; Tinian.

122ND BATTALION

Milne Bay; Hollandia; Samar.

123RD BATTALION

Oahu; Midway; Leyte and Samar.

WHERE THE SEABEES WORKED AND FOUGHT

124TH BATTALION
Adak, Amchitka and Tanaga in the Aleutians.

125TH BATTALION
Oahu and Okinawa.

126TH BATTALION
Engebi, Parry, Japtan, and Hawthorne Islands in the Marshall Group; Oahu and Okinawa.

127TH BATTALION
Maui; Oahu; Leyte; Samar.

128TH BATTALION
Oahu and Guam.

129TH BATTALION
Oahu and Samar.

130TH BATTALION
Oahu and Okinawa.

131ST BATTALION
Inactivated without overseas duty.

132ND BATTALION
Inactivated without overseas duty.

133RD BATTALION
Oahu and Iwo Jima.

235

134TH BATTALION

Guam.

135TH BATTALION

Oahu; Tinian; Okinawa.

136TH BATTALION

Oahu and Guam.

137TH BATTALION

Okinawa.

138TH BATTALION

Attu; returned to States. Inactivated in 1945.

139TH BATTALION

Okinawa.

140TH BATTALION

Manus and Los Negros.

141ST BATTALION

Oahu; Hawaii; Kwajalein.

142ND BATTALION

Maui; Samar.

143RD BATTALION

Samar.

144TH BATTALION

Guam.

WHERE THE SEABEES WORKED AND FOUGHT

145TH BATTALION

Russells; Okinawa.

146TH BATTALION

Iceland; England; Utah Beach; Cherbourg; returned to States. Second tour: Okinawa.

147TH BATTALION

Okinawa.

148TH BATTALION

Okinawa.

301ST BATTALION (Harbor developing specialists)

Midway; Oahu; Kwajalein; Guam; Saipan; Tinian; Pelelieu; Iwo Jima; Okinawa.

302ND BATTALION (Pontoon specialists)

Kwajalein; Pelelieu; Guam; Saipan; Tinian; Angaur; Leyte; Luzon.

The Seabee stevedore battalions are called "special" battalions. Here is the record of where the "special" battalions were employed during the war. As with the construction battalions, the record is complete to September 1, 1945.

1ST SPECIAL BATTALION

Guadalcanal; New Zealand; Noumea; Espiritu Santo.

2ND SPECIAL BATTALION

Noumea; Guadalcanal; Guam; returned to States and inactivated in July, 1945.

FROM OMAHA TO OKINAWA

3RD SPECIAL BATTALION

Espiritu Santo; Okinawa.

4TH SPECIAL BATTALION

Noumea; Guadalcanal; Okinawa.

5TH SPECIAL BATTALION

Dutch Harbor; Adak; returned to States. Second tour: Milne Bay; Tacloban on Leyte; Samar.

6TH SPECIAL BATTALION

Guadalcanal; Bougainville; Treasury; Ulithi; Leyte; Samar; returned to States. Inactivated in 1945.

7TH SPECIAL BATTALION

Clatskanie, Oregon; Dutch Harbor; Adak.

8TH SPECIAL BATTALION

Attu; Dutch Harbor; Kodiak; Clatskanie, Oregon.

9TH SPECIAL BATTALION

Tulagi; Guadalcanal; Bougainville; Green; Munda; Sasavele, New Guinea.

10TH SPECIAL BATTALION

Milford Haven and Penarth, Wales; Plymouth, Falmouth, Dartmouth, Exeter and Fowey, Southern England.

11TH SPECIAL BATTALION

Russell Islands; Guadalcanal; Noumea; Okinawa.

WHERE THE SEABEES WORKED AND FOUGHT

12TH SPECIAL BATTALION
Russells; Okinawa.

13TH SPECIAL BATTALION
Oahu; Saipan; Guam; Eniwetok.

14TH SPECIAL BATTALION
Oahu; Funafuti; Tarawa; Kwajalein; Eniwetok; Japtan.

15TH SPECIAL BATTALION
Kwajalein and Eniwetok.

16TH SPECIAL BATTALION
Oahu; Eniwetok; Guam.

17TH SPECIAL BATTALION
Banika; Emirau; Guam; Samar.

18TH SPECIAL BATTALION
Oahu; Ulithi; Pelelieu; Samar.

19TH SPECIAL BATTALION
Woendi and Biak, Netherlands East Indies; Leyte and Samar.

20TH SPECIAL BATTALION
Manus.

21ST SPECIAL BATTALION
Manus; Subic Bay in the Philippines.

22ND SPECIAL BATTALION
Manus; Los Negros.

23RD SPECIAL BATTALION

Oahu; Iwo Jima; Okinawa.

24TH SPECIAL BATTALION

Milne Bay; Tacloban; Subic Bay; Manila.

25TH SPECIAL BATTALION

Milne Bay; Palawan.

26TH SPECIAL BATTALION

Oahu.

27TH SPECIAL BATTALION

Oahu; Tinian; Okinawa.

28TH SPECIAL BATTALION

Oahu; Leyte; Samar.

29TH SPECIAL BATTALION

Guam.

30TH SPECIAL BATTALION

First Section: Rosneath, Scotland, and Exeter, England. Second Section: Leyte and Samar.

31ST SPECIAL BATTALION

Saipan.

32ND SPECIAL BATTALION

Leyte; Samar.

WHERE THE SEABEES WORKED AND FOUGHT

33RD SPECIAL BATTALION

Milne Bay; Leyte; Samar.

34TH SPECIAL BATTALION

Oahu; Guam.

35TH SPECIAL BATTALION

Oahu.

36TH SPECIAL BATTALION

Okinawa.

37TH SPECIAL BATTALION

Oahu.

38TH SPECIAL BATTALION

No overseas service.

41ST SPECIAL BATTALION *

Hollandia.

* Organization of the 39th and 40th Specials was halted by the sudden end of the war.

TO THE SEABEES

by CAPT. JOHN E. ESTABROOK, USMC

Up from the beach the long road winds,
Over the distant hill—
Born of the sweat and toil of men,
Born of a dauntless will.
Swept by the rains of tropic skies;
Scorched by the burning sun;
Bearing its burden the long road lies
'Til the work of war be done.

> So we'll sing the song
> Of the brave and strong—
> Of Hunkies and Swedes and Micks—
> Of hammers and nails
> And girders and rails,
> Of shovels and blades and picks.
> We'll sing a song
> Of the brave and strong—
> Battalions, proud and great—
> That paved the way
> To the Glory Day
> And dared the hand of fate.

Up from the beach the long road bears
The panoply of war—
Up from the beach where dust clouds hide
The shattered palms and shore.
That fighting men may live and fight
The road must wind away
And builders build where the long road ends
And death has had its day.

TO THE SEABEES

Here's to the men who builded well—
Sweated and bled and died—
Who fought the jungle, swamp and Hell,
Their fighting men beside.
Here's to the docks and camps and dumps;
Here's to the roaring strips;
Here's to the men who turn to war
The treasure trove of ships.

Down to the beach some day will wind
The road that led to war
And men will turn the long way back
As men have turned before
And ships that wait will sail away
And eyes will brim with tears
For roads of war lead back again
From out the bitter years.

So we'll sing the song
Of the brave and strong—
Of Hunkies and Swedes and Micks—
Of hammers and nails
And girders and rails,
Of shovels and blades and picks.
We'll sing a song
Of the brave and strong—
Battalions, proud and great—
That paved the way
To the Glory Day
And dared the hand of fate.

INDEX

Ada, Okla., 46
Adak, 112
Admiralty Islands, 193
Agana, 135, 139, 143
—— Air Base, 154
—— Beach, 143-4
—— Field, 136, 138
—— Springs, 139
Agat, 145-6
Agnew, Richard J., 196
Ahlberg, Edward C., 206
Ahoskie, N. C., 57
Airdromes, 214
Airfields
  North—Guam, 137-8
  North—Iwo Jima, 60
  —— Tinian, 76
  Northwest—Guam, 137-8
  South—Iwo Jima, 51
  West Field, Tinian, 87
  Central—Iwo Jima, 59, 62
  Depot—Guam, 136, 138
Airplanes (individual)
  Big Boots, 108
  Black Cat, 107
  Coral Queen, 107
  Gooney Bird, 107
  Indian Maid, 109
  Lucky Lady, 107, 109
  Mad Russian, 109
  Tamerlane, 109
Airplanes (type)
  B-24, 90
  B-29, 51, 59, 62-3, 69, 76-7, 92, 101,
    106-7, 111, 124, 136, 155
  Betty, 59
  Black Widow, 59
  C-47, 76, 124, 207
  Hellcat, 83
  Helldiver, 155
  Mustang, 51, 59, 216
  NAT, 106
  Night fighter, 51
  P-38, 197
  Piper Cub, 84

Zeros, 142
Aisenberry, L. F., 153
Akutan Island, 97-8
—— Pass, 97
Alabama City, Ala., 51
Alaska, 97
Alaska-Aleutian projects, 25
Albert Park (N. Z.), 141
Alcohol, 198
Aleutians, 97, 99, 107, 121
Alexander, H. F., 142
Allison Park, Pa., 43
Allston, Mass., 102
Almagordo, N. M., 18
Almagosa Springs, 139
Alvee, John, 124
Amarillo, Tex., 85, 204
Amato, Sam C., 208
Ameche, Don, 118
Amphtrack, 73, 83
Amphibious Corps, 219
  5th, 35
Amtracks, 40, 143
Anchorage, Alaska, 45
Anchors Aweigh, 122
Andrews Lagoon, 112
Anna from Agana, 146
Anzio, 36
Appleton, Wis., 49
Apra harbor, 135, 137-8
Archer, E. E., 143
Arcturus, 111
Ardmore, Okla., 205
Argentia, Newfoundland, 116
Argentina, 118
Armstrong, R. L., 150
Army Engineer battalions, 214
Arromanches, 171, 173, 178, 187
Arzew, 112
Ashburn, Ga., 143
Asia, 25
Aslito airstrip, 97
Atkins, Eugene E., 96
Atlanta, Ga., 17-18
Atlantic City, N. J., 140

245

INDEX

246

INDEX

Bridgewater, Me., 48
Bristol Channel, 172, 183, 186
British Channel, 169
British East India Co., 70
British Royal Engineers, 172-3, 179
Broadway, 112
Brockton, Mass., 90
Bronx, N. Y., 142, 183, 206
Bronze Star, 88, 97, 142-3
Brooklyn, N. Y., 38, 48, 62, 210
Brown, A. H., 144
——, Nellie, 152
Brunk, Grover E., 110
Brunner, W. J., 30
Brunswick, Jerome A., 44
Bryan, Allen O. (Dead-eye), 210
B-24, 90
Bubble Harbor, 175
Buffalo Bill, 157
——, N. Y., 20
Bulldozer, 36, 39, 50, 52, 76, 83, 88, 142, 144, 190, 198, 214, 216
—— Boys, 24
Bunkie, La., 49
Bunn, John C., 111
—— Mattress Renovating Co., 111
Burbank, Cal., 44
Burgettsville, Pa., 145
Burkart, E. W., 122
Burnett, Ignatius, 210
Butte, Mont., 94
Butts, John C., Jr., 45
Byfield, L. J., 53
Byrne, Lt. Comdr. William G., 94

C-47, 76, 124, 207
Cairn Head, 172-6, 185
Calera, Ala., 50
Calicoan, 192, 203-4
California, 154
California, 161
Callender, Ia., 53
Calvados Reef, 187
Cameron, Homer W., 109-10
——, Roy E., 45
Camp Churo, 87
—— Forrest, 131
—— Tarawa, 49, 84
Can Do!, 23, 25, 36, 126, 161, **168**
Cape Girardeau, Mo., 183
—— Sansapor, 207
Captains Courageous, 111
Carabao, 203, 205
Carline, Lt. Col. John C., **173-4**
Carlisle, Pa., 140

Carlson, R. W., 105
Carrick (ex-Marine), **153-4**
——, John W., 151
Carryall, 52
Carson, Dr. A. B., 122
—— City, Nev., 145
Carter, Eugene F., 206
Cash, Hollis, Jr., 50
Cashatt, J. E., 45
Cat-eye rings, 119
Cat Island, 128
Cats, 45-7, 50, 94, 144-5, 203, **205**
Catt, Carl L., 82
Cattle boat, 99, 103
Causeways, 218
Cavite, 211
Centerville, Tex., 84
Central airfield, Iwo Jima, 60, 62
—— Pacific route, 25
Chagrin Falls, O., 125
Chamorros, 126-7, 135, 146-7, **152**, 154-7
Champagne, Donald E., 196
Channel ports, 169
Chanutte, Kan., 206
Charleston, N. C., 112
Charlotte, N. C., 45
Cherbourg, 169, 171, 187
Cherrypicker, 41, 99, 150
Chicago, 47, 57, 76, 103, 105, 146-7, 208
Chico, Cal., 152
Childress, Tex., 47
Chillicothe, Miss., 13
China, 77, 158-9
Chinese 19th Route Army, 159
Chmielewicz, F. J., 97
Christ in Japan, 166
Churchill, Winston, 170, 175-6
Cincinnati, O., 125, 153
CINCPAC, 138, 155
Clanton, Ala., 144
Cleveland, Okla., 39
Clifton, Tenn., 84
Coal, 82
Coaster, 173
Coca-Cola, 101
Collins, Richard D., 94
Colorado Springs, Col., 49
Colucci, "Mayor" Thomas A., 112
Columbia River, 122
Columbus, O., 206
Compton, Cal., 84
Concord, N. H., 38
Conover, P. G., 98

247

INDEX

Cooper, H. A., 85
——, Harold Lee Reed, 112
Coral, 70, 77-9, 90, 154, 191, 219
Corden, A. H., 122
Cordes, Bernard R., 13, 62
Corpus Christi, Tex., 150
Corregidor, 62
Cotentin Peninsula, 171
Cousineau, R. N., 103
Covington, Ky., 122
Coweta, Okla., 210
Cox, W. W., 144
Cranford, N. J., 44
Crittendon, Gerald L., 208
Crockett, Davey, 163
Crowley, Michael J., 102
Cuba, 80
—— Street, Battle of, 81
Culver City, Cal., 47
Cumberland, Md., 204

Dairen, 159
Dalin, Russell G., 46
Dallas, Lieut. Comdr. Bill, 75
——, Tex., 18, 20, 111, 155, 204
Dams
  Boulder, 61, 77, 213
  Grand Coulee, 24, 77, 150, 153
  Shasta, 77
  TVA, 61, 77
Dancing, 98
Danley, Noah E., 84
Dare, R. G., 183
Davenport, Iowa, 122
Davidson, Lt. J. D., 204
Davis, D., 43
——, Sam, 142
Day, Nelson A., 43
Dayton, O., 201
Dean, R. T., 146
Decatur, Ala., 144
——, Mich., 104
Decker, George E., 153
Decorations, 85, 87-8, 90
Delmar, N. Y., 82
Delmore, F. J., 210
De Luca, John, 75
Deming, N. M., 98
Dengue Bowl, 154
—— fever, 84, 123. 155
Deniston, Tex., 208
Denver, Colo., 104, 154
Depot Field, 136
De Ramus, William, 50
Detroit, Mich., 42, 219

Diegoli, E. W., 90
Dieppe Raid, 170-1, 188
Diesel marine engines, 92-3
Dingle, R. E., 41
Diseases
  Dengue, 84, 123, 155
  Malaria, 84, 135
  Venereal, 24, 212
Dismore, Jack, 117
Disney, Walt, 127
Ditching machine, 99
"Ditty koy," 55-6
Dixie, 192
Dollar Line, 159
Doodlebug, 74-5
Doyle, William L., 125
Driggers, E. R., 90
Duck, 36, 38-40, 43, 143, 183
Duffy, T. J., 38-9
Dulag, 191, 193
Dunkirk, 170
Dunlap, Iowa, 123
Dunn, Benjamin Franklin, 85-7
——, Floyd, 95
Dupre, Henri, 47
Dupuis, Norman V., 47
Dutch Harbor, 52, 97, 102, 121-3, 139, 215

East Boston, Mass., 195
East Machias, Me., 41
Eastern Island (Midway), 103
Ecuador, 117
Edinburgh, 164
Efate, 161
Elder Point, 122
Elgin, Ill., 43
——, Tex., 75, 82
Elizabeth, N. J., 98
Elkton, Va., 75
Ellenboro, N. C., 144
Elliott, Jim, 98
Ellis, H., 197
——, Monroe, 145
Elmwood, Ill., 194
El Paso, Tex., 53
Emirau Island, 190, 192-3, 203
England, 61
Eniwetok, 17, 21, 88-91, 99-101, 105, 113
—— Kickapoo Juice, 90
Erskine Point, 121
Escanaba, Mich., 45
Espiritu Santo, 161
Esquire, 108

248

INDEX

INDEX

INDEX

251

INDEX

254

INDEX

INDEX

The Naval Institute Press is the book-publishing arm of the U.S. Naval Institute, a private, nonprofit, membership society for sea service professionals and others who share an interest in naval and maritime affairs. Established in 1873 at the U.S. Naval Academy in Annapolis, Maryland, where its offices remain today, the Naval Institute has members worldwide.

Members of the Naval Institute support the education programs of the society and receive the influential monthly magazine *Proceedings* and discounts on fine nautical prints and on ship and aircraft photos. They also have access to the transcripts of the Institute's Oral History Program and get discounted admission to any of the Institute-sponsored seminars offered around the country.

The Naval Institute also publishes *Naval History* magazine. This colorful bimonthly is filled with entertaining and thought-provoking articles, first-person reminiscences, and dramatic art and photography. Members receive a discount on *Naval History* subscriptions.

The Naval Institute's book-publishing program, begun in 1898 with basic guides to naval practices, has broadened its scope in recent years to include books of more general interest. Now the Naval Institute Press publishes about one hundred titles each year, ranging from how-to books on boating and navigation to battle histories, biographies, ship and aircraft guides, and novels. Institute members receive discounts of 20 to 50 percent on the Press's nearly six hundred books in print.

Full-time students are eligible for special half-price membership rates. Life memberships are also available.

For a free catalog describing Naval Institute Press books currently available, and for further information about subscribing to *Naval History* magazine or about joining the U.S. Naval Institute, please write to:

Membership Department
U.S. Naval Institute
291 Wood Road
Annapolis, MD 21402-5035
Telephone: (800) 233-8764
Fax: (410) 269-7940
Web address: www.usni.org